Paid Care

in Australia:

Politics, Profits, Practices

Edited by Debra King and Gabrielle Meagher

SYDNEY UNIVERSITY PRESS

Published 2009 by SYDNEY UNIVERSITY PRESS
www.sup.usyd.edu

© Individual authors 2009
© Sydney University Press 2009

Reproduction and Communication for other purposes

Except as permitted under the Act, no part of this edition may be reproduced, stored in a retrieval system, or communicated in any form or by any means without prior written permission. All requests for reproduction or communication should be made to Sydney University Press at the address below:

Sydney University Press, Fisher Library F03, The University of Sydney,
NSW 2006 AUSTRALIA, Email: info@sup.usyd.edu.au

National Library of Australia Cataloguing-in-Publication entry

Title:	Paid care in Australia : politics, profits, practices / editors, Debra King and Gabrielle Meagher.
ISBN:	9781920899295 (pbk.)
Notes:	Bibliography.
Subjects:	Older people--Care--Australia.
	Older people--Care--Australia--Costs.
	Older people--Services for--Australia.
	Older people--Care--Economic aspects--Australia.
	Older people--Care--Government policy--Australia.
	Public welfare--Australia--Finance.
	Child care--Australia
	Child care--Australia--Costs.
	Child care--Government policy--Australia.
	Mothers--Employment--Australia.
Other Authors/Contributors:	
	King, Debra, 1959-
	Meagher, Gabrielle
Dewey Number:	362.610994

Cover design by Miguel Yamin, the University Publishing Services
Printed in Australia at the University Publishing Services,
The University of Sydney

Contents

About the authors ix
Preface and acknowledgements xiii

1. **Introduction: politics, profits and practices in child and aged care** 1
   Debra King and Gabrielle Meagher

   References 9

2. **The political economy of for-profit paid care: theory and evidence** 13
   Gabrielle Meagher and Natasha Cortis

   Mapping the territory 15
   Profit and care: arguments for and against 18
       Arguments for for-profit paid care 18
       Arguments against for-profit paid care 20
       Arguments that for-profit status doesn't matter 23
   Evidence from social care systems 25
       Residential aged care 26
       Child care 28
       Home care for the elderly and people with disabilities ... 31
   Taking stock 34
   References 36

3. **For-profit organisations in managed markets for human services** 43
   Bob Davidson

   Human services 44
   Managed markets 49
   Forms of managed markets 52

For-profit organisations 56
For-profit organisations in managed markets for human services 58
    Incentives for entry 58
    Barriers to entry 60
    Entry and market type 61
    Market power 62
    The effect of history, politics, and place 63
    Contract failure theory 64
Relational approaches in regulating entry 69
A future scenario? 71
Conclusion 72
References 73

4. **Outsourcing of elder care services in Sweden: effects on work environment and political legitimacy** 81
Rolf Å Gustafsson and Marta Szebehely

The context of the study 83
New public management in Swedish elder care 84
Social infrastructure and public employers 87
Working in Swedish elder care: a case study 89
    Private and public employment and the psychosocial work environment 90
    Perceptions of local politicians in purchaser-provider systems 94
    Who wants more outsourced elder care? 97
Summary and conclusions 105
    Work environment 105
    Political control 106

    Opinions for and against outsourcing............................ 106
    Internal legitimacy and social infrastructure 107
References 108
Appendix 112

5. **Caring for profit? The impact of for-profit providers on the quality of employment in paid care** 113
Debra King and Bill Martin

Caring for-profit? Or caring for *profit*? 115
The data 120
Working in aged care 123
    The workplace: flexibility and the staffing mix 124
    The work: caring for residents 128
    The workers: attitudes, opinions and job satisfaction ... 133
Does ownership type really matter? 138
References 141

6. **Blurred boundaries: how paid careworkers and care managers negotiate work relationships** 145
Jane Mears

Paid careworkers in Australia 146
What do we know of the experiences of careworkers? 147
The research project: method and participants 149
The research project: results 152
    Providing good care 152
    Transcending boundaries 154
    Care managers' perspectives 155
    Careworkers' perspectives 158
    Points of tension between managers and careworkers .. 161
    The role of policies and guidelines 161

Conclusion 163

References 165

7. **Parents as consumers of early childhood education and care: the feasibility of demand-led improvements to quality** 167
   Jennifer Sumsion and Joy Goodfellow

   Market rationality, imperfections and intervention mechanisms 169

   Demand- and supply-side imperfections 170

   Demand- and supply-side intervention mechanisms 172

   The feasibility of demand-led improvements to quality 175

   Developing the typology: an explanatory note 176

   A. Parents as uninformed, undiscerning consumers, focused on private benefits with limited agency/power 180

   B. Parents as potentially informed and discerning consumers, focused on private benefits with some agency/power 182

   C. Parents as informed, discerning, community-focused consumers with considerable agency/power 184

   D. Parents as informed, discerning consumers, focused on private benefits with considerable agency/power 187

   E. Parents as informed, discerning, activist citizen-consumers, focused on social benefits with considerable agency/power 189

   Concluding thoughts 195

   References 197

8. **Improving quality in Australian child care: the role of the media and non-profit providers** 203
   Bronwen Dalton and Rachel Wilson

Evaluating child care: quality versus quantity measures 204
The child care quality assurance regime in Australia 205
Factors influencing parental decisions about child care 207
The role of the media in influencing parental understandings of quality child care 210
Content analysis of media coverage of child care 211
    Method 212
    Analysis 212
    Results 213
Discussion of findings 217
Improving quality in Australian child care: the role of non-profit providers 218
From service providers to advocates? Strategies for making an impact 221
    Strategic communication 222
Conclusion 223
References 225

9. **The giant in the playground: investigating the reach and implications of the corporatisation of child care provision** 231
Frances Press and Christine Woodrow

Prologue 231
Introduction 232
Market domination 234
Interrelationships 237
Professional identity 239
Curriculum 242
Policy impact 244
Conclusion 247
References 249

1

Introduction: politics, profits and practices in child and aged care

Debra King and Gabrielle Meagher

On an average day in Australia in 2006 there were approximately 145,000 people over 65 years of age living in nursing homes. In 2004–05, a further 562,000 older Australians received some kind of formal, publicly funded care at home—25 per cent more than three years before. In 2005–06, approximately 157,000 people with disabilities received government-funded services to assist with their daily activities either in residential or non-residential settings. In 2006, nearly 700,000 Australian children were in some kind of formal child care, about three-fifths of them in long day care, while the proportion of children using formal child care increased from 14 to 23 per cent between 1996 and 2005. Around 174,500 workers in the social care labour force were employed to care for the recipients of these services in 2006—up nearly 10 per cent from two years earlier. In other welfare service fields, such as child welfare and family support, service use and provision is also rising.[1]

Clearly, then, a significant and increasing number of Australians use social care services, and so receive the services of a growing number of paid careworkers. The reasons for growth in provision

---

1 With the exception of the figure used to calculate the rate of growth of the social care (community services) workforce, for which see Australian Institute of Health and Welfare (2005, p. 381), these data are derived from the Australian Institute of Health and Welfare (2007). For data on nursing home residents, see Table 3.13 (p. 120); on home care for the elderly, see Table 4.13 (p. 183); on service use by people with a disability, see Table 4.8 (p. 177); and on child care, see Table 2.11 (p. 38) and growth in use (p. 39). The workforce data for 2006 come from Figure 7.4 (p. 331).

and employment in social care services are complex—and well documented. Changes to the social and family roles of women, population ageing, and the increasing incidence of disability all affect demand for social care services (Australian Institute of Health and Welfare 2007, pp. 30–31, 82, 165, 455). It is now also well established that public social care services, along with health and education services, contribute to improving living standards and alleviating social inequality (Maricale et al. 2006).

Providing high quality social care on a large scale throws up significant policy and practical challenges, and concerns about availability and quality are central. In the Australian context, where the demand for care outstrips supply, the availability question has been addressed largely by opening care services up to the market. By 2006 for-profit providers of care ran 71 per cent of long day care places for children and 31 per cent of residential facilities for the aged (Davidson 2009, pp. 72–73). Significantly, what we might call increasing 'marketisation' of care services has also involved experiments in 'corporatisation', that is, the emergence—and sometimes withdrawal and even crash—of large corporate entities in care provision.

For-profit providers compete for care funding and care places with non-profit (charitable, religious, community) organisations and government services, and they have acquired a significant voice in shaping government policy regarding their regulatory environment. This shift in the economic structure of care provision may not have occurred had greater consideration been given to public opinion; to the voices of those using the services. As Gabrielle Meagher (2007, 2008) illustrates in her analysis of the Australian Survey of Social Attitudes, Australians prefer governments to not only fund but also to deliver care. In child care, aged care and services for the disabled, people ranked for-profit provision as the least desirable option for formal care. Obviously there is widespread disagreement between the government and its citizens about how paid care might best be organised.

Concerns about the market orientation of care policy often focus on what is often referred to as the 'inherent tension' between the purpose of the market and the purpose of care. Particular concerns arise with corporate care provision, because corporations are, by law, required to put the needs of shareholders first. Where does this leave the children, the aged, and people with a disability? How can families and governments ensure that the needs of those requiring care are being met? While quality in care provision is often taken to be about meeting measurable outputs such as staffing ratios, it is also about the less tangible elements of care such as the quality of interactions and the feeling of being cared about. These are the relational aspects of care and the types of care that develop and sustain human capabilities. Such care requires continuity, consistency and the capacity to interact with others in an 'attentive, responsive and respectful manner' (Engster 2005, p. 55). In many ways, the quality of care depends on the skills and experience of the careworker, and how their work is organised, which means the qualities of the workforce and the quality of jobs are also critical factors. In turn, these depend upon how provider organisations are funded and the policy framework within which organisations operate. Within paid care, then, the issues of availability and quality are intertwined with the politics of regulation and the profits and practices of care providers.

It would be foolhardy to suggest that these issues about quality are isolated to the for-profit sector; or that they are indicative of all care providers in the for-profit sector. Indeed, some would argue that market principles have also spread to care providers run by not-for-profit organisations and government bodies through practices associated with the 'New Public Management' (NPM). Modes of management which emphasise cost minimisation, risk aversion, efficiency and objective measurements of outcomes are now widespread across care providers. Within this framework, accreditation becomes a metaphor for quality and economic considerations come before those of the people using the services. Yet there are differences between service providers—and these may not always be a consequence of whether or not they are for-profit. The need to develop a competitive edge in a field of large corporate and non-profit entities means that smaller service providers, whether owner-operated for-profit, or community-managed non-profit, are likely to offer something different, and are often well placed to offer services that emphasise those intangible elements of care.

Proponents of NPM argue that market orientation, via competition and enhanced 'customer focus', will maintain or drive up quality, while containing or reducing costs (Osborne & Gaebler 1992). However, relying on the market alone to improve quality is likely to be a limited strategy. This begs the question of how pressure can be put on governments to improve the quality of service provision within the care sector. Although governments remain the major source of funding for care services, and implement the regulatory framework, there is a risk that the colonisation of care by the market and market logic will result in paid care being depoliticised. In other words, the quality and quantity of care services and care work jobs may come to be (seen as) outside the domain of democratic deliberation and active policy intervention. For care advocates (for example, peak body organisations) and the families and consumers of care services, a big question is the extent to which they have information about the quality of services upon which to base campaigns to improve services and jobs (Folbre 2006). The absence of publicly available, comparable information is partly an effect of the difficulty in measuring the kinds of inputs and outputs that genuinely indicate the quality of care. But detailed information about care services is also unavailable because care providing organisations have no incentive to provide it, beyond meeting government requirements or shareholder needs. Trying to engage in political processes without good information would be extremely difficult and probably unproductive.

Another source of pressure for quality improvement could come from careworkers (Folbre 2006). In Australia careworkers have traditionally been advocates of the value of the relational and more intangible aspects of care. This is a central component of their job satisfaction, regardless of the kind of ownership structure they are employed under (Moskos & Martin 2005). However, the extent to which they can influence the quality of care beyond their own practices—to politicise issues relating to quality—is unclear. How marketisation of care can depoliticise careworkers is evident in countries such as Sweden. Historically, universal welfare and care regimes have been the norm, and governments have been responsive to the needs of citizens, resulting in care systems characterised by high quality and universal availability (Szebehely 2005). However, as market influences have been introduced into the care sector within these regimes, evidence suggests that employee-citizens working in for-profit organisations are less likely to see government intervention as relevant and important for how care is organised and delivered (see Gustafsson & Szebehely 2009).

Which strategies might counter the depoliticisation of careworkers, consumers and families, and who might pursue them, are cross-cutting themes throughout this volume. Our purpose is to explore, though analysis of child care and aged care systems in Australia, how economic and organisational changes, most notably the expansion of private sector providers into social care, are affecting the politics and practices of paid care.

Chapters 2 and 3 provide the context for thinking about questions relating to the institutional and policy arrangements within which paid care—in particular for-profit provision of paid care—is organised. In chapter 2, Gabrielle Meagher and Natasha Cortis map the care terrain and delineate the territory within which for-profit providers of paid care operate. Based on analysis of existing research, and mindful of debates about the 'inherent tension' between maximising profit and providing quality care, they carefully examine the strengths and weaknesses of for-profit provision of care and what the similarities and differences are in various fields of social care. Meagher and Cortis argue that, while there may be some evidence against for-profit provision of care, overall the distinction between for-profit and non-profit is too 'coarse-grained' to be useful.

In chapter 3, Bob Davidson gives some insight into why this may be so, with an analysis of the managed market framework through which social care is delivered in Australia. The government uses managed markets to encourage competition between care providers in the process of distributing funds for care provision. Davidson argues that how markets are managed has implications for the emergence of for-profit organisations, the power of users in the 'market', and the behaviour of both for-profits and non-profits in providing a service. Given this, the government has both the power and responsibility to ensure that markets are managed to achieve good service quality, rather than being focused on the micro-management of short-term outputs. Davidson reiterates the findings of Meagher and Cortis in noting differences within types of ownership as well as between them.

Both these chapters indicate the need to take account not only of the type of ownership, but also of differences in the sector within which care is being provided—aged care, child care, child protection, care of people with a disability—and whether or not the care is being provided in an institution or within a private home. These all have implications for the delivery and quality of service provision, various aspects of which are taken up in each of the remaining chapters. As noted above, the two sectors of care provision we address throughout this book are aged care and child care, with the main focus being on care provided within an institutional setting (but see Gustafsson and Szebehely's contribution for a comparison of home-based and residential aged care).

In chapter 4, Rolf Gustafsson and Marta Szebehely lead the section on the organisation and experience of aged care work. The first two chapters in this section analyse data gathered in surveys with careworkers (including nurses and personal carers) to see what differences, if any, that ownership type means for their quality of work. In contrast to Australia, Sweden is generally regarded as a prime example of a welfare state with universal provision of public social services. However, in recent years there has been a trend toward outsourcing aged care (called elder care in Sweden) through competitive tendering, which has resulted in the emergence of for-profit providers. Gustafsson and Szebehely explore whether workers in publicly- and privately-owned elder care facilities assess their work environments differently. They also analyse workers' views on the role of the state in the provision of elder care. Here they find quite stark differences between workers in public and private organisations, and their findings illustrate how marketisation can lead to depoliticisation.

In chapter 5, Debra King and Bill Martin also analyse the impact of ownership type on the experience of aged care workers, this time in residential aged care facilities in Australia. They find that for-profit facilities have fewer staff per bed, younger personal care assistants, higher vacancies (particularly for registered nurses), more use of agency staff, and higher staff turnover. Like Gustafsson and Szebehely, King and Martin also find that ownership type had little impact on workers' experience of, or satisfaction with, 'doing' aged care work. They argue that this apparent contradiction between the objective and subjective assessment of for-profit organisations might be partially explained by management practices which enable workers to achieve a reasonable balance between caring for their aged residents, caring for their children and working in a caring environment (that is, good relationships between coworkers).

In the final chapter in this section on aged care work, Jane Mears examines some of these management practices from the perspectives of both care managers and careworkers in a non-profit organisation. In discussing how working relationships are negotiated, Mears identifies several tensions around the boundaries of care work: in particular the extent to which the emotional and relational dimensions of care work can be enacted within an organisational context. Her research illustrates a central dilemma in paid care work between care and employment and Mears sensitively addresses both sides of the issue.

The three chapters in the section on child care continue the discussion about the relationship between quality care and the market provision of care, but are more focused on outcomes for care recipients: children. The first two chapters examine the factors that influence parents' ability to shape the quality of early childhood education and care. In chapter 7, Jennifer Sumsion and Joy Goodfellow begin from the premise that the market-oriented system of childcare provision in Australia has led to an emphasis on availability rather than quality. The difficulty of shifting the focus to quality is evident in their analysis of the barriers to effective intervention arising from demand- and supply-side imperfections in the child care market. Nevertheless, they argue that demand-led improvements in child care quality are feasible, although they require a more complex understanding of parents as consumers. In developing their ideas further they formulate a useful typology of parents' capacity to advocate for change based on variations in parent knowledge/perceptiveness, parent motivation/focus and parent agency/power.

In chapter 8, Bronwen Dalton and Rachel Wilson draw attention to the role of the mass media in shaping parents' knowledge about and perceptions of child care. Their empirical analysis of newspaper articles about child care reveals that the media overwhelmingly report on market issues such as the supply, demand and financial aspects. Where quality is reported, it was likely to be about issues relating to structural quality, such as staffing ratios and health and safety, rather than about process quality. This lack of emphasis on process—which includes issues such as staff skill levels, curricula and learning opportunities—means that parents are rarely provided with opportunities to consider quality in these terms. In recognising the issues for demand-led improvements in child care, Dalton and Wilson argue that small non-profit childcare providers have a key role in advocating with, and on behalf of, parents to improve the quality regime.

In the final chapter on child care, Frances Press and Christine Woodrow trace the impact of corporatisation of children's services, raising questions about whether the market-led approach to child care has resulted in positive outcomes for the process dimensions of care quality or for the professional identities of childcare workers. Written at a time when ABC Learning, and its related companies, was the 'giant' in the childcare playground, they ask whose interests were being met by creating and supporting such large and complex corporate identities in a care sector. One outcome of the corporatisation of child care has been the diminution of the public space within which issues such as quality can be raised and debated. As with the authors of chapters 7 and 8, Press and Woodrow seek to extend that public space to provide a forum through which parents, teachers, careworkers, non-profits and owner-operated facilities can participate on their own terms about issues that concern them.

While it is common for edited collections from Europe to cover multiple care sectors (see, for example, Anttonen et al. 2003; Boddy et al. 2006; Lewis 1998; Sipilä 1997), it is far less common in Australia. Perhaps this reflects the ways in which different sectors of care are segregated into specific departments and policy areas in this country. Nevertheless, we believe that there are advantages to be had from combining them. We hope to encourage the cross-fertilisation of ideas across sectors and, perhaps, to help initiate what Stone (2000) calls a 'new care movement'.

References

Lewis, J. ed. 1998, *Gender, Social Care and Welfare State Restructuring in Europe*, Ashgate, Aldershot.

Anttonen, A., Baldock, J. & Sipilä, J. eds. 2003, *The Young, the Old and the State: Social Care Systems in Five Industrial Nations*, Edward Elgar, Cheltenham.

Australian Institute of Health and Welfare 2005, *Australia's Welfare 2005*, Australian Institute of Health and Welfare, Canberra.

Australian Institute of Health and Welfare 2007, *Australia's Welfare 2007*, Australian Institute of Health and Welfare, Canberra.

Boddy, J., Cameron, C. & Moss, P. 2006, *Care Work: Present and Future*, Routledge, London.

Davidson, B. 2009, 'For-profit organisations in managed markets for human services', in *Paid Care in Australia: Politics, Profits, Practices*, eds D. King & G. Meagher, Sydney University Press, Sydney.

Engster, D. 2005, 'Rethinking care theory: The practice of caring and the obligation to care', *Hypatia*, vol. 20, no. 3, pp. 50–74.

Folbre, N. 2006, 'Demanding quality: Worker/consumer coalitions and 'high road' strategies in the care sector', *Politics & Society*, vol. 34, no. 1, pp. 1–21.

Gustafsson, R. Å. & Szebehely, M. 2009, 'Outsourcing of eldercare services in Sweden: Effects on work environment and political legitimacy', in *Paid Care in Australia: Politics, Profits, Practices*, eds D. King & G. Meagher, Sydney University Press, Sydney.

Maricale, F., d'Ecole, M.M., Vaalavuo, M. & Verbist, G. 2006, Publicly-provided services and the distribution of resources, OECD Social, Employment and Migration Working Papers No. 45, Organisation for Economic Co-operation and Development, Paris.

Meagher, G. 2007, 'Contested, corporatised and confused? Australian attitudes to child care', in *Kids Count: Better Early Childhood Education and Care in Australia*, eds E. Hill, B. Pocock & A. Elliott, Sydney University Press, Sydney.

Meagher, G. 2008, Australian attitudes to provision of services for the elderly and people with disabilities: Who should deliver and why should the government subsidise them?, paper presented at the workshop on Social care for people with a disability and frail aged people: Perspectives from Australia, Scandinavia, Canada and the UK, Social Policy Research Centre, University of New South Wales, February.

Moskos, M. & Martin, B. 2005, What's best, what's worst? Direct carers' work in their own words, report prepared by the National Institute of Labour Studies for the Department of Health and Ageing, Canberra.

Osborne, D. & Gaebler, T. 1992, *Reinventing Government*, Addison-Wesley, Reading, MA.

Sipilä, J. ed. 1997, *Social Care Services: The Key to the Scandinavian Welfare Model*, Ashgate, Aldershot.

Stone, D. 2000, 'Why we need a care movement', *The Nation*, 13 March, pp. 13–16.

Szebehely, M. 2005, 'Care as employment and welfare provision—Child care and elder care in Sweden at the dawn of the 21st century', in *Dilemmas of Care in the Nordic Welfare State: Continuity and Change*, eds. H.M. Dahl & T.R. Eriksen, Ashgate, Aldershot.

2

The political economy of for-profit paid care: theory and evidence

Gabrielle Meagher and Natasha Cortis

In recent decades, for-profit provision of social care—care for children, the elderly and people with disabilities—has increased, particularly in Australia, the United Kingdom and the United States.[1] This growth has precipitated much debate about the role of for-profit organisations in providing care, because for-profit provision of care seems to involve a clash of images, values and interests. The pursuit of 'fat-trimming' cost efficiency by self-interested shareholders seems to fit ill with the image of care as other-oriented service to those in need. That said, the rising cost of and demand for social care services does seem to demand mechanisms that contain costs and promote innovation—mechanisms many economists and policy-makers believe that markets best supply. This paper explores theoretical debates about the compatibility of profits and care, to document the potential strengths and weaknesses of for-profit provision of care. A brief survey of evidence from several social care fields attempts to establish the actual strengths and weaknesses of care as enterprise.

Two main policies have facilitated growth in for-profit provision of social care services in OECD countries in recent years: vouchers or

---

[1] Choosing a collective term for these services is not straightforward. In Australia, the term 'community services' was used to classify official statistics on such activities (Australian Bureau of Statistics 1993; 2001), but has recently been replaced by two terms, 'residential care services' and 'social assistance services' (Australian Bureau of Statistics 2006). Our preferred alternative, 'social care' is more commonly used in the United Kingdom, and includes both these domains of practice. See Kendall and colleagues (2006) for an extensive definition.

rebates to individuals seeking care services, and government contracting (Gilbert 2005). These policy changes have taken place in the context of expanding demand for paid care and an ideological backlash against public provision, particularly in liberal welfare states.

Policies that allocate cash, vouchers or rebates to individuals bolster consumers' purchasing power and choice, in turn creating opportunities for (subsidised) profit that attract private providers of social care services. In Australian child care, for example, the extension of fee relief to users in the early 1990s allowed the number of child care places and the for-profit sector to expand, with for-profit growth compounded by the removal of operating subsidies for competing non-profit, community-based long day care centres in 1996 (Brennan 2007). Similarly in the United States, tax credits combined with reduced federal regulation in the 1980s stimulated growth in for-profit child care. Chain-affiliated for-profits targeted the middle and upper income families benefiting from tax credits, while obtaining advantages by lowering staff-child ratios and salaries in response to deregulation (Tuominen 1991, p. 461).

For-profit provision of social care services has also been stimulated by government contracting, as governments have sought either to privatise public services or to expand service provision without expanding the public sector. The typical mode of contracting in the social care field is purchaser-provider arrangements, which aim to create arms-length market-type relations by separating public funding from service provision. Under these arrangements public purchasing decisions are based on provider performance, and so are, ideally, neutral to ownership or providers' organisational form. In the United Kingdom, for example, the NHS and Community Act (1990) facilitated both growth in domiciliary care and growth in for-profit providers, as local authorities increasingly contracted with private organisations (Scourfield 2006). In the United States, the sweeping reforms to income support programs under the Personal Responsibility and Work Opportunity Reconciliation Act 1996 included provisions that made for-profits eligible to contract for an expanded range of associated services, including welfare case management, children's services, mental health, and residential or outpatient care (Dias & Maynard-Moody 2006; Gibelman & Demone 2002).

Mapping the territory

Our aim is to investigate what might be specific about the dynamics and consequences of *care* delivered in particular relationships and institutional settings, namely care provided by *paid* workers employed

Figure 2.1: For-profit paid care: mapping the territory

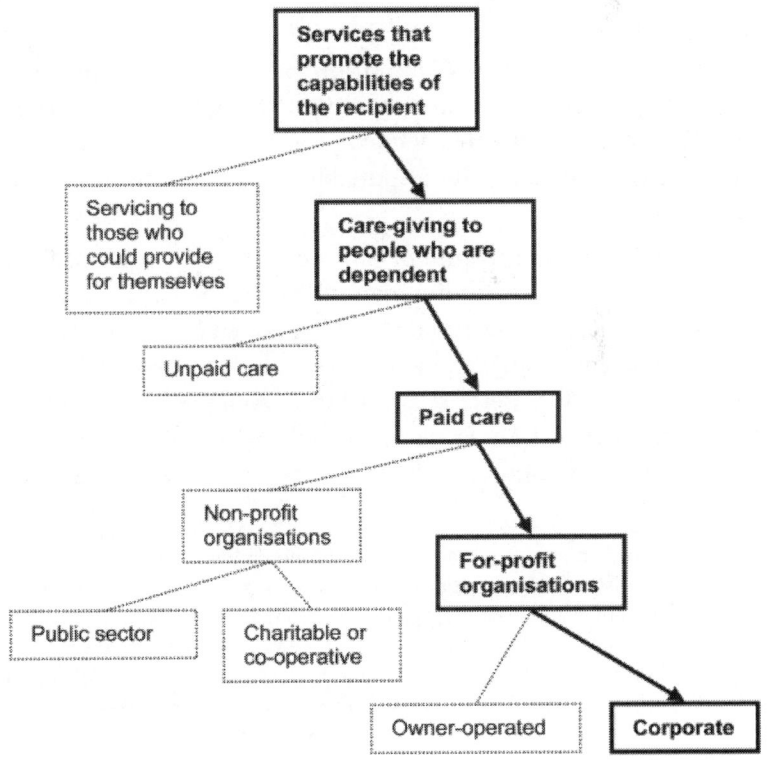

by *for-profit* organisations. Before we begin to examine the arguments and evidence about for-profit paid care, we need to define our focus by establishing some key conceptual distinctions (see Figure 2.1).

First, as many theorists of care and care work have noted, the concept of care is complex. One reason is its diverse meanings in ordinary language, as a noun to denote both *activities* (such as nurturance) and *feelings* (such as worry and affection), and as the related verbs *to care for* (one's hair, spouse, friends) and *to care about* (one's appearance, children, students, or world poverty). Researchers on care work usually define care more narrowly; England and colleagues, for example, define it as 'a face-to-face service that develops the capabilities of the recipient' (2002, p. 455). But even on this more narrow definition, which clearly excludes the personal toilette and political commitments, social policy analysts need to distinguish 'care-giving' to people who are dependent, from 'servicing' those who could otherwise perform the relevant activities themselves (see Wærness 1984). Our focus is on care, defined as services that promote the capabilities of recipients who are unable to provide those services for themselves.

Complexities remain. The kind of care we focus on is practised in a range of relationships, including natural (parent and child), chosen (friend and friend), professional (teacher and student), commercial (employee and customer), or mandated (statutory social worker and foster child). In all of these relationships, money may or may not change hands between the carer and cared-for[2] so we need to make some further distinctions, of which the first is between unpaid and

---

[2] Even parents are sometimes paid for caring for their children under, for example, personal care assistant schemes that provide cash to people with disabilities to purchase care from whomever they please, including family members. Indeed, some forms of home child care payments can be understood as 'payments for care' to parents of able-bodied children. Meanwhile, in many paid care interactions, a third party pays for the care services provided to the recipient: nurses are typically employed by hospitals, not patients, for example. The carer is paid, but not by the recipient.

paid care. Although unpaid and paid care share many features (see Himmelweit 1999), they also differ (Meagher 2006), and our interest is in paid care. Theorists of paid care have debated whether paying for care will 'crowd out' carers' altruistic motivation (England 2005; Folbre & Nelson 2000; Nelson 1999). One persuasive claim to emerge from this debate is that the effect of payment on motivation depends on whether payment is perceived as controlling or acknowledging careworkers' intrinsic orientation towards care. Writing about nurses, Nelson and Folbre argue that, in the first case, 'overly regimented work and payment structures ... can, indeed, lead to reduced feeling of vocation' (2006, p. 129). In the second, they argue, 'If high pay is given in such a way that nurses feel respected and rewarded for their care and professionalism, feelings of vocation can be reinforced and expanded' (2006, p. 129).

These arguments are about how *individuals* respond to payments, but they make clear reference to the impact of *institutional or organisational arrangements* on how payment affects carer motivation. And care work takes place in many institutional settings, including families, community networks, non-profit agencies, fee-for-service arrangements, corporations, and public institutions. It is reasonable to conjecture that the impact of institutional structure and practice on the organisation, experience and practice of care might differ systematically between these institutions. We are particularly interested in any difference that *for-profit* institutional structure and practice might make to the quality and experience of care for both workers and recipients.

Defining precisely what we mean by 'for-profit' is important, because all sorts of arrangements in which money changes hands for care have been labelled as 'commodification' or 'marketisation' of care (see, for example, Ungerson 1997), and these terms easily blur with the more specific concept of for-profit provision. Production for profit involves the systematic creation of a revenue stream from private capital ownership. This revenue is distributed to capital owners, who have an interest in the revenue being as large as is sustainable.[3] In competitive markets, private firms stay profitable by using the resources they have at their disposal, including labour, in the most productive ways possible. As we shall see in the following section, both its champions and critics respectively emphasise what they see as the benefits and risks of the dynamic process of production for profit. For-profit organisations take two primary forms—owner-operated firms, typically on a small scale; and corporations, in which ownership and management are separated, and ownership may be dispersed among many shareholders. Some evidence suggests that in the social care field, at least, these two types of for-profit organisations may operate quite differently (Morris 1999).

A final distinction we need to make is one between *actual* for-profit organisations (firms), and the extension of the *discourses and practices* of for-profit organisations into the public and third sectors, without necessarily changing their ownership structures. This extension has been a key element of the 'New Public Management', along with actual privatisation and the growth of a for-profit social care sector. Our focus is on actual private sector organisations—although as we shall see, there is debate about whether it really makes a difference if organisations are 'actual' or 'discursive' private businesses.

Profit and care: arguments for and against

Arguments for for-profit paid care

Both moral and economic arguments for private, for-profit provision of paid care exist, and both kinds of arguments share an assumption that care is like any other good or service, best—or at least not harmed by being—produced and distributed through markets.

---

[3] Theories of the origin of profit are notoriously controversial in economics, both orthodox and heterodox. However, most economists would agree that firms seek to maximise profit.

Proponents of the moral value of markets see anonymous, profit-motivated market exchanges to have 'civilising' potential, as they encourage the moral virtues of efficiency and enterprise, and promote social order through cooperation among strangers (Fourcade & Healy 2007, p. 304). From this perspective, the pursuit of profit is an intrinsic human freedom, with private exchanges perceived to offer autonomy and choice to both producers and consumers (Dowding & John n.d.).

More commonly, proponents of for-profit provision draw arguments from economic rather than moral theory. Arguments about the economic benefits of for-profit care focus on three areas: for-profits' incentives to efficiency, innovation and growth; the responsiveness and sustainability of private investment compared with government borrowing or charitable donations; and the capacity of for-profits to complement non-profit and government activity.

First, orthodox theories of the market treat profit as the reward for efficient and effective production. Competition for profit share is thought to filter out inefficient or low quality providers and drive costs down. The pursuit of profit can also be argued to promote innovation, with competition requiring providers to specialise in response to consumer preferences (Le Grand 1998). Further, profit can provide incentives for growth, with growth leading to further cost advantages (and benefits for consumers) through economies of scale like collective purchasing and flexible deployment of resources (including labour) across sites (Davis 1993; Holden 2005).

Second, for-profit provision can be argued to overcome constraints on government and non-profit performance and resourcing. Unlike public providers, for-profits operate at arms length from political processes, so can focus completely on cost and quality (Le Grand 1998). For-profits also have freer access to sources of investment. Private investment is argued to be more sustainable and responsive than government borrowing, private donation or sponsorship, offering a way to reduce the cost of government where this is a political goal (Le Grand 1998; Pearson & Martin 2005).

A third set of economic arguments highlight roles for private providers in mixed markets, on the basis that for-profits can supplement and complement government and non-profit activity. For-profits may play a supplementary or 'gap filling' role, by offering different products to non-profits, and operating in separate market niches (Abzug & Webb 1999). For-profits may also play a complementary role, comfortably co-existing with (or even enhancing) government or non-profit agencies, where they are operated as subsidiaries and can subsidise their 'parent' organisations' social missions (Salaman 1999). Alternatively, for-profits may comfortably co-exist with other organisations under quasi-market arrangements, by competing with non-profits to deliver services on behalf of governments, and complying with government regulation (Le Grand 1998).

Arguments against for-profit paid care

Unlike arguments for for-profits, which treat care as a generic product, critics frame care as a social good with general benefits for the economy and society, and focus on the relational characteristics that differentiate care from other activities and products. As well as the physical activities of 'caring for', care work involves ways of feeling and regarding another, with human virtues of affection, commitment, intimacy, and attentiveness argued to produce a sense of support and wellbeing in others (Lynch 2007; Stone 2005). As we noted above, critics argue that marketisation has a corrosive impact on these moral and emotional dimensions of care, seen as essential for human flourishing. A subset of arguments against marketisation or commodification relates specifically to the impact of for-profit provision on the organisation, practice and experience of care services. In many of these arguments, moral and economic dimensions are inextricably linked.

Objections to for-profits highlight problems of inefficiency, poorer quality, inequity and lack of accountability. First, profit is seen as a poor economic incentive for achieving social goals. Care is a public good, better produced and distributed according to human need than skewed by investors' self-interest (Schmid 2001). Critics raise concerns that because for-profits are controlled by owners of capital, provision will be guided by expectations of investment returns, so will be 'auctioned to the highest bidder' rather than guided by social needs or priorities. For-profits will gravitate to the most profitable end of the market, the impact being to 'cream' the least disadvantaged clients, to divert resources from the neediest needy people to (not needy) shareholders, and to crowd out the pursuit of collective goals (Gibelman & Demone 2002). In addition, for-profits may routinely under-serve or maintain 'excess demand' to stabilise high occupancy or placement rates, and to elevate prices and profits (Davis 1993). Second, it is not clear that, in the end, private provision is actually efficient, since governments often need to offer citizens significant fiscal incentives to take up private services, and the cost of these incentives may be so large as to eliminate the fiscal gains of reducing direct expenditure in the first place (Pearson & Martin 2005, p. 31).

Other critics question the 'trustworthiness' of for-profits where markets are imperfect. Care recipients do not fit the model of fully rational consumers able to exercise choice, accurately assess quality, choose between alternatives, and exit the market when a product fails to satisfy (Hirschmann 1970). Care recipients, and those purchasing care on their behalf can access only imperfect information, as care takes place over extended periods of time and is highly personal, making it difficult (and expensive) to monitor quality (Folbre & Nelson 2000). This raises risks that opportunistic for-profits will exploit consumers' inability to fully monitor services by charging high prices but skimping on those aspects of quality which consumers find difficult to observe and respond to (Hirth 1997, p. 419; Morris & Helburn 2000). That is, for-profits may 'sell low-quality care as if it were of high quality' (Morris 1999, p. 142). Compounding this, for-profits lack organisational values and social missions against which they can be held to account (and which offer symbolic assurance of quality); and they have less thorough public reporting requirements and democratic accountability, and may shy from evaluation of their outcomes (Gibelman & Demone 2002, p. 395).

Another set of arguments highlights the supposedly negative implications of growth. Pursuing profit exposes care services to speculative investment as well as mergers and takeovers, processes which risk reducing the competition supposed to keep service provision efficient, and exposing care provision to the possibility of collapse (Scourfield 2007; Salaman 1999). Profit-seeking growth also increases the dominance of chains which, controlled by off-site management and shareholders, are seen as more aggressive profit-maximisers than smaller, independent for-profits (Morris 1999). Further, increased concentration may make care markets difficult to regulate, as large profit-seeking providers can entrench their interests by influencing regulation and shaping the terms of the market (see Press & Woodrow 2009; Scourfield 2007).

A final set of arguments against for-profits highlights working conditions and the organisation of work. Crucial here is the idea that 'profitable care' and 'quality care' conflict. Workers are the major determinants of care quality—and the major component of costs. Because care involves relationship-building, any increases in productivity will reduce quality (Morris 1999; Himmelweit 2007). Quality declines as the need to minimise costs causes for-profits to circumscribe the time available for the relationship-building at the heart of good care. The risk here is that 'caring' motivation (a guarantee of quality and effectiveness) will be squeezed out, with care instead performed 'lovelessly', impersonally and to minimum standards (King 2007, p. 203; Folbre & Nelson 2000). As Lynch puts it:

> When a "care" relationship is set within a system of social relations focused on profit or gain in particular, it is self-evident that the care dimension of this relationship is likely to be either precluded, subordinated, or made highly contingent on the profit-margins expected (2007, p. 563).

For-profits' imperative to minimise costs places pressure on labour, lowering staff-to-client ratios, wages, skills, training and professional development, and contributing to problems in recruiting and retaining staff (Schmid 2001). Profit also provides an incentive to produce those more physically visible, measurable aspects of care, which are easiest to clearly codify in contracts to be bought and sold. The main consequence is reduced professional discretion and therapeutic work in for-profits and a tendency to squeeze out those more fluid interpersonal aspects of labour processes which seem to yield few tangible results, like attentiveness and friendship, and, at an organisational level, participation of workers and consumers in decision-making (Scourfield 2007; Schmid 2001).

Arguments that for-profit status doesn't matter

A third set of arguments holds that organisational form matters little to care. Some we have already canvassed treat the involvement of *money*, not profits *per se* as the key problem for care provision (Stone 2005), so that many of the organisations included in Figure 2.1, not just for-profits, would engender the same problems. This is because, as Stone puts it, paying for care compels third-party purchasers to 'count it, monitor it, define it, and limit it' (2005, p. 282–83), and to prioritise the physical acts or 'doing' of care over the less tangible 'being' of care. In this frame, it is not (only) the pursuit of profits, but paying for care, contracting for care, and bureaucratising care that risks reducing care to mundane, physical, measurable elements.

By contrast, some analysts see concerns about for-profit status as exaggerated. They claim that real world markets and organisations do not operate according to the competitive and profit-maximising ideal, but instead involve complex social relationships and institutions, and the profit motive can be bounded and controlled (Folbre & Nelson 2000). Some feminist economists, for example, have questioned dualisms between self-interested behaviour in supposedly impersonal markets, and virtuous motivation in the non-market sphere, pointing out for-profit provision can embody a range of values and strategies (Folbre & Nelson 2000; Nelson & England 2002). Some for-profits may pursue only small profits alongside social goals rather than being driven by 'financial gain above all else' (Nelson & England 2002, p. 5). These arguments suggest it is how care services are delivered, not the ownership structure of the delivering organisation, that matters most. As motivations for care are complex and layered, the pursuit of profit will not, inevitably, squeeze moral virtue or quality out of care.

Another set of arguments highlights pressures towards organisational 'isomorphism' which obviate the differences between organisations with different ownership structures (Estes & Swan 1994). Some emphasise the importance of institutional networks, and their structure, over ownership (Perry 1998, p. 414; Le Grand 1998). On this view, government contracting can neutralise differences in for-profit and non-profit behaviour, with regulation and quasi-market competition driving providers both to mimic each other and to emulate the government agencies on which they depend (see also Estes & Swan 1994, p. 279). When obliged to conform to the same regulations and outcome standards, contractors, regardless of organisational form, are expected to develop similar service delivery structures and technologies (Schmid & Nirel 2004). In this frame, organisations are dynamic. Rather than ownership determining behaviour, organisations respond to each other in competitive environments, and to regulation.

The disability rights movement's call for 'nothing about us without us', and for the rights of people with disabilities to live independently, also imply that ownership structure is not a critical determinant of service quality and access. What matters is that users 'have *choice* over … who provides assistance and control over when and how that assistance is provided' (Carmichael & Brown 2002, p. 805, emphasis in original).[4]

---

[4] Thanks to Helen Meekosha, who pointed this out at the workshop on 'Social care for people with a disability and frail aged people: Perspectives from Australia,

Control may also be important to service providers as well as service users, and may eclipse profit-maximising as a primary goal, particularly among small, owner-operated, for-profit providers. When autonomy and a modicum of professional satisfaction replace profit maximising as an organisational goal, some of the consequences feared by critics of the provision of care for profit may not materialise (Kendall 2001; Matosevic et al. 2007; 2008). These are the 'dwarves of capitalism', and suggest that when it comes to the impact of ownership on services, size matters (Davidson 2009).

Professionalism can, in theory, also play a role in reducing the differences between for-profit and non-profit providers. Professionalism has been posited as a 'third logic', beside the logic of markets and bureaucracies (Freidson 2001, cited in Evetts 2003). On this view, where professionals provide services, they adhere to norms and practices defined by their occupation rather than by the organisations for which they work, regardless of ownership. There are, of course, positive and negative views of professionalism: proponents see professionalism as offering a framework for the development and practice of norms that support high-quality care, based on specialised expertise and commitment to professional ethics, while critics see professionalism as the paternalistic exercise of power by self-interested members of state-sanctioned monopolies (Evetts 2003; Knijn & Verhagen 2007; Meagher 2006).

Evidence from social care systems

Many arguments for and against for-profit provision—and some that are indifferent—rest on theoretical claims about ideal typical behaviours and organisations. Yet whether or not organisational form makes a difference to the quality and accessibility of paid care services is an empirical question. In this section we consider

---

Scandinavia, Canada and the UK' at the Social Policy Research Centre, University of New South Wales, in February 2008.

research evidence on whether the quality of care is different in for-profit organisations in three social care sectors: residential aged care, child care, and home care for the aged and people with disabilities.

Residential aged care

With few exceptions (for example, Castle & Shea 1998), studies show inferior standards of quality in for-profit residential aged care (Aaronson et al. 1994; Castle & Engberg 2007; Davis 1993; Harrington et al. 2001; Martin 2005). Staffing is a consistent theme. In the United States, a study of over 13,000 federally regulated nursing homes revealed investor-owned homes had lower staffing ratios than non-profits or public homes, with chain ownership associated with the lowest levels of quality (Harrington et al. 2001). Similarly, in Canada, for-profit status is associated with lower levels of staff-client contact than in non-profits, with studies showing they deliver fewer hours of direct nursing care (Berta et al. 2005; McGrail et al. 2007; McGregor et al. 2005).

In Australia's residential care sector, too, for-profits have been found to have fewer aged care workers per bed than non-profits and government operated facilities, higher staff turnover, higher staff vacancy rates (especially for registered nurses), and higher use of agency staff (Martin 2005). However, despite this discrepancy, when asked about various aspects of their work, such as pressure to work harder, ability to spend enough time with each resident, level of freedom to decide how to do their work, and capacity to use their skills, workers in non-profit and for-profit facilities gave very similar answers (King & Martin 2009).

In terms of care outcomes, for-profits appear to have poorer health outcomes. In a study of 449 nursing homes in Pennsylvania, Aaronson and colleagues (1994) found that residents of for-profit homes had higher risks of pressure sores than residents of non-profits, and for-profits used restraints on the elderly more often. Another study of 422 hospices across the United States found that patients in for-profit facilities received a narrower range of care services than in non-profits, controlled for a range of confounding factors (Carlson et al. 2004).

Hospitalisation rates provide further evidence of poorer outcomes of for-profit nursing home care. A study of more than 43,000 residents of subsidised nursing homes in British Columbia (McGregor et al. 2006) found for-profits had higher hospitalisation rates for some conditions (pneumonia, anaemia and dehydration) although differences were not significant for falls, urinary tract infections or gangrene. In that large study, the lowest hospitalisation rates came from non-profit facilities attached to a hospital or health authority (presumably due to their proximity to health professionals), or those that were multi-site, with the latter tending to be better staffed and to have better access to health professionals (who may, for example, be shared between sites).

Other studies point to the negative impact of growth and concentration in the residential care sector. In the United Kingdom in particular, mergers and acquisitions have compounded concentration in aged care since the late 1990s. These processes, it is argued, allow more aggressive profiteering, as they have shifted political power from regulators to the largest for-profits and, in the process, have limited scope for choice, service user involvement and professional discretion (Drakeford 2006; Holden 2005; Scourfield 2007).

While there is little evidence that quality standards are higher in private for-profit residential care, studies into care-home providers' motivations (potentially a proxy for quality) suggest ownership status may not make a significant difference. A series of English studies has found that regardless of whether they were operating as public, private or voluntary providers, care-home managers reported aspiring to professional goals, and the desire to meet older people's needs (intrinsic motivators), over any desire for personal income or profit (extrinsic motivators) (Matosevic et al. 2007; 2008). Moreover, private providers should not be assumed to be profit-maximisers—the desire for autonomy and independence are also important motivators among the small-business operators of care homes who participated in Kendall's English study (2001). The findings of these studies are interesting, but not entirely comparable with the studies we discuss above. One problem is that providers' attitudes may not be a reliable and valid measure of service quality, because they may not directly translate into organisational policy and behaviour. Matosevic and colleagues surveyed 'managers' of public, voluntary non-profit and for-profit care homes, and more than a third of respondents from for-profit homes were neither owners nor owner-managers. These respondents probably worked in the corporate sector.[5] How much scope these managers have to set organisational policies and service standards on the basis of their own motivations for working in aged care is not established.

Child care

Studies of child care also contribute a considerable body of evidence to support the argument that for-profit organisations are more likely to provide services of inferior quality. And like for-profit residential aged care, staffing and staffing ratios are recurrent themes in studies of the quality of child care.

In a study of 325 child care centres in Canada, for example, Cleveland and Krashinsky (2005) found a statistically significant difference in the quality of the environment and of care in for-profit and non-profit centres, with for-profit centres over-represented among poor quality services. However, much depends on the type of non-profit or for-profits (with chain-affiliated centres performing the worst),

---

5 Matosevic and colleagues (2007, p. 114) gathered data from 58 homes, of which 28 were private for-profit, 21 were voluntary non-profit, and nine were local-authority managed. Among for-profit homes, ten were small, six were medium-sized, and 12 were corporate. Among respondents, 40 were managers, four owners, and 14 acted as both manager and owner. Given the organisation types included in the sample, logic suggests that all eighteen of the owners and owner-managers operated in the for-profit sector, mostly in small and medium homes, leaving ten non-owning managers of for-profit homes, most probably in the corporate sector.

and on the character of licensing and regulation (Morris & Helburn 2000). In a study of 401 centres in four representative states of the United States, Morris and Helburn (2000) found higher staff ratios in independent and church-affiliated non-profits, and in public child care centres, and lower ratios in those centres operated by for-profits, but also in those operated by community agencies and churches. Morris found for-profits skimp on staff wages and qualifications, instead spending more on facilities than non-profits (1999, p. 138).

As well as operating with lower staff ratios and lower paid staff, there is evidence that for-profit child care centres may be less likely to publicly state their staffing standards. A study of 115 American child care centres (Gelles 2000) found that, in the absence of strong regulation, for-profit centres were less likely to state their staff-child ratios in written advertising material (19 per cent of for-profits did compared with 44 per cent of non-profits). As well as failing to state standards against which they could be held accountable, for-profits were more likely to regroup children throughout the day, temporarily lowering staffing ratios at the expense of stability in children's care environment, and without parents' knowledge (Gelles 2000, p. 240). In addition, Gelles (2000) found patterns of volunteering (which offers a way for parents to monitor the centre's internal operations) differed significantly between for-profit and non-profit child care centres. Only one per cent of for-profits reported seven or more volunteer hours a week, compared with 30 per cent of non-profits. Together, these practices make it more difficult to monitor for-profit performance, and to hold them to account.

Some studies explicitly test the theory that for-profit child care centres are less 'trustworthy' than non-profits, exploring whether they will exploit consumers' inability to accurately assess quality by enhancing superficial aspects of quality in attempts to lower cost without losing business (Morris 1999). Morris and Helburn (2000) examined whether for-profit child care centres were more likely to direct effort to 'easy to observe' aspects of quality (like centre appearance) while skimping on supervised learning programs and staff-child interactions, which involve more highly trained staff and higher staff-to-child ratios. They confirm that skimping on the hard to observe aspects of quality occurs where lower licensing standards allow staff ratios and staff training to fall (in their multi-state study, this was in North Carolina). For-profits affiliated with chains, in particular, were found to skimp on activities undertaken while parents were not present (including meals, supervision of creative play, supervision of fine motor activities, staff cooperation and staff professional development opportunities). Compared with independent for-profits, chain-affiliated for-profits focused their efforts more strongly on greeting and departing, personal grooming, furnishings, child-related displays, space, equipment, and provisions for parents (such as meeting areas). Community agencies also provided lower hard-to-observe quality for preschoolers, which the authors attributed to either managerial laxness or shirking where agencies had long contracts with government departments (Morris & Helburn 2000).

Further evidence of poorer performance by for-profits relates to equity, with for-profits found to serve smaller proportions of low-income children and children with special needs (Cleveland & Krashinsky 2005; Morris & Helburn 2000). Preston (1993) also found that, in the absence of regulation in the United States, non-profits provided services with higher levels of 'social externalities', measured in terms of service to children who were black, minority, or from poor or single parent families. That study also found lower levels of extra early childhood and counselling services in for-profit child care centres. However, minority participation levelled where centres were subject to stringent regulation, although non-profits maintained advantages in terms of staff quality and provision of extra early childhood services.

There is also some evidence to support the argument that size matters when it comes to for-profit provision of child care (Rush 2007; Morris & Helburn 2000). For example, one Australian study of centre-based child care quality, based on a survey of 578 childcare workers, found significant differences on most main measures of service quality between (large) corporate chains on one hand and (small) owner-operated for-profit providers and non-profit providers on the other (Rush 2007).

Home care for the elderly and people with disabilities

Evidence about for-profits in home care is mixed, with several studies pointing to the potential for regulation to neutralise differences in behaviour deriving from organisational form.

One study of 750 home care clients in Ontario (where providers are required to meet specific standards) found that, for the most part, there were no differences in the care provided by for-profits and non-profits, although clients of for-profits were slightly more satisfied with their care, and had slightly better mental health outcomes than those of non-profits (Doran et al. 2007). However, other Ontario studies draw evidence from home care workers, showing lower wages and working conditions in the for-profit sector. Aronson and colleagues (2004) examined the consequences of layoffs of 317 non-profit home care support workers in 2002, finding that most who stayed in the sector were absorbed by for-profits and suffered deterioration in their wages and conditions. A third Ontario study draws evidence from 835 home care workers (Denton et al. 2007). Denton and colleagues identify problems of job satisfaction and staff turnover, but attribute this to the character of managed competition, which, rather than for-profit status, they argue, reduces job security, erodes organisational and peer support, and shifts organisational values from 'caring' to business priorities. Thus, overarching market structures, which engender organisational isomorphism among providers with different ownership structures, may de-differentiate the quality of care and work, bringing both down by 'spreading the bads' between providers of different ownership status (see also Gustafsson & Szebehely 2009).

Researchers in the United Kingdom also emphasise the importance of regulatory arrangements. In a study of 155 providers in eleven

English local authorities, Forder and colleagues (2002) highlight how the type of contract between purchasers and providers, rather than ownership *per se*, influences how home-care organisations pursue profit. They found that regardless of ownership structure, recipients of grants (lump sums with broad service specifications) placed a lower priority on profit-making than those engaged on contracts for specified quantities of service, or those contracting on the basis of price per case. This adds weight to arguments that the character of contracts and regulation may be more important influences on organisational behaviour than ownership or organisational form.

The case of home care also offers support for arguments downplaying the role of ownership, showing how regulation can neutralise the effects of ownership differences. A ten-year longitudinal study examined the growth of Israeli home care services, which was facilitated by the introduction of social insurance contributions (Schmid 2001). That study showed government contracting caused the strategic, structural, administrative and human behaviour of for-profits and non-profits to blur. Both non-profits and for-profits became more dependent on government resources, adopted similar service technologies and similar pricing, financing and marketing strategies, and transmitted professional norms. Professional communication networks minimised differences, and executives moved across sectors, transmitting policies and processes as they went (Schmid 2001).

Nevertheless, Schmid (2001) found that private providers did perform worse than non-profits in the first few years of contracting, although distinctions lessened over the decade. For-profits 'caught up' by establishing links with governments, adhering to standards, setting up quality control systems, formalising work roles and systems, investing more in training, and reducing staff turnover. After ten years, for-profits were virtually indistinguishable from non-profits in terms of service effectiveness and client satisfaction, causing the author to call for research and policy to focus on the key problem not of *who* provides services, but on *how* care is organised and provided (Schmid 2001).

British studies of the motivations of domiciliary care providers find that they are, like the motivations of residential care providers, mixed, with the desire to make money co-existing with the desire for professional satisfaction and to help others. The balance between intrinsic and extrinsic motivations may differ by ownership type, but so does the capacity to express intrinsic motivations, which depends much on the external environment. The researchers stress the role of contract specification and the experience of day-to-day relationships with local authority purchasers in determining whether motivations that support high-quality care are crowded in—or out (Kendall et al. 2003).

Given the theoretical potential for professionalism to support high-quality care, Knijn and Verhagen's (2007) study of the impact of payments for care on professionalism in home care offers a further useful insight into the dynamic effects of the emergence of markets in home care services. These researchers argue that professionalism in home care has been put under significant pressure by one key method of promoting a market in home care services; viz. direct payments to service users. Direct payments push care out of the public sector, into the private domains of the family and market. In many European countries, for example, service users can pay family members to provide care. One result of this is that home care, as a 'weak profession', is poorly placed to resist perceptions that it is not clearly distinguishable from what family members can offer, more cheaply, and more warmly. Further, direct payment systems typically decouple public funding from public provision, opening up private markets for home care, markets in which pressures for cost-cutting are strong, thereby undermining the quality of both care and employment in the sector.

Taking stock

Abstract principles from economics and moral theory are invoked by some participants in the debate about for-profit care. However, the debate takes place in a specific historical context, in which several trends converge to create demand for paid care services and in which for-profit paid care becomes one way of meeting that demand.

Population ageing, changing family structures and increasing participation in the labour market by women are increasing demand for provision of care services outside the family. Writing about Western Europe, but making arguments also applicable in the English-speaking liberal welfare states, Fargion argues that these changes 'reduce … the practical possibilities for inter-generational cooperation, thereby increasing the difficulties in the performance of caring functions within the primary network' (Fargion 2000, p. 61).

Increasing demand is expressed as increasing expectations by citizens that social care services will be provided in some form by governments. But the emergence of new care needs has coincided with concern that claims on the welfare state need to be constrained, and that the size of the public sector needs to be contained, and if possible, reduced. Thus, privatisation of social care has emerged as a solution—the institutional size of the public sector has been contained in English-speaking countries, while service provision can be expanded through public subsidies to private sector (both for-profit and non-profit) organisations.

Because the changes that have 'defamilialised' informal care and 'privatised' social care have been so profound and contested, it is not surprising that the debate about for-profit paid care is caught up in wider debates about the nature of the good society. These debates canvass questions about the appropriate scope of the market (as a domain of freedom or exploitation, depending on one's point of view), the proper role of governments and the public sector (as an inefficient and coercive institution or as an expression of collective responsibility, again depending on one's point of view), and the place of women in the public sphere.

That the debate about for-profit care reflects broader ideological divides is one reason why assessment of the evidence is so crucial in this rather fraught field of social policy. Several points stand out from our survey of evidence on for-profit provision of paid care.

First is that the weight of evidence seems to fall on the side of critics of for-profit provision, particularly in residential aged care and in child care, and particularly in North America. However, the case against for-profit provision in any and all situations is not overwhelming, which brings us to a second point: that the distinction between 'for-profit' and 'non-profit' may be too coarse-grained. As Morris and Helburn (2000) show in their study of child care in the United States, the categories 'for-profit' and 'non-profit' can each include different kinds of organisations, such that quality outcomes do not vary entirely systematically with auspice. Further, Shmid's study of home care for the aged in Israel (2001) shows how differences between for-profit and non-profit services can decline over time, as environmental factors and organisational learning engender a process of institutional isomorphism. Meanwhile, professionalism is a set of values and practices that can be mobilised in both non-profit and for-profit settings, and so may also mitigate differences between the performance of different kinds of organisations.

Third is that the policy context, including regulation and contracting conditions, is a critical environmental factor affecting the performance of organisations providing social care. Regulation can put a 'floor' under the quality of care services (and care work jobs), or fail to do so, enabling skimping on unmeasured or hard-to-measure aspects of quality. Regulation can also 'spread the bads' in purchaser-provider or consumer choice systems, as the dynamic consequences of competition play themselves out in pressures on providers to cut costs and to fragment and routinise care work practices. Thus, when the motivations of care providers include both intrinsic and extrinsic elements, policy makers need to design social service systems that enable expression of the intrinsic motivations that support quality care. This suggests that the fate of professionalism as a normative and organisational framework for maintaining and improving the quality of care is also ultimately policy-dependent.

Fourth, it seems that the care sector matters too. Evidence suggests that the impact of for-profit organisation differs in home care services compared to institutional care services for children and the elderly (specifically centre-based child care and nursing homes). Why this might be is worth further investigation.

These findings mean that the search for models of social care provision in which the quality of both care and jobs is high, and access to services is equitable, remains open—in wealthy, English-speaking democracies, at any rate. Clearly, further research and policy experimentation are required.

References

Aaronson, W., Zinn, J. & Rosko, M. 1994, 'Do for-profit and not-for-profit nursing homes behave differently'?, *The Gerontologist*, vol. 34, no. 6, pp. 775–86.

Abzug, R. & Webb, N. 1999, 'Relationships between non-profit and for-profit organizations: A stakeholder perspective', *Nonprofit and Voluntary Sector Quarterly*, vol. 28, no. 4, pp. 416–31.

Aronson, J., Denton, M. & Zeytinoglu, I. 2004, 'Market-modelled home care in Ontario: Deteriorating working conditions and dwindling community capacity', *Canadian Public Policy* vol. 30, no. 1, pp. 111–25.

Australian Bureau of Statistics 1993, *Australian and New Zealand Standard Industrial Classification (ANZSIC), 1993*, Cat. No. 1292.0, Australian Bureau of Statistics, Canberra.

Australian Bureau of Statistics 2001, *Community Services, Australia, 1999–2000*, Cat. No. 8696.0, Australian Bureau of Statistics, Canberra.

Australian Bureau of Statistics 2006, *Australian and New Zealand Standard Industrial Classification (ANZSIC), 2006*, Cat. No. 1292.0, Australian Bureau of Statistics, Canberra.

Berta, W, LaPorte, A, & Valdemanis, C. 2005, 'Observations on institutional long-term care in Ontario: 1996-2002', *Canadian Journal of Aging*, vol. 24, no. 1, pp. 70–84.

Brennan, D. 2007, 'The ABC of child care politics', *Australian Journal of Social Issues*, vol. 42, no. 2, pp. 213–26.

Carlson, M., Gallo, W. & Brady, E. 2004, 'Ownership status and patterns of care in hospice: Results from the National Home and Hospice Care Survey', *Medical Care*, vol. 42, no. 5, pp. 432–38.

Carmichael, A. & Brown, L. 2002, 'The future challenge for direct payments', *Disability & Society*, vol. 17, no. 7, pp. 797–808.

Castle, N. & Engberg, J. 2007, 'The influence of staffing characteristics on quality of care in nursing homes', *Health Services Research*, vol. 42, no. 5, pp. 1822–47.

Castle, N. & Shea, D. 1998, 'The effects of for-profit and not-for-profit facility status on the quality of care for nursing home residents with mental illnesses', *Research on Aging*, vol. 20, no. 2, pp. 246–263.

Cleveland, G. & Krashinsky, M. 2005, *The Quality Gap: A Study of Nonprofit and Commercial Childcare Centres in Canada*, Toronto, Child Care Resource and Research Unit.

Davidson, B. 2009, 'For-profit organisations in managed markets for human services', in *Paid Care in Australia: Politics, Profits, Practices*, eds D. King & G. Meagher, Sydney University Press, Sydney.

Davis, M. 1993, 'Nursing home ownership revisited: Market, cost and quality relationships', *Medical Care*, vol. 31, no. 11, pp. 1062–68.

Denton, M., Zeytinoglu, I., Kusch, K. & Davies, S. 2007, 'Market-modelled home care: Impact on job satisfaction and propensity to leave', *Canadian Public Policy*, vol. 33, no. 1, pp. 81–100.

Dias, J. & Maynard-Moody, S. 2006, 'For-profit welfare: Contracts, conflicts, and the performance paradox', *Journal of Public Administration Research and Theory*, vol. 17, no. 2, pp. 189–211.

Doran, D., Pickard, J., Harris, J., Coyte, P., Macrae, A., Laschinger, H., Darlington, G. & Carryer, J. 2007, 'The relationship between characteristics of home care nursing service contracts under managed competition and continuity of care and client outcomes: Evidence from Ontario', *Healthcare Policy*, vol. 2, no. 4, pp. 97–113.

Dowding, K. & John, P. n.d., 'The value of choice in public policy', [Online], Available: http://www.ipeg.org.uk/papers/D+J_value_of_choice_in_public_policy290906.pdf [2008, Sep 10].

Drakeford, M. 2006, 'Ownership, regulation and the public interest: The case of residential care for older people', *Critical Social Policy*, vol. 26, no. 4, pp. 932–44.

England, P. 2005, 'Emerging theories of care work', *Annual Review of Sociology*, vol. 31, pp. 381–99.

England, P., Budig, M. & Folbre, N. 2002, 'Wages of virtue: The relative pay of care work', *Social Problems*, vol. 49, no. 4, pp. 455–73.

Estes, C. & Swan, J. 1994, 'Privatization, system membership, and access to home health care for the elderly', *Milbank Quarterly*, vol. 72, no. 2, pp. 277–98.

Evetts, J. 2003, 'The sociological analysis of professionalism: Occupational change in the modern world', *International Sociology*, vol. 18, no. 2, pp. 395–415.

Fargion, V. 2000, 'Timing and the development of social care services in Europe', *Western European Politics*, vol. 23, no. 2, pp. 59–88.

Folbre, N. & Nelson, J. 2000, 'For love or money—Or both?' *Journal of Economic Perspectives*, vol. 14, no. 4, pp. 123–40.

Forder, J., Knapp, M., Hardy, B., Kendall, J., Matosevic, T, & Ware, P. 2004, 'Prices, contracts and motivations: Institutional arrangements in domiciliary care', *Policy & Politics*, vol. 32, no. 2, pp. 207–22.

Fourcade, M. & Healy, K. 2007, 'Moral views of market society', *Annual Review of Sociology*, vol. 33, pp. 285–311.

Gelles, E. 2000, 'The role of the economic sector in the provision of care to trusting clients', *Nonprofit Management & Leadership*, vol. 10, no. 3, pp. 233–49.

Gibelman, M. & Demone, H. 2002, 'The commercialization of health and human services: Neutral phenomenon or cause for concern?' *Families in Society: The Journal of Contemporary Human Services*, vol. 83, no. 4, pp. 387–97.

Gilbert, N. 2005, *The 'enabling state?' from public to private responsibility for social protection: Pathways and pitfalls*, OECD Social Employment and Migration Working Papers No. 26, OECD Publishing, Paris.

Gustafsson, R. Å. & Szebehely, M. 2009, 'Outsourcing of eldercare services in Sweden: Effects on work environment and political legitimacy', in *Paid Care in Australia: Politics, Profits, Practices*, eds D. King & G. Meagher, Sydney University Press, Sydney.

Harrington, C., Woolhandler, S., Mullan, J., Carrillo, H. & Himmelstein, D. 2001, 'Does investor ownership of nursing homes compromise the quality of care?', *American Journal of Public Health*, vol. 91, no. 9, pp. 1452–55.

Himmelweit, S. 1999, 'Caring labor', *Annals of the American Academy of Political and Social Science*, vol. 561, pp. 27–38.

Himmelweit, S. 2007, 'The prospects for caring: Economic theory and policy analysis', *Cambridge Journal of Economics*, vol. 31, no. 4, pp. 581–99.

Hirschmann, A. 1970, *Exit, Voice and Loyalty: Response to Decline in Firms, Organizations, and States*, Harvard University Press, Cambridge, Mass.

Hirth, R. 1997, 'Competition between for-profit and nonprofit health care providers: Can it help achieve social goals?' *Medical Care Research and Review*, vol. 54, no. 4, pp. 414–38.

Holden, C. 2005, 'Organizing across borders: Profit and quality in internationalized providers', *International Social Work*, vol. 48, no. 5, pp. 643–53.

Kendall, J. 2001, 'Of knights, knaves and merchants: The case of residential care for older people in England in the late 1990s', *Social Policy & Administration*, vol. 35, no. 4, pp. 360–75.

Kendall, J., Matosevic, T., Forder, J., Knapp, M., Hardy, B. & Ware, P. 2003, 'The motivations of domiciliary care providers in England: New concepts, new findings', *Journal of Social Policy*, vol. 32, no. 4, pp. 489–511.

Kendall, J., Knapp, M., & Forder, J. 2006, 'Social care and the non-profit sector in the Western developed world', in *The Nonprofit Sector: A Research Handbook*, eds W. Powell & R. Steinberg, Yale University Press, New Haven.

King, D. 2007, 'Rethinking the care-market relationship in care provider organisations', *Australian Journal of Social Issues*, vol. 42, no. 2, pp. 199–212.

King, D. & Martin, B. 2009, 'Caring for-profit? The impact of for-profit providers on the quality of employment in paid care', in *Paid Care in Australia: Politics, Profits, Practices*, eds D. King & G. Meagher, Sydney University Press, Sydney.

Knijn, T. & Verhagen, S. 2007, 'Contested professionalism: Payments for care and the quality of home care', *Administration & Society*, vol. 39, no. 4, pp. 451–75.

Le Grand, J. 1998, 'Ownership and social policy', *The Political Quarterly*, vol. 69, no. 4, pp. 415–21.

Lynch, K. 2007, 'Love labour as a distinct and non-commodifiable form of care labour', *Sociological Review*, vol. 55, no. 3, pp. 550–70.

Martin, B. 2005, *Residential aged care facilities and their workers: how staffing patterns and work experience vary with facility characteristics*, National Institute of Labour Studies, Flinders University.

Matosevic T., Knapp, M., Kendall, J., Henderson, C. & Fernández, J. 2007. 'Care home providers as professionals: Understanding the motivations of care home providers in England', *Ageing and Society*, vol. 27, pp. 103–26.

Matosevic, T., Knapp, M. & Le Grand, J. 2008, 'Motivation and commissioning: Perceived and expressed motivations of care home providers', *Social Policy & Administration*, vol. 42, no. 3, pp. 228–47.

McGrail, K. McGregor, M., Cohen, M., Tate, R. & Ronald, L. 2007, 'For-profit versus not-for-profit delivery of long-term care', *Canadian Medical Association Journal*, vol. 176, no. 1, pp. 57–58.

McGregor, M., Tate, R., McGrail, K., Ronald, S., Broemeling, A. & Cohen, M. 2006, 'Care outcomes in long-term care facilities in British Columbia, Canada: Does ownership matter?' *Medical Care*, vol. 44, no. 10, pp. 929–35.

McGregor, M., Cohen, M., McGrail, K., Broemeling, A., Adler, M., Schulzer, M., Ronald, L. Cvitkovich, Y. & Beck, M. 2005, 'Staffing levels in not-for-profit and for-profit long-term care facilities: Does type of ownership matter?' *Canadian Medical Association Journal*, vol. 172, pp. 645–49.

Meagher, G. 2006, 'What can we expect from paid carers?' *Politics and Society*, vol. 34, no. 1, pp. 33–54.

Morris, J. 1999, 'Market constraints on child care quality', *Annals of the American Academy of Political and Social Sciences*, vol. 563, pp. 130–45.

Morris, J. & Helburn, S. 2000, 'Child care centre quality differences: The role of profit status, client preferences, and trust', *Nonprofit and Voluntary Sector Quarterly*, vol. 29, no. 3, pp. 377–99.

Nelson, J. 1999, 'Of markets and martyrs: Is it OK to pay well for care?' *Feminist Economics*, vol. 5, no. 3, pp. 43–59.

Nelson, J. & England, P. 2002, 'Feminist philosophies of love and work', *Hypatia*, vol. 17, no. 2., pp. 1–18.

Nelson, J. & Folbre, N. 2006, 'Why a well-paid nurse is a better nurse', *Nurse Economics*, vol. 24, no. 3, pp. 127–30.

Pearson, M. & Martin, J. 2005, Should we extend the role of private social expenditure? *OECD Social Employment and Migration Working Papers No. 23*, OECD Publishing.

Perry 6. 1998, 'Ownership and the new politics of the public interest services', *The Political Quarterly*, vol. 69, no. 4, pp. 404–14.

Press, F. & Woodrow, C. 2009, 'The giant in the playground: Investigating the reach and implications of the corporatisation of childcare provision', in *Paid Care in Australia: Politics, Profits, Practices*, eds D. King & G. Meagher, Sydney University Press, Sydney.

Preston, A. 1993, 'Efficiency, quality, and social externalities in the provision of day care: Comparisons of nonprofit and for-profit firms', *Journal of Productivity Analysis*, vol. 4, nos 1–2, pp. 165–82.

Rush, E. 2007, 'Employees' views on quality', in *Kids Count: Better Early Childhood Education and Care in Australia*, eds E. Hill, B. Pocock & A. Elliott, Sydney University Press, Sydney.

Salaman, L. 1999, 'The nonprofit sector at a crossroads: The case of America', *Voluntas: International Journal of Voluntary and Nonprofit Organizations*, vol. 10, no. 1, pp. 5–23.

Schmid, H. 2001, 'Nonprofit organizations and for-profit organizations providing home care services for the Israeli frail elderly: A comparative analysis', *International Journal of Public Administration*, vol. 24, no. 11, pp. 1233–65.

Schmid, H. & Nirel, R. 2004, 'Ownership and age in nonprofit and for-profit home care', *Administration in Social Work*, vol. 28, no. 3–4, pp. 183–200.

Scourfield, P. 2006, '"What matters is what works"? How discourses of modernization have both silenced and limited debate on domiciliary care for older people', *Critical Social Policy*, vol. 26, no. 1, pp. 5–30.

Scourfield, P. 2007, 'Are there reasons to be worried about the "cartelization" of residential care?' *Critical Social Policy*, vol. 27, no. 2, pp. 155–80.

Stone, D. 2005, 'For love nor money: The commodification of care', in *Rethinking Commodification: Cases and Readings in Law and Culture*, eds M. Ertman & J. Williams, New York University Press, New York, pp. 271–90.

Tuominen, M. 1991, 'Caring for profit: The social, economic and political significance of for-profit child care', *Social Service Review*, vol. 65, no. 3, pp. 450–67.

Ungerson, C. 1997, 'Social politics and the commodification of care', *Social Politics*, vol. 4, no. 3, pp. 362–81.

Wærness, K. 1984, 'The rationality of caring', *Economic and Industrial Democracy*, vol. 5, no. 2, pp. 185–211.

3

For-profit organisations in managed markets for human services

Bob Davidson

The provision of human services, including paid care, relies substantially on government funding. Increasingly over the last 25 years, in Australia and elsewhere, that funding has been distributed using 'competitive' market mechanisms. The result has been a widespread development of managed markets, also known as 'quasi-markets', in human services. There are many variants of managed markets, but they are all distinguished from conventional markets[1] primarily by the fact that government is the source of much, if not all, of the purchasing power of the users of services. This enables government to dictate how these markets operate in ways that go well beyond the powers of government in most conventional markets. In turn, government action in shaping the particular form of each managed market will substantially influence the types of service provider organisations that operate in that market, including the extent to which for-profit organisations (FPOs) are present.

This chapter reviews some key characteristics of human services, managed markets, and FPOs, as a basis for examining the type of service providers that should and do operate in these markets, particularly in terms of the growing role of FPOs. This analysis can assist in establishing whether there may be justification for limiting or encouraging the participation of some types of providers in these

---

[1] We use the term 'conventional markets' to refer to markets where there is no or minimal government funds to purchase the product; that is, the type of market assumed in standard economic theory.

markets—and if so, under what circumstances and on what terms. There are, of course, more fundamental concerns about the validity of marketising human services, but the chapter assumes that, in the foreseeable future, governments will continue to use managed markets to support the provision of these services. Thus the focus is on how these markets work and how they might be made to work to maximise the achievement of social objectives, rather than examining the broader concerns.

The chapter draws on developments from a range of services and market types. Its findings should be regarded as an attempt to identify general trends and issues that then need to be tested in sector-specific or cross-sector studies, rather than as a claim to lay down a theory or prescription that fits all situations. Two key points emerge from the chapter. First is the importance of ensuring that the initial entry of all service providers is closely monitored given the inherent tension between profit maximisation and service quality, coupled with the lack of perfect information for service users and their agents in these markets. Second is the blurring of the boundaries between non-profit organisations (NPOs) and FPOs in these markets, such that we need to go beyond this simple dichotomy to establish which types of organisation can best provide services in each situation.

Human services

Zins (2001, pp. 6–7) defines human services as 'institutionalised systematic services' aimed at 'meeting human needs ... required for maintaining or promoting the overall quality of life' of service users. While this covers a diverse range of fields and programs, including education, health, child care, residential and at-home care for the aged, disability, family support, early intervention, homelessness, and job search assistance for the disadvantaged, most share common features that can make their provision via a 'market' somewhat problematic. That said, it is important not to overstate the distinct features of human services and to recognise that some of these features have traditionally been ascribed to all services, including services provided through conventional markets.

Economic analysts (for example, Productivity Commission 2002a; Miles & Boden 2000; Miles 1995; Bureau of Industry Economics 1980; Akehurst & Gadrey 1987; Baumol 1967) have identified that services are more likely to have the following core characteristics:

(i) *Simultaneity of production and consumption*, as shown, for example, in the way that the assistance given by a carer in bathing an aged person is 'consumed' at the same time it is 'produced'.

(ii) *Intangibility*, in that 'the output tends to disappear at the point of delivery, leaving no lasting physical manifestation' (Saunders 1999, p. 40).

(iii) *The central importance of labour in production*, so that, for example, the capacity of each individual carer largely determines the quality of care provided.

(iv) *The consumer as an active agent in determining the final product*, as shown by the way a teacher adapts a lesson to suit the individual students in a class.

In turn, these factors mean that with services there is more likely to be:

(v) *Heterogeneity in a given 'product'*, such that there is variation both between different suppliers and by a single supplier over time. For example each doctor's consultation, carer's act of bathing an aged person, and lesson by a teacher will be distinct in some way.

(vi) *Limits to improving labour productivity*, in that there is limited scope to reduce the amount of labour needed for a given level of output.

(vii) *Complexities with measurement* of output, quality, and productivity.

(viii) *Asymmetry of information* whereby one player or set of players in a market, usually the suppliers, has more information about the production process and the final product.

(ix) *Buyer uncertainty about the product before purchase,* given that there is likely to be nothing tangible to inspect before buying.

Early economists regarded labour used in services as 'unproductive' (Smith 1991, pp. 294–96), and thus the foundations of modern micro-economics were largely developed on the basis of the production and distribution of *goods*, and in denial of the characteristics and economic value of services based on labour (Tucker 1977, pp. 13–16; Channon 1978, p. 1). Hence, the gap between the standard core assumptions of micro-economic theory, such as homogenous products and full information for all buyers and sellers, and the complexity of economic reality is even more pronounced in relation to services.[2] While developments in computerised technology and integrated systems over the last 25 years have transformed some service industries, including communications and retail (Triplett & Bosworth 2003), the distinct characteristics set out above all remain very relevant—and accentuated—in human services where the 'product' being supplied is largely dependent on the quality of the human interaction. Nowhere is this clearer than in the care sectors, and England and Folbre (2003), Fine (2007), and Himmelweit (2007) provide an insight into the special features of caring and paid care that illustrate a number of the points made in this section.

We now consider what factors distinguish human services from other services, especially in terms of why greater government intervention is necessary. First, because human services aim to meet basic devel-

---

2 Of course, subsequent developments in mainstream economics (from Coase (1937) onwards) have recognised these issues. However, the use of the term 'cost disease' to describe Baumol's argument that the inherent nature of services limits productivity improvements illustrates a common view among economists that labour-intensive services are aberrant problems rather than simply different forms of economic activity. It must be noted, however, that Baumol himself actually said that many of these services are ones 'that do so much to enrich our existence' (Baumol 1967, p. 422).

opment and care needs of *people*, there are strong moral and public policy imperatives to ensure at least some minimum level of service for everyone and to avoid poor service to anyone. A wide range of quality from Armani to Target may be acceptable in consumer items, but not in human services. Second, the effective delivery of human services is more likely to require an extended set of individual service transactions over time. This has major cost implications for each user, while also making it more difficult to assess the quality and outcomes of a service, especially in the shorter term. Third, on the demand side, the end users of human services generally have vulnerability or limited capacity in some respect and thus *agents* who make decisions on behalf of users are an important feature of human services. Agents may be family members, personal associates, government agencies, or paid brokers. For example, parents make decisions about child care for their children, and adult children may make decisions about aged care for their parents. Importantly, however, agents are rarely able to observe the service being provided. Fourth, many of the end users of human services, and their family agents, have limited, if any, funds to buy the services they need.

Having identified core differences between services and goods, and then between human services and other services, our next step is to identify the main sources of difference between various types of human services. Propper (1993, p. 40), writing about health and social care services, noted that those services differ in 'the technology of production, the nature of demand, and the information of actors in these industries', and this observation can be applied more generally across all human services. Thus, for example, residential aged care differs from at-home community care for the aged because it requires substantially more capital and buildings, because it has to provide service for longer periods each day and for less able users, and because buyers of residential care are less likely to have information about the full production process.

The above analysis has implications for the way in which human services are provided and the organisations—and *types* of organisations—that become service providers in each market. First, given that many services are largely unobserved by buyers—who are buying on behalf of others—and the quality and outcomes are difficult to measure, there is much potential for opportunistic behaviour both through adverse selection and moral hazard.[3] Hence there is a greater need for trust between the buyer (service user or agent) and seller (service provider), with the motivation, values and commitment to client needs of the provider being critically important.

Second, to the extent that trust is lacking, there will be transaction costs for all parties, both *ex ante* (prior to approval of a provider) and *ex post* (monitoring and assessing the services)—and these costs can be large. Indeed, Williamson (1975; 1998; 2000), a seminal writer in the field of contracting, points out that the limits on an individual's capacity to gather and process all relevant information, which economists called 'bounded rationality', make it impossible to specify all the contingencies that may arise in the future, and hence 'all complex contracts are unavoidably incomplete' (Williamson 2000, p. 599).

Third, because *people* are central to the production and delivery of human services, a provider is limited in the extent to which it can genuinely increase measured productivity (Baumol 1967; Himmelweit 2007). The quality of a service is critically dependent on the personal and professional skills of staff and the relationships they develop with users, and thus significantly reducing the number or quality of staff or the time they spend with clients can fundamentally alter the nature of the service that is provided. Larger organisations have been able to effect economies of scale and scope in human services, but these often arise from strategies in management, marketing, and 'back-office' functions rather than enhancing the direct production of the service.

Fourth, there are limits to standardisation of a service, since too

---

3 *Adverse selection* is where the buyer makes a wrong choice because the provider does not reveal everything about itself. *Moral hazard* is where the provider puts in less resources and produces lower quality products than has been agreed.

close a specification of processes and outputs may reduce the quality of service for each user by ignoring his/her individuality. Fifth, it is likely that the 'provider profile', that is, the mix of different types of provider organisations, will vary between different human services.

An important implication of the above analysis is the inherent tension between commercial imperatives and the quality of human services, especially in relation to staff. A common lesson from studies of specific human services is that the major drivers of quality are lower user-staff ratios (variously described as case load, class size, et cetera), higher staff qualifications, an overall staff profile that has a high proportion of people who have significant qualifications and experience, and adequate remuneration to ensure the attraction and retention of good staff. However, these are precisely the major cost drivers for human service providers, for whom staff can represent over 80 per cent of total costs in some sectors. Thus there will be continuing pressure to control these staff costs (Wade 2007). FPOs will rightly argue that they will lose 'customers' or their contract if quality is perceived to fall, but a fine balance between limiting costs and an acceptable level of quality can be maintained, especially where information to customers can be restricted and marketing techniques used to shape customer expectations (Press & Woodrow 2005, pp. 282–83). This does *not* mean that there is no role for FPOs and the profit motive, but it does suggest that profit *maximisation* does not sit easily with ensuring high quality services.

Managed markets

Managed markets are distinguished from most other forms of public funding because they require external bodies that provide direct services for the public to directly compete against each other to obtain the funds. Managed markets are distinguished from conventional markets primarily because government provides much of the purchasing power for users.

From an economic perspective, government involvement is necessary in human services because of the prevalence of *market failure*—the 'provision by a competitive market of an output quantity which is not socially optimal' (Maddala & Miller 1989, p. 619)—or, more precisely in some cases, because *no* market has formed given the limited finances of the people who need the services. It is thus somewhat ironic that market mechanisms are now being used to fund services in sectors where historically the market has not worked.

The concept of *contestability* is central to the establishment and operation of managed markets. Formally, contestability is about the ease of entry into and exit from a market. In a *perfectly contestable market*, entry and exit are 'costless', in the sense that there are no additional costs for new entrants or 'departees' above the normal costs of establishing and operating the enterprise (Baumol 1982; Baumol et al. 1982). The core premise of contestability is that by making service providers subject to merely the *threat* of competition (and thus to the threat of loss of revenue), the overall quality and efficiency of all providers will be improved, both by attracting new providers and by driving improved performance by incumbents. Whether this logic is valid for managed markets in human services and whether it varies by the type of service, the form of the market or the type of provider are empirical questions to be answered in each situation.

Managed markets as a means of distributing government funds are not unique to human services nor are they a recent innovation (for example, tendering for public infrastructure has long been used). Further, governments can and do shape *all* markets, through policy statements, through general laws on corporations, competition, taxation and fair trading, and through the regulation of specific industries. However, because it provides a high proportion of the 'consumer purchasing power' in managed markets, government has greater power to shape these markets.

Bartlett and Le Grand (1993, pp. 13–19) identify the core objectives that governments have in establishing managed markets in social policy, namely to promote greater effectiveness, efficiency, choice, responsiveness to client needs, and equity.[4] There will be trade-offs in achieving these objectives; for example, increasing choice can mean a loss of efficiency. Bartlett and Le Grand (1993, pp. 19–34) also identify five key prerequisites of managed markets if these objectives are to be achieved: some level of competition between providers; appropriate motivations and incentives for both buyer (whose focus should be the welfare of the users) and provider (who should in part be motivated by financial considerations so that they respond to market signals); symmetry in the information available to buyers and providers; minimal transaction costs; and avoidance of 'creaming'.[5]

In a managed market, government can substantially dictate the way that the market functions, by making decisions about key features of the four core elements of a market:

(i) *Product*: What is the service to be funded? What aspects of the service will be funded?

(ii) *Buyer (users or agents)*: Who is eligible to use the subsidised product? How much is the subsidy? Do some users get a higher subsidy than others? Is any additional payment by the buyer required or possible? Can the subsidy cover all costs or is an additional co-payment by the buyer required or possible? Are there limits on the total dollars (or places) available to the whole population?

(iii) *Sellers, or service providers*: Who can sell to those buyers supported by government funds? On what basis do they have to operate? What, if any, minimum standards are mandated for

---

4 Bartlett and Le Grand (1993) only list four objectives, conflating effectiveness and efficiency into efficiency.

5 'Creaming' involves limiting services to 'less difficult' clients rather than assisting those with more complex needs who require more resources and represent a greater operational risk. The term 'residualisation' is also used to describe this process (Press & Woodrow 2005, p. 284).

providers to enable entry to the market? What mechanism determines who can service clients: tender or licensing? How often is the market 'opened' to new providers and is it open periodically or continuously? Is the right to operate tradeable? What performance targets and requirements are in place, and how are performance standards monitored and enforced?

(iv) *Means of exchange*: How do buyers and sellers interact? How do providers obtain individual clients? What is the basis of payment of the government funds: inputs, outputs, or outcomes, and how are these measured? Are payments made to providers or to users? What method of payment does the government use?

In an unregulated conventional market, most of these factors are irrelevant or not directly the business of government, with buyers and sellers subject only to general laws. Even in a regulated conventional market, government action in any single market will usually be limited to only some aspects of the four elements. In a managed market, however, government may have at least five distinct roles: policy-maker, regulator, banker, direct buyer, and service provider. Different agencies or even jurisdictions may take on each of these five roles in a specific market, but it is not uncommon for all roles to be administered from within the same agency.

Forms of managed markets

There are many potential variants of managed markets, each emerging as the outcome of government decisions on the factors listed above in specific cases. Governments, however, do not necessarily make *explicit* decisions about all of these factors. Indeed, in some cases, the ad hoc and implicit nature of some 'decisions' can mean that some elements of a program are inconsistent with other elements, or even with the overall objectives of the program. Further, 'In practice, the way a service is delivered ... may be more a product of political dogma than of an assessment of relative efficiency or equity' (Burchardt 1997, p. 5).

Three major forms of managed markets using non-government providers, both FPO and NPO, can be identified:

- *Competitive tendering and contracting (CTC)*: A government agency chooses who will be the service provider(s) for a designated group of users.
- *Licence-subsidy (LS)*: Entry is possible for any provider who meets a set of minimum requirements and standards (*licence*). Licensed providers then 'compete for customers' with the government substantially meeting much, possibly all, the costs of service for approved users (*subsidy*). Subsidies may be paid either to users or providers. If paid to users, they may be paid by cash, 'vouchers', tax deductions or tax credits.
- *Hybrids of CTC and LS models*: A limited number of providers are chosen via a CTC process, and then these providers 'compete for customers', with various possible limitations placed on the buyer-seller interaction and/or the use of mechanisms that ensure a minimum level of activity for all providers.

There are two main advantages of using CTC instead of a LS system. First, CTC better facilitates the planning of limited resources to ensure coverage of all areas and groups, greater stability in the overall supply of services, and greater stability for individual providers (which in turn can promote more investment in resources to improve the quality of services). Second, CTC allows closer monitoring of the quality of services. Against this, CTC is a costly and time-consuming process for both government and providers, offers little opportunity for users to select or have a choice of providers, and gives only limited signals from users as to which organisations provide the best service. Users generally have no exit option and very limited voice options to influence how a service operates (Hirschmann 1970). Thus LS is likely to be used where there is a desire to increase market signals, consumer sovereignty, choice, and provider responsiveness, and to reduce administration costs. In practice, however, there is much variation in LS systems between service types, regions, and individual providers in the extent to which users can actually influence the form and operation of the service they receive (Press & Woodrow 2005, pp. 281–82).

Hybrid systems have emerged in response to the disadvantages of CTC. They aim to draw on the best aspects of both systems by limiting providers to the best ones, ensuring better planning of limited resources, and giving a greater guarantee of quality, while giving users some greater choice and generating market signals. The major disadvantage of the hybrids is that they retain the complexities and costs of the CTC process.

One argument for the introduction of managed markets has been that they will give users more information and make the allocation of public funding more transparent. But in practice, under all three forms, the notion of 'commercial-in-confidence' has often been used to restrict the information available to users.

For both the users and providers of services, LS markets operate more like a conventional market, although governments still make most of the critical decisions about the features of a market listed above. There is no clear-cut boundary between a LS managed market and a conventional market, but even where a high proportion of the providers' revenue comes from user contributions, government licensing and funding can still drive the involvement and operation of major providers in the market.[6] LS systems are also referred to as 'quasi-vouchers' (Lyons 2001, p. 186), 'demand-side subsidies', or 'consumer-directed payments', but it is important to use a term that also acknowledges the critical supply-side licensing element, which limits the organisations to which service users can present their 'subsidies' and requires providers to comply with regulations that are continuously monitored and enforced.

---

6 For example, the corporate FPO, ABC Learning Centres, stated that a key element of its 'successful child care model' is to 'maximise government funding [to] underwrite income sources' (ABC Learning Centres 2005).

Under a LS system, any organisation that meets the minimum licensing requirements can provide services that attract government funds, whereas under CTC an organisation may meet the minimum service standards required of all tenderers, but still not be able to service approved users if it is not selected in the tender process. Under CTC, the competition between providers is to gain *entry* to the market and the user typically has no direct say about who the providers will be. Under LS, the competition between providers is to *attract consumers*. In other words, under CTC providers compete *for* markets, while under LS they compete *within* markets. Both forms of competition exist under hybrid systems. Under both CTC and hybrids, generally no new provider can enter in the shorter term to respond to emerging client needs. Two observed effects in some CTC markets (for example, the Job Network)[7] are that after an influx of new providers with the initial introduction of contestability, the market becomes more closed over time with fewer providers and the larger ones increasingly dominant.

The type of managed market used has no necessary connection, theoretically or empirically, with the type of service. A given service may be supported by any of the managed market variants, depending on the jurisdiction. For example, the use of various LS systems to support 'consumer-directed' at-home personal care for aged people has been widespread in western nations for some years (Evers et al. 1994; Keigher 1999; Ungerson & Yeandle 2007), but this approach has had limited use in Australia where CTC continues to be primarily used. On the other hand, LS systems have been supported by proponents of markets in Australia for the last quarter of a century and are used for child care and residential aged care, while there is currently strong support from some users for voucher-type systems for disability programs (Hughes 2006). The Productivity Commission (2002b, pp. 11.1–11.6) has also argued for the introduction of

---

[7] This national program was established in 1998 to replace a service system formerly provided by the government's Commonwealth Employment Service (CES).

a licence system for the Job Network; in response, van Dyke (2002) argues that this would lead to wasted resources in marketing and more providers than are needed or efficient.

In practice, CTC is used more for services that focus on a limited group of disadvantaged people, while LS systems are used for more universal services. The larger the target group, the greater the pressure for a more decentralised approach, while universality is more likely to involve more informed and affluent users who want greater choice. Services may begin as a grant or CTC system and evolve to a hybrid or LS system, as has happened with the Job Network and child care in Australia. Once the Rubicon is crossed to a LS system for any service, history shows that such a change can lead to a major shift in the profile and behaviour of providers, including the increased presence of FPOs.

For-profit organisations

Historically, human services have largely been provided by government or by non-profit organisations (NPOs) motivated primarily by social and altruistic objectives seeking to fill gaps in service systems. With the growth of managed markets, however, there has been increasing involvement of FPOs in human services. In Australia, this change has been particularly evident in fields such as child care, at-home community care, and job search assistance for the disadvantaged unemployed.

There is diversity among the FPOs involved in human services. At one level, there is diversity of legal structure and size, with public companies (that is, those traded on the stock exchange), transnational companies (both Australian- and overseas-based), large private equity firms, other incorporated firms with single owners or multiple shareholders, and unincorporated sole traders all now having a presence in one or more of the various services types. All of these forms are present in the at-home community care sector in Australia.

More importantly, there is also diversity in motivation and objectives.

A core assumption of micro-economic theory and most models of the behaviour of the firm is that FPOs are organised around maximising profit or the personal benefits of the people who own or manage the organisation. However, this can paint an overly simplistic picture, even for conventional markets. Some firms become involved in activities with altruistic or broader social aims as strategies to increase benefits in the long-term. Fligstein's sociological analysis of markets (2001) assumes that suppliers fundamentally want stability in the market as the basis for ensuring their continuing prosperity. Other FPOs have owners or managers who aim for some threshold of financial surplus but are then prepared to forsake extra profit in order to increase the social contribution of what they produce.

Marceau (1990) also identified a group in mainstream business (in manufacturing) that she described as the 'dwarves of capitalism'. These are people who own small operations, including many whose core objective is to be independent rather than wealthy. The 'dwarves of capitalism' have a very strong presence in human services, and include people who have left employment with large NPOs or government because of their concern about the constraints of the bureaucratic and increasingly commercial culture in these organisations. Further, in an age of outsourcing, FPOs (including self-employment) 'may offer the only alternative to professionals seeking to continue to practice their face-to-face-support skills' (Taylor & Hoggett 1994, p. 191). Some of these 'dwarves' represent a distinct and positive feature of FPOs, enabling experienced and capable people to provide services in ways, often very innovative, that focus on social and human objectives rather than organisational and commercial imperatives. While many very effective operators prefer to remain small, a number of major enterprises in human services that operate at national and international level began as 'dwarves'.

Thus one needs to be cautious in generalising about FPOs that provide human services, as Rush (2006) showed in distinguishing between large corporates and small FPOs in the quality of child care each provides. Nor is there a straightforward association between motivation and size—large FPOs may be more likely to be focused on profitability, but large FPOs can also have objectives other than to maximise profits (Martin et al. 1998) and small FPOs can have owners who see them as cash cows and the first step to a commercial empire.

This chapter is not seeking to systematically assess the advantages and disadvantages of FPOs, and whether they do in fact achieve greater efficiency, innovation, choice, responsiveness, and better outcomes as proponents claim (for which, see Meagher & Cortis 2009). The evidence on this is mixed and varies with each case. However, some situations highlight the intrinsic potential for a clash of interests between clients and profit-maximising FPOs in human services. First, the board and management of public companies are required by law to ensure that the interests of shareholders are pre-eminent (Bakan 2004). Second, with regard to license-subsidy systems, basic micro-economic theory shows that part of any subsidy for consumers is likely to be captured by suppliers in the form of a price increase (albeit generally less than the subsidy).[8] This has occurred with child care in Australia (Hill 2007), but such price increases are avoidable in the absence of increased costs, and simply represent the capacity of a profit-maximiser to take advantage of an increase in demand.

For-profit organisations in managed markets for human services

In this section, we consider the economic and other factors that determine the entry and the potential market power of FPOs in managed markets for human services.

Incentives for entry

FPOs can have a range of motivations, but the major incentive for many to enter any sector is the potential *level of profitability*.

---

8 This assumes no increase in supply, while the proportion captured by suppliers depends largely on the elasticities of demand and supply for the product.

In managed markets this is substantially affected by government decisions about the design of the managed market.

On the revenue side, a major driver is the *scale of the market*, which will be largely determined by policy and budgetary decisions about the universality of the service, the number of places available, and the size of the subsidy. FPOs will also be more present where there is the *scope to build market share*, which, in turn, depends on three design features of a managed market. First, there needs to be scope to attract more 'customers', as is possible under hybrid and LS systems. Second, licences and contracts need to be tradeable, for example through the sale of a licence or by a takeover. Third, the level of revenue in a managed market will be affected by whether providers are allowed to charge a co-payment if the subsidy does not meet the full cost of the service, or users want more or higher quality service. For some human services, the contribution by clients is negligible, for example, in programs for homeless people. But for others, such as child care and residential aged care, there can be substantial scope for an additional payment, particularly where the users/agents are more affluent and/or can draw on other sources of government support, such as family allowances or the aged pension.

Two factors that impact on profitability will vary with each case depending on the decisions by government about the structure of payments. First, higher need clients involve higher costs and risk for providers and usually attract higher payments. Where the payments are relatively high, this is an important niche for some FPOs; in other sectors, providers do not consider the extra payment justifies the extra costs or risk, and 'creaming' occurs. Second, the way subsidies are paid under a LS system can affect the relative presence of FPOs via a range of possible mechanisms. For example, in child care, a change from tax deductions to direct payment to providers could have a number of possible effects on the relative use of NPOs and FPOs, and the viability of individual providers.[9]

---

9 For example, tax deductions require parents to wait for reimbursement. This will constrain the demand for child care from some less affluent families, leading some

Barriers to entry

A number of the possible barriers to entry in conventional markets (Bain 1956; Carlton & Perloff 2005, pp. 73–82), such as patents or exclusive access to key inputs, have limited relevance in human services. On the other hand, the use of franchises is much more central to managed markets, because government is effectively issuing a franchise to some providers such that only they can access government funds. Indeed, for some programs, whole classes of providers, for example FPOs or government, are formally excluded. These barriers are less severe in LS systems because, while the need to meet licensing regulations can delay entry of a provider, it cannot ultimately prevent entry as can occur under a CTC or hybrid system.

Another difference between managed markets in human services and conventional markets involves access to capital. The need for capital in any sector depends substantially on the nature of the product; where economies of scale exist, size matters and the inability to obtain investment capital for buildings or management systems and technology is a barrier for some organisations. With managed markets, the significant share of revenue provided by government may be perceived by investors as either 'government-guaranteed', which is more likely if the program is well established; or as *less* secure because it ultimately depends on decisions by very few people in government rather than on decisions by many individual customers. The significant involvement of NPOs in managed markets for human services is a further difference in relation to access to capital. In general, FPOs have an advantage in obtaining capital (Krashinsky 1986, p. 116; Weisbrod & Schlesinger 1986, p. 146), although this can be offset by tax concessions available to NPOs (Gjems-Onstad 1994). As well, the removal of direct capital assistance to NPOs in some sectors and the expectation that providers will incorporate

---

to seek to switch to lower cost NPOs and reducing the incentive for FPOs to set up in some communities.

capital costs in their overall 'price' has worked against the growth of community-based NPOs and to the advantage of FPOs.

An important perspective on barriers to entry into any market—but especially valuable here—comes from Demsetz (1982), who argued that underlying most standard barriers to entry is imperfect information, which can affect decisions by all participants, including producers, consumers, and providers of capital. In the absence of perfect information, which is more likely to occur where the product is a human service, the reputation of incumbent providers and the trust they have developed is central in giving them an advantage with both investors and buyers. The notion of 'commercial-in-confidence' can be used to further restrict the information available to competitors and consumers, and a means by which incumbents can entrench their advantage.

Finally, for any industry, entry is also partly determined by whether there are barriers or incentives to *exit*. Hence, for example, an organisation is less likely to enter if there is a high level of asset-specificity in production (that is, they cannot easily transfer the assets to another product or industry) or if the contract/licence to operate is not tradeable. While asset-specificity is clearly important with physical plant (for example, specialised machinery), it can also be very relevant in human services in determining the extent to which a provider will invest in obtaining and training quality staff.

Entry and market type

A key determinant of the presence of FPOs in a sector is the type of managed market, that is, whether a CTC, LS, or hybrid system is used. FPOs are more common under LS systems, a result of fewer barriers to entry, higher potential profitability, and greater opportunity for FPOs to use their relative advantages (in, for example, marketing and capital-raising) to expand and increase market share. However, while a LS system may give greater scope for small operators to enter the market, ultimately it may also lead to a smaller number of large

FPOs, since a LS system allows greater scope for takeovers and amalgamations.[10] Thus, while aimed at increasing choice for users, a LS system may end up reducing the choice—as indeed has happened in the child care sector in a number of Australian communities.

While FPOs are likely to be more common in LS systems, they may also be significant in those sectors using CTC and hybrid systems, where more of the key contracted outcomes are stated in quantifiable and observable terms. This is the case in the Job Network, where the number of jobs obtained by disadvantaged clients is a key outcome required of providers.

Market power

Once an organisation is in a market, it is potentially in a position to exercise market power to improve its position relative to other providers and to limit the entry of new providers. The theory of conventional markets is that the market power of an incumbent derives from the extent to which there are barriers to entry. Its power will be a function of its size and market share and will be reflected in its capacity to set price above marginal cost and limit the total quantity of output so as to maximise profit.

In CTC and hybrid markets, a provider's power over price and quantity will be substantially constrained given that the government agency offering the contract may have the power of a monopsonist (that is, a single buyer) to force down price and require greater output and accountability from providers. Hence, competition between providers is likely to be focused more on quality and costs. However, the buyer's power will be more limited where there are large multi-service providers, such as nation-wide religious NPOs, which always have the option of transferring resources to another program and type of service.

---

10 For example, the Productivity Commission (2002b, p. 11.5) noted that the introduction of a LS system in the Job Network would be 'likely to lead to some consolidation in the industry'.

There is more potential in LS markets for providers to exert power over price and quantity, but the nature of human services noted earlier means that these markets will tend to have two characteristics that limit this power. First, *differentiated* (or *monopolistic*) *competition* will be common, whereby there is a number of suppliers (many quite small), each with a slightly different version of a core product (Chamberlin 1933; Robinson 1933). Second, competition between suppliers will tend to be centred on a local area or a segment of customers (Hotelling 1929).

There are two other major sources of power for suppliers in conventional markets, namely that a supplier has the capacity to shape the expectations of consumers (Galbraith 1958) and to use 'political' power to shape the market by influencing government decisions on regulation and incentives. These two sources of power are potentially even more important in managed markets for human services. Governments have great power to shape managed markets, and suppliers have ample opportunity to shape consumer expectations by exploiting the asymmetry of information and the lack of observable outputs prevalent in human services.

The effect of history, politics, and place

The impact of the design of a managed market on the type of providers and the presence of FPOs in that market is limited by other factors related to *history, politics,* and *place*. In sectors where large NPOs are long established, inevitably there will initially be fewer opportunities for FPOs when funding for any service becomes contestable. This situation is likely to be exacerbated by the contracting decisions made by government agencies wishing to minimise early problems and choosing larger NPOs as major providers. Politics is important and every sector has its stories of lobbying government at both the political and bureaucratic levels, to open up opportunities and close off competitors. Thus in some cases, causality may be in the opposite direction from that generally assumed, if the market has been shaped to favour certain players, rather than the players responding to the market.

The differing effects of history, politics and place on the profile of providers of a service are very evident in paid care in Australia. Tables 3.1 and 3.2 show the profiles of providers in each state in child care and residential aged care. While the data in the tables must be approached with caution,[11] they suggest some significant differences in the presence of FPOs between states and service types. Both nationally and in every state and territory, FPOs are more prevalent in child care, a sector where government funding was not available for FPOs twenty years ago. There are also major differences between jurisdictions for each service, with the proportion of places provided by FPOs in aged residential care ranging from 11.8 per cent (Tasmania) to 43.5 per cent (Victoria), and the proportion of FPO providers in child care ranging from 26.2 per cent (Northern Territory) to 82.5 per cent (Queensland). There are also differences in the type of NPOs in each sector: over 30 per cent of aged care places nationally are provided by religious organisations, a group that has a negligible presence in child care. In part, these differences in the provider profiles are driven by local circumstances including the size, structure, and location of the target group and the history of NPOs in the state, and by the development strategies of major providers. But they also reflect differing policy and practice of state and territory governments, with for example, the licensing function in child care being carried out by state authorities.

Contract failure theory

The theory of contract failure,[12] initially developed by Henry Hansmann (1980; 1987; 1996), is the theory most often cited

---

11 See notes on Tables 3.1 and 3.2. There is also a different base for each table, with Table 3.1 showing the number of *places* managed by each type of provider and Table 3.2 showing the number of *providers* of each type.

12 The term 'contract failure' has the potential to create some confusion. The meaning of 'contract' here is not restricted to formal agreements as in CTC, but includes implicit understandings between buyers and sellers.

Table 3.1: Aged care residential places in Australia and each state/territory, proportion of places by type of provider, June 2005*

Type of Provider	NSW	VIC	QLD	WA	SA	TAS	ACT	NT	Total
Religious	32.5	17.2	43.7	33.6	28.6	38.4	23.5	55.6	30.4
Community-based	15.6	16.0	12.3	12.1	13.0	25.1	6.7	15.3	14.7
Charitable	19.8	6.0	14.1	15.5	26.2	21.8	47.9	17.4	15.8
Private-for profit	29.3	43.5	23.8	34.1	23.4	11.8	21.9	11.6	31.2
State/territory govt	1.4	14.6	5.3	0.6	6.6	2.6	-	-	5.9
Local government	1.3	2.7	0.8	4.1	2.2	0.4	-	-	1.9
Total	100	100	100	100	100	100	100	100	100
Total places	55,027	40,708	28,173	13,418	15,319	4,270	1,556	430	158,901

* Excludes multi-purpose services and flexibly funded services.

Source: Steering Committee for the Review of Government Service Provision (2006, Table 12A.4)

Table 3.2: Centre-based long day care child care providers in Australia and each state/territory, proportion of providers by type of provider, 2004-05*

Type of Provider	NSW	VIC	QLD	WA	SA	TAS	ACT	NT	Total
Community-managed	22.4	23.7	15.5	34.8	51.2	48.7	68.4	73.8	25.7
Private-for profit	77.6	64.6	82.5	62.5	46.5	29.5	31.6	26.2	71.0
Government **	na	11.7	2.0	2.6	2.3	21.8	-	na	3.3
Total	100	100	100	100	100	100	100	100	100
Total providers	1,938	913	1,197	531	258	78	98	65	5,078

*The Steering Committee for the Review of Government Service Provision notes that its data on child care services by provider type 'needs to be interpreted with care because the scope of data collection varies across jurisdictions' (2006, p. 14.13).

** Includes local government owned services, but excludes Australian government supported services.

Source: Derived from Steering Committee for the Review of Government Service Provision (2006, Tables 14.2, 14A.33, 14A.42, 14A.51, 14A.60, 14A.69, 14A.78, 14A.87, 14A96)

to explain the relative presence of NPOs and FPOs in any field. Essentially, Hansmann argues that where there is asymmetry of information between seller and buyer because the delivery of the service is largely unobservable by the buyer and/or the outcomes are largely unmeasurable, there is a need for buyers to put great trust in the service provider. In such situations, Hansmann argues, NPOs will be more prevalent because they are more trusted, and they are more trusted because they face a non-distributional constraint (that is, their financial surplus does not get distributed to shareholders). In brief, the argument is that where trust is required, NPOs are chosen because they are not 'in it for the money'. Hansmann further argues that 'The distinction between the for-profit and the non-profit form becomes blurred when the organisations in question are small in scale. The non-distributional constraint ... has real meaning only when an enterprise is of sufficient scale to develop large earnings' (1980, pp. 870–871).

In the context of this theory, how do we explain the growing (and in some cases dominant) presence of FPOs, especially large ones, in human services? Under CTC and hybrid systems, why do government agencies choose FPOs; and under hybrid and LS systems, why do individual users (or their agents) choose FPOs? Let us examine the two major premises of Hansmann's theory.[13]

Hansmann's first major premise is that where outcomes cannot be easily observed or measured, a buyer's decision is based on the trust they have in the seller. However, this will be less of a concern for those buyers who believe they can accurately assess the quality and outcomes of a service. Thus, a government agency may put great faith in 'objective' performance indicators, or users/agents trust their own judgement. This confidence may or may not be justified, especially if the assessment is based on only on a partial view of the

---

13 Note that Hansmann's original article (Hansmann 1980) focused largely on overseas aid, where donors (or 'buyers of aid services') have few means of checking on the supplier. He explicitly noted that his analysis needs further development to cover 'mixed market' situations where NPOs directly compete with FPOs.

service—but we are here trying to explain 'buying decisions', not the objective reality of the service. Press and Woodrow (2005, p. 282) note that several studies have found that parents tend to overestimate the quality of child care.

Another caveat to the first premise rests on the way that many decisions are made, which is not by a simultaneous balancing of all the variables in a single function, but a series of filter decisions (Mannion & Smith 1998, pp. 128–29). Buyers may first seek to ensure a minimum threshold level of quality, after which locality, price, efficiency, and other factors will be successively taken into account in the calculus of decision-making about human services to determine the 'best value-for-money'. In these ways, the commercial advantage of large organisations and FPOs can come into play, especially in more capital-intensive sectors, providing there is an acceptable base level of quality.

Hansmann's second major premise is that NPOs are trusted more because of the non-distributional constraint. In practice, however, this needs to be qualified by considerations as to *how* trust is gained—or lost. On the one hand, FPOs can gain greater trust in a number of ways. They can employ well-qualified, experienced staff with good reputations. They can provide a better level of service than the minimum required by a contract or regulations. They can undertake non-profit maximising activities, such as building local social capital. They can also use their marketing efforts to mould the attitudes and expectations of buyers. On the other hand, NPOs as a group can lose some of their 'trust advantage' when some adopt corporate strategies and processes aimed at maximising financial surplus, organisational growth, and the 'market-based' remuneration of senior employees,[14]

---

14 Note that the non-distribution constraint does not normally apply to remuneration for employees in defining an organisation as 'non-profit'. However, this has been an issue in the United States, where some states have sought to limit the level of remuneration payable to NPO employees if the organisation is to retain its tax exemptions.

while reducing the conditions and rights of staff (Horin 2007). This is associated with *mission drift* (Weisbrod 2004) and *institutional isomorphism* as NPOs move away from their original purpose and are perceived to operate more like FPOs or their funders (Taylor & Hoggett 1994, p. 193; Di Maggio & Powell 1983; Smith & Lipsky 1993). This 'blurring of the boundaries' between NPOs and FPOs means that one cannot predict organisational *behaviour* simply on the basis of ownership, but that subtler and more complex models are needed (Austin et al. 2006; Crossan et al. 2005) to identify how well each provider balances its social and commercial objectives in a market environment.

Relational approaches in regulating entry

Given the difficulty of observing performance and the potential for opportunism where human services have been marketised, two major focuses of action are to ensure more rigorous government and self-regulation of provider behaviour, and to continually improve instruments to assess performance, especially for service quality and client outcomes. These are clearly important strategies and action on these fronts needs to be sustained.

However, in establishing the processes and requirements for contracting, licensing, and regulation, rigorous requirements relating to the *initial entry* of providers into a managed market are also necessary. Such requirements are not incompatible with contestability, and can lead to gains in both efficiency and service quality. Baumol (1982) and Baumol and colleagues (1982) point out that the assumption of perfect competition requiring many sellers is not essential for maximum efficiency, providing that there is at least one potential efficient entrant that can enter and exit costlessly. Indeed, an excess number of suppliers can lead to a loss of efficiency even if it might be argued that some users are overall better off because they have wider choice. Further, we can look to the *theory of the second best* (Lipsey & Lancaster 1957), which essentially holds that where all of the conditions for an efficient market cannot be met, the most efficient outcome may be achieved by ensuring that one or more of the other conditions is *not* met. Thus Le Grand and Bartlett note that if 'purchasers have inadequate information, it may be preferable to have providers that are not motivated by financial considerations' (1993, p. 34).

Dyer (1997, cited in Horton 2005) provides an interesting lesson from the private sector for the operation of managed markets in human services. He examined different approaches to contracting for the supply of parts for the manufacture of cars, and showed that Japanese manufacturers essentially used *relational contracting*, by which they chose suppliers based on common values, and then used longer-term contracting and less detailed checking of production processes. By contrast, US manufacturers used *competitive transactional contracting*, which involved micro-management of the supplier's processes and intermediate outputs. Even in this most tangible and commercial activity, the relational approach produced significantly superior results in productivity, reliability, sales and profit.

With the expansion of managed markets, governments in Australia and elsewhere have often moved much more towards competitive transactional approaches in working with external bodies. Yet given the nature of human services, a stronger relational approach, with a closer focus on the overall organisation in determining who can gain entry to a managed market seems more appropriate. A relational approach, of course, is not without its dangers—for example, corruption, a 'closed shop', or monopoly power for incumbents—especially where 'public money' is used. Accordingly, the case for and against a relational contracting approach, and how it might be operationalised, needs close examination in each case. Such an approach, however, can increase effectiveness and produce better outcomes, as well as saving substantial resources that would otherwise be applied to monitoring and enforcement.

While it is unlikely to be politically feasible to retrace the steps in well-established managed markets, there are other fields still to be opened up and in which there may be significant expansion in coming years. The next section takes a brief look at how one type of paid care service might develop without adequate regulation of the initial entry of providers.

A future scenario?

The major program under which home-based care for older people and people with disabilities is currently provided in Australia is the Home and Community Care (HACC) program. HACC is funded by both national and state governments and administered by the states through a CTC system, with providers winning contracts for specific areas or groups of clients. While government providers are still very significant and most non-government providers are NPOs, FPOs have been contracted under HACC. In addition, a range of other FPOs, including specialist employment agencies (Perrett 2005) and US corporates (Horin 2006), either work with HACC providers or provide home-based care outside HACC through other government programs or on an unsubsidised basis.

Home-based care is very likely to expand in the future, given the ageing of the population and policy support for this type of care as a much more cost-effective alternative to residential care (Fine 2007, p. 102–68). If significant extra money starts flowing, it is also very likely that there will then be much greater interest from FPOs and strong pressures to introduce a LS system, which (as noted earlier) operates in a number of Western nations. In this event, we might also see the use within HACC and other government-funded home care programs of the standard FPO franchising models for home-based services. Under this model, a large corporate would gain a licence, and sell a 'franchise' to individuals operating their own business—that is, a variant of Jim's Mowing or XYZ Cleaning Services. The individual would pay a significant fee in return for the benefits of the corporate brand, marketing and back-office support;

the corporate could earn substantial revenue, while having shifted much of the risk, responsibility, and costs to the individual service provider and the service user. This model is already being used for home care that is not funded by government.

We can presume that franchisees will be required to meet all of the conditions of the licence—staff qualifications, work processes, and so on—and that the corporate franchisers will need to provide training and back-up. It will undoubtedly produce some very good services, enabling skilled and experienced people dedicated to good caring to operate their service independently of the bureaucratic constraints of larger organisations; and enabling many users and their agents to have a greater influence on the service. How it will work across *all* providers and the *whole* population is not so clear, especially in ensuring consistent quality. Issues of *privity of contract*, which are already intrinsic to CTC systems, may also arise, whereby 'service recipients, who are not parties to the contract, are unable to take steps to enforce it even though they may be clearly affected by the contractor's breach' (Administrative Review Council 1998, pp. 87–89). The corporate franchise approach may not be allowed initially, but it could gradually evolve and become accepted, just as many previously 'unthinkable' approaches for providing public services are now mainstream.

Conclusion

Governments have the power to substantially shape managed markets. If they propose to continue—or extend—the use of managed markets in human services, they need to use this power strategically to maximise the achievement of social objectives. Two key points emerge from this chapter to guide to how this might be done.

First, it is important to ensure that the initial entry of all service providers to these markets is closely monitored, given the distinct features of human services, the inherent tension between profit maximisation and service quality, and the lack of perfect information for service users and their agents in these markets. Further, the requirements set should include an assessment of the overall objectives, values and behaviour of the organisation, to ensure that all providers have a fundamental concern with the welfare of users rather than with maximising the personal benefits of the owners or managers of the provider organisations. This also implies a greater use of relational approaches in admitting providers to the market.

Second, there has been a blurring of the boundaries between NPOs and FPOs in the provision of human services, which in part helps to explain the growth of FPOs in this field. While it still remains more likely that NPOs will have strong social motivation and FPOs will have a strong focus on commercial objectives, the situation is now far more complex than a simple dichotomy in those terms. While there may be a need to limit the entry of certain providers in some situations, it is necessary to recognise that different forms of FPOs operate, and to focus on the behaviour of providers rather than simply on their ownership in determining these limits.

Finally, it is important to emphasise that the most appropriate form of managed market and entry requirements, and the type of providers that should be admitted, will vary in each case, depending on the factors outlined in this chapter.

References

ABC Learning Centres 2005, ABC Learning Centres Ltd: So much more than childcare [Online], Available: http://www.childcare.com.au/index.htm [2006, March 12].

Administrative Review Council 1998, *The Contracting Out of Government Services: Report to the Attorney General,* Administrative Review Council, Canberra.

Akehurst, G. & Gadrey, J. (eds) 1987, *The Economics of Services*, Frank Cass and Co, London.

Austin, J., Stevenson, H. & Wei-Skillern, J. 2006, 'Social and commercial entrepreneurship: Same, different, or both?', *Entrepreneurship: Theory and Practice*, vol. 30, no. 1, pp. 1–22.

Bain, J. S. 1956, *Barriers to New Competition: Their Characters and Consequences in Manufacturing Industries*, Harvard University Press, Cambridge Mass.

Bakan, J. 2004, *The Corporation: The Pathological Pursuit of Profit and Power*, Constable, London.

Bartlett, W. & Le Grand, J. 1993, 'The theory of managed markets', in *Quasi-Markets and Social Policy*, eds J. Le Grand & W. Bartlett, Macmillan, London, pp. 13–34.

Baumol, W. J. 1967, 'Macroeconomics of unbalanced growth: The anatomy of urban crisis', *American Economic Review*, vol. 57, no. 3, pp. 415–26.

Baumol, W. J. 1982, 'Contestable markets: An uprising in the theory of industrial structure', *American Economic Review*, vol. 72, no. 1, pp. 1–15.

Baumol, W. J., Panzar, J. C. & Willig, R. D. 1982, *Contestable Markets and the Theory of Industry Structure*, Harcourt Brace Jovanovich, San Diego.

Burchardt, T. 1997, *Boundaries between public and private welfare: a typology and map of services*, Centre for Analysis of Social Exclusion, London School of Economics, Case Paper 02, November [Online], Available: http://eprints.lse.ac.uk/6534/ [2008, Sep 5].

Bureau of Industry Economics 1980, *Features of the Australian Service Sector*, Research Report 5, Bureau of Industry Economics, Canberra.

Carlton, D. W. & Perloff, J. M. 2005, *Modern Industrial Organisation*, Pearson-Addison-Wesley, Boston.

Chamberlin, E. H. 1933, *The Theory of Monopolistic Competition*, Harvard University Press, Cambridge, Mass.

Channon, D. F. 1978, *The Service Industries: Strategy, Structure, and Financial Performance*, Macmillan, London and Basingstoke.

Coase, R. 1937, 'The nature of the firm', *Economica*, vol. 4, no. 16, pp. 386–405.

Crossan, D., Bell, J. & Ibbotson, P. 2005, Towards a classification framework for social enterprises, paper presented to the Australian Social Policy Conference, University of New South Wales, July.

Demsetz, H. 1982, 'Barriers to entry', *American Economic Review*, vol. 72, no. 1, pp. 47–57.

Di Maggio, P. & Powell, W. W. 1983, 'The iron cage revisited: Institutional isomorphism and collective rationality in organizational fields', *American Sociological Review*, vol. 48, no. 2, pp. 147–60.

Dyer, J. 1997, 'Effective inter-firm collaboration', *Strategic Management Journal*, vol. 18, no. 7, pp. 535–56.

England, P. & Folbre, N. 2003, 'Contracting for care', in *Feminist Economics Today*, eds M. A. Ferber & J. A. Nelson, University of Chicago Press, Chicago.

Evers, A., Pijl, M. & Ungerson, C. (eds) 1994, *Payments for Care: A Comparative Overview*, Avebury, Aldershot.

Fine, M. 2007, *A Caring Society: Care and the Dilemmas of Human Service in the 21st Century*, Palgrave MacMillan, New York.

Fligstein, N. 2001, *The Architecture of Markets: An Economic Sociology of Twenty-First Century Capitalist Societies*, Princeton University Press, Princeton New Jersey.

Galbraith, J. K. 1958, *The Affluent Society*, Houghton-Mifflin, Boston.

Gjems-Onstad, O. 1994, 'Money pouring out of its ears: On the taxation of really profitable non-profit organisations in Australia', *Australian Journal of Social Issues*, vol. 29, no. 2, pp. 146–61.

Hansmann, H. B. 1980, 'The role of nonprofit enterprise', *Yale Law Journal*, vol. 89, no. 5, pp. 835–901.

Hansmann, H. B. 1987, 'Economic theories of nonprofit organisations', in *The Nonprofit Handbook*, ed. W. W. Powell, Yale University Press, New Haven, pp. 27–42.

Hansmann, H. B. 1996, *The Ownership of Enterprise*, Harvard University Press.

Hill, E. 2007, 'Making child care count is not just about cost', *The Sydney Morning Herald*, 13 November.

Himmelweit, S. 2007, 'The prospects for caring: Economic theory and policy analysis', *Cambridge Journal of Economics,* vol. 31, no. 4, pp. 581–99.

Hirschmann, A. 1970, *Exit, Voice and Loyalty*, Cambridge University Press, Cambridge, Mass.

Horin, A. 2006, 'Giant US care franchise will visit Gran for $60', *The Sydney Morning Herald*, 4 May.

Horin, A. 2007, 'Workers are in trouble when the rot sets in at Vinnies', *The Sydney Morning Herald*, 28 July.

Horton, J. 2005, Contracts: Homage to an economic innovation, paper presented to the NSW Branch of the Australian Economic Society, Sydney, 14 September.

Hotelling, H. 1929, 'Stability in competition', *Economic Journal*, vol. 39, no. 153, pp. 41–57.

Hughes, V. 2006, 'The empowerment agenda: Civil society and markets in disability and mental health', Institute of Public Affairs Backgrounder, February, vol. 18, no. 1.

Keigher, S. M. 1999, 'The limits of consumer directed care as public policy in an aging society', *Canadian Journal of Aging,* vol. 18, no. 2, pp. 182–210.

Krashinsky, M. 1986, 'Transaction costs and a theory of the nonprofit organisation', in *The Economics of Nonprofit Institutions: Studies in Structure and Policy*, ed. S. Rose-Ackerman, Oxford University Press, New York, pp. 114–32.

Le Grand, J. & Bartlett, W. (eds) 1993, *Quasi-Markets and Social Policy*, Macmillan, London.

Lipsey, R. G. & Lancaster, K. 1957, 'The general theory of the second best', *Review of Economic Studies*, vol. 24, no. 1, pp. 11–32.

Lyons, M. 2001, *Third Sector: The Contribution of Nonprofit and Cooperative Enterprise in Australia*, Allen & Unwin, Sydney.

Maddala, G. S. & Miller, E. 1989, *Microeconomics : Theory and Applications*, McGraw-Hill, Singapore.

Mannion, R. & Smith, P. 1998, 'How providers are chosen in the mixed economy of community care', in *A Revolution in Social Policy: Quasi-*

Markets Reform in the 1990s, eds W. Bartlett, J. A. Roberts & J. Le Grand, Policy Press, Bristol, pp. 111–31.

Marceau, J. 1990, 'The dwarves of capitalism: The structure of production and the economic culture of the small manufacturing firm', in *Capitalism in Contracting Cultures,* eds G. Redding & S. Clegg, de Gruyter, Berlin.

Martin, J., Knopoff, K. & Beckman, C. 1998, 'An alternative to bureaucratic impersonality and emotional labour: Bounded emotionality at the Body Shop', *Administrative Science Quarterly,* vol. 43, no. 2, pp. 429–70.

Meagher, G. & Cortis, N. 2009, 'The political economy of for-profit paid care: Theory and evidence', in *Paid Care in Australia: Politics, Profits, Practices,* eds D. King & G. Meagher, Sydney University Press, Sydney.

Miles, I. 1995, *Services Innovation, Statistics and Conceptual Issues,* Group of National Experts on Science and Technology Indicators, OECD, Paris, DSTI/EAS/STP/NESTI, (95)23.

Miles, I. & Boden, M. 2000, 'Introduction: Are services special?' in *Services and the Knowledge-Based Economy,* eds M. Boden & I. Miles, Continuum, London and New York, pp. 1–20.

Perrett, J. 2005, 'Finding the people who'll look after us', *The Sydney Morning Herald,* 1 July.

Press, F. & Woodrow, C. 2005, 'Commodification, corporatisation, and children's spaces', *Australian Journal of Education,* vol. 49, no. 3, pp. 278–91.

Productivity Commission 2002a, *Australia's Service Sector: A Study in Diversity,* Productivity Commission Staff Research Paper.

Productivity Commission 2002b, *Independent Review of the Job Network: Inquiry Report,* Report No. 21, Productivity Commission, Canberra.

Propper, C. 1993, 'Quasi-markets, contracts and quality in health and social care: The US experience', in *Quasi-Markets and Social Policy,* eds J. Le Grand & W. Bartlett, Macmillan, London, pp. 35–67.

Robinson, J. 1933, *The Economics of Imperfect Competition,* Macmillan, London.

Rush, E. 2006, Child care quality in Australia, *Discussion Paper No 84,* The Australia Institute, Canberra, April.

Saunders, P. 1999, 'Changing work patterns and the community services workforce', *Australia's Welfare 1999: Services and Assistance*, Australian Institute of Health and Welfare, Canberra, pp. 38–87.

Smith, A. 1991 (1776), *The Wealth of Nations*, Everyman, London.

Smith, S. R. & Lipsky, M. 1993, *Non-profits for Hire*, Harvard University Press, Cambridge Mass.

Steering Committee for the Review of Government Service Provision 2006, *Report on Government Services 2006*, Productivity Commission, Canberra.

Taylor, M. & Hogget, P. 1994, 'Quasi-markets and the transformation of the independent sector', in *Quasi-Markets in the Welfare State*, eds W. Bartlett, C. Propper, W. Wilson & J. Le Grand, SAUS Publications, Bristol, pp. 184–206.

Triplett, J. E., & Bosworth, B. B. 2003, 'Productivity measurement issues in services industries: "Baumol's Disease" has been cured', *FRBNY Economic Policy Review*, vol. 9, no. 3, pp. 23–33.

Tucker, K. A. 1977, 'The nature and size of the service sector', in *The Economics of the Australian Service Sector*, ed. K. Tucker, Croom Helm, London, pp. 13–52.

Ungerson, C. & Yeandle, S. 2007, *Cash for Care in Developed Welfare States*, Palgrave Macmillan, Basingstoke.

Van Dyke, J. 2002, Submission to the Productivity Commission Independent Review of the Job Network, prepared for the Leichhardt Community Youth Association, April, [Online], Available: http://www.pc.gov.au/inquiry/jobnetwork/subs/subdr077.pdf [2005, October 25].

Wade, M. 2007, 'It costs a bundle to give a damn', *The Sydney Morning Herald*, 27 June.

Weisbrod, B. A. & Schlesinger, M. 1986, 'Public, private, nonprofit ownership and the response to asymmetric information: The case of nursing homes', in *The Economics of Nonprofit Institutions: Studies in Structure and Policy*, ed. S. Rose-Ackerman, Oxford University Press, New York, pp. 133–51.

Weisbrod, B. A. 2004, 'The pitfalls of profits', *Stanford Social Innovation Review*, vol. 2, no. 3, pp. 40–47.

Williamson, O. 1975, *Markets and Hierarchies*, The Free Press, New York.

Williamson, O. 1998, 'Transaction cost economics: How it works; where it is headed', *De Economist*, vol. 146, no. 1, pp. 23–58.

Williamson, O. 2000, 'The new institutional economics: Taking stock, looking ahead', *Journal of Economic Literature*, vol. 38, no. 3, pp. 595–613.

Zins, C. 2001, 'Defining human services', *Journal of Sociology and Social Welfare*, vol. 28, no. 1, pp. 3–21.

4

Outsourcing of elder care services in Sweden: effects on work environment and political legitimacy

Rolf Å Gustafsson and Marta Szebehely

In Sweden, as in other parts of the world, a number of market-inspired institutional and organisational changes in welfare services are taking place.[1] These developments are often summarised in the concept New Public Management (NPM), and involve shifts in both the way services and work are organised (praxis) and represented (discourse) (Hood 1998; Pollitt & Boucaert 2000). NPM has been compared to a 'shopping basket' in which the important ingredients are competition, contracts, freedom of choice and cost control (Pollitt 1995); and Swedish elder care[2] is definitely affected by these trends.

Debate about the impact of NPM in Swedish elder care has focused on quality and efficiency: do these policies improve the quality of care and contain costs? We seek to raise two other issues central to the provision of elder care as a welfare service: working conditions and democratic control. This approach highlights the perspectives of *careworkers* (both as employees and citizens) and the roles of *politicians* (both as public employers and decision-makers) in the evolution of elder care in Sweden.

Our approach is informed by a theoretical perspective that recognises differences in the goals and dynamics of public and private

---

1 This chapter presents findings previously discussed in Gustafsson and Szebehely (2007).
2 Editors' note: we have maintained the authors' use of the term 'elder care', rather than standardising usage to the typical Australian expression 'aged care'.

organisations. Public employers do not own their organisations. They operate on behalf of vote-holding citizens who collectively own the buildings and other assets used to provide services. In Sweden, many of those entitled to vote are also public employees in various types of welfare services. Welfare services personnel, then, participate in the election of their own employers. This means that the power of public employers is democratically delegated and, therefore, conditional. Private employers, by contrast, operate on behalf of shareholders within the framework of private ownership rights. Thus, private employers who obtain contracts to provide welfare services must serve two masters: on the one hand, they serve the politicians who steer their operations to meet social targets on behalf of citizens, and on the other, they serve their shareholders, for whom they are required to pursue financial profit.

The institutional history of the public sector as an employer is, no doubt, a marginal and rare topic in social and historical research in Sweden and elsewhere (Kolberg 1991; Gustafsson 2000). There has been, for instance, very limited interest in the fact that municipal and county council politicians are the employers of almost a quarter of the total Swedish labour force, among them the vast majority of the elder care personnel. This has probably contributed to the lack of theoretical perspectives that could further an analysis of differences in the socio-political roles of public and private employers.

Inspired by Michael Mann (2006, p. 59), we raise the issue of conceiving elder care as a part of the local state's infrastructural power and we examine perspectives that, to date, have not received much attention in either public discourse or research. Our research foci have evolved through the merging of three perspectives that are usually treated in theoretical and empirical isolation from each other. This article presents a broad empirical investigation into the outsourcing of publicly financed elder care services in Sweden. Specifically, we consider:

- how the careworkers in both private and public elder care in Sweden assess their *work environment;*

- how the careworkers in both private and public elder care experience the *influence of local politicians;*
- and whether, in turn, these two aspects have any connection with the careworkers' *opinions for or against continued outsourcing of elder care.*

The context of the study

Care of elderly people occupies a central position within the Swedish welfare model. In Sweden, unlike many countries of continental Europe, adult children have no legal obligation to provide care or financial support for their parents (Millar & Warman 1996). Formal responsibility lies with municipal governments, which have a statutory duty to meet the needs of elderly people. From an international perspective, Swedish (and in fact all Scandinavian) elder care is usually labelled 'universal' and is characterised by comprehensive, high quality services. The same services are directed towards, and used by, all social groups (Sipilä 1997; Anttonen 2002). Services are almost entirely publicly financed: about 85 per cent of the cost for elder care services is covered by municipal taxes, 10 per cent by national taxes (state grants) and only 5 per cent by user fees (National Board of Health and Welfare 2007a). Until recently services were also almost entirely publicly provided. During the postwar expansion of tax-financed elder care, the welfare state not only acted as the financer of welfare services, but also as employer of all the personnel.

A high degree of autonomy of the local vis-à-vis central government (including the right to levy taxes locally) is typical in Scandinavian municipalities. Within the limits prescribed by legislation, locally elected politicians set income tax rates and decide on budgets, and thus also decide on the priority given to elder care in relation to other services. More specifically, they also decide on local guidelines for the organisation of elder care work. Not surprisingly, there are large municipal differences in the coverage and organisation of elder care. Using a concept from Kröger (1997), it has been argued that when it comes to care of the elderly it is more appropriate to talk of many different 'welfare municipalities' than one uniform welfare state (Trydegård 2000).

Sweden is a big welfare spender (Organisation for Economic Co-operation and Development 2005), but in spite of the rising proportion of older people in the population, the amount of public funds allocated to elder care on a per capita basis has been falling. Public resources for elder care in relation to the proportion of persons in the population 80 years and older was 15 per cent lower in fixed prices in 2000 than it was in 1990 (SOU 2004:68, p. 147). Further, declining resources are targeted to the neediest, while those with less extensive care needs are increasingly left without public support. Between 1980 and 2006, the share of Swedish older persons (80 years or older) receiving publicly financed elder care has decreased from 62 to 37 per cent (Szebehely 2009).

New public management in Swedish elder care

In 1992, a new Local Government Act in Sweden increased the latitude of local politicians to explore the institutional and organisational changes typical of the NPM. The new Act allowed municipalities to enter contracts with private providers—even for-profit companies—which had earlier been explicitly forbidden by law. These 'alternative actors' are allowed to organise and run the publicly financed elder care services on their own terms, provided that content and costs stay within the framework of the locally established contracts and the law. The Local Government Act allows municipalities two possibilities when relinquishing responsibility for these services to private organisations. They can either outsource services to external providers after a process of competitive tendering, or develop a system of 'consumer choice' to allow elderly citizens to choose the organisation, public or private, from which they receive publicly subsidised services.

It should be noted that, in the 1990s, public discourse in Sweden on the future of the welfare state was markedly ideological, and came to be labelled 'the system shift debate'. This debate was particularly intense during the time the right-wing parties held government from 1991–94. The prevailing side in the debate criticised bureaucratic organisations as inflexible and authoritarian. Competition was supposed to bring about creative entrepreneurship and thus revitalise the field (Antman 1994; Gustafsson 1996; see also Vabø 2006).

Arguments for different purchaser-provider models—which were a central theme in a debate where only shifts of nuance could be observed between the Social Democratic and the right-wing positions—all included an appeal for individual choice in order to improve the quality of services. Under a choice model, 'consumers' would be able to vote with their feet, complementing their voices as citizens who choose elected representatives to the municipal councils. A subsidiary theme was the promise of an improved work environment for elder care personnel. In strained municipal economies, however, opening elderly care to competition increasingly led to demands for inproved productivity and cost effectiveness.

Since the introduction of the Local Government Act, the purchaser-provider model of outsourcing has been applied widely. In 1993, 10 per cent of Swedish municipalities used this model; by 2003, the share had grown to 82 per cent (National Board of Health and Welfare 2004a). Private employers' share of publicly financed elder care services has also increased steadily and almost continuously. According to the latest official statistics, in 2005 almost 15 per cent of all employees working with care of the elderly and the disabled had private employers: 11 per cent worked in for-profit establishments (mostly for large international companies) and 3.5 per cent worked in non-profit organisations (Szebehely & Trydegård 2007). This means a fourfold increase nationally since 1993, although inter-municipal variation is great. Some municipalities around Stockholm have more than half their elder care in private hands, compared to less than one per cent in around one-third of all Swedish municipalities (National Board of Health and Welfare 2007b).

The majority of privately run elder care is in the form of outsourcing although the number of municipalities that have introduced a consumer-choice model has increased from 10 in the year 2003 to 27 in 2006 (of a total of 290 municipalities in Sweden) (National Board of Health and Welfare 2007a).[3]

A common feature of organisational changes in Swedish welfare services during the 1990s has been the lack of follow-up and empirical research on the impact of changes on service and job quality (Palme et al. 2003). A review of the limited research shows, however, that there is probably little difference in the quality of care between the privately and publicly run establishments (National Board of Health and Welfare 2004b). Further, there are indications that opening elder care to competition has led to higher, rather than lower, municipal costs (National Board of Health and Welfare 2004b). When it comes to the working environment in elder care, research has not established whether privatisation has led to advantages or disadvantages for elder care personnel (this applies also to health care services in general, see further Blomqvist 2005; Gustafsson 2005). In the Nordic region generally, there is a lack of systematic research on the working conditions of elder care personnel under public versus private operation (Trydegård 2005).[4] One aim of this chapter is to contribute some empirical research on this question.

---

3 Since the re-election of a centre-right coalition in 2006, there is an increasing state-initiated push towards more consumer-choice models in Swedish elder care (Ministry of Health and Social Affairs 2007). So far, however, the Swedish municipalities still possess self-government in this matter, whereas a purchaser-provider split combined with a consumer-choice model in home-care services is mandatory, by legislation, in all Danish municipalities since 2003 (Vabø 2005).

4 There is extensive research on private forms of care in the international literature. The most wide-ranging overviews that we are aware of indicate a number of negative experiences of privately run or privately financed care; see further Rosenau and Linder (2003). However, this research is difficult to relate to Swedish conditions since labour legislation and social policies in Sweden differ in many ways from those in the countries where these studies have been conducted.

Social infrastructure and public employers

One central line of reasoning among Swedish advocates for purchaser-provider models during the 1990s was that new and possibly more efficient (private) providers should be invited to participate in competitive tendering. At the same time, the discretion and power of local politicians should be preserved, and even strengthened, in their new purchasing role. Inherent in this line of reasoning is the assumption that the relationship between employers and employees is similar in the public and in the private sectors (du Gay 2000). Yet history shows that politically appointed employers in the field of 'welfare production' answer to different constituencies and are responsible for different tasks, compared with private employers.

One important difference between private and public employers is that the latter often have more or less explicit mandates to change either the society they govern, or some individuals therein. This applies particularly to welfare services; examples are improvements in the levels of education, public health, democracy and social integration. Private employers, historically speaking, have not had such responsibilities (even if some have done so) and must be subjected to political regulation if this is to be the norm. If such regulation is implemented, it has to work alongside the priorities chosen by the shareholders, within the framework of market conditions.

Most welfare service work involves creating and maintaining relationships between at least four parties: employer, employee, the welfare service recipients, and their next of kin. Further, in practical terms, all these actors are also members of the same political community, which means that their civil and social rights are connected to their political rights as voting citizens. Thus welfare services are something more than, and different from, work and service in the established senses of the words. A service provided under the Schools Act in Sweden is not only aimed at ensuring an economically efficient transfer of knowledge from teachers to pupils under the control of an employer, but also at creating a democratic mindset in future citizens. In elder care services, ageing Muslims, Mosaics, Lutherans or atheists, whether rich or poor, are to meet frailty, dependency and finally death with equal dignity.

Achieving these goals requires a complex interaction in the social network around the employer (the local politician), the employee (the teacher, the caregiver) and the citizen (the pupil, the parents, the elderly). This unique characteristic of welfare work makes particular demands on the public employer. Welfare services have a moral, political and cultural content, and can thus be conceptualised as the *social infrastructure* of a society. Many of the intangible benefits created by welfare services have effects that transcend time and space. Some of the children in publicly funded child care will perhaps, in 30 or 40 years, be candidates for the post of UN Secretary-General; others will perhaps be international criminals. If the 50-year-olds of today begin to worry about what will happen to elder care services in 25–30 years (or to their parents' elder care today), their own work and consumption patterns, as well as gender relations, will be affected.

All this means that the public employer faces a problem of democratic legitimacy private employers do not. This becomes clear when we distinguish between the external and internal legitimacy of welfare systems. The *external* legitimacy of welfare systems— that is, the strength of political support among the citizens and taxpayers—has been the object of considerable empirical research in Sweden (Svallfors 2003). Compared with citizens of other countries, Swedes tend to favour the public financing of welfare systems and to accept high taxes. The *internal* legitimacy of the welfare system refers to corresponding issues in the inner life of the welfare-service producing organisations. The internal legitimacy of welfare policy builds on—or is undermined by—the views and perspectives of welfare services personnel on the political control of their own working conditions. In light of the ongoing outsourcing movement, we ought to differentiate between *direct* internal legitimacy issues (concerning the majority of elder care provision that is still run by public employers), and the *indirect* internal legitimacy that is at stake when private providers are contracted. This has seldom been discussed, and applies not only to financing, but also to organisational matters. Who makes decisions for whom? How are the rewards and burdens of the work distributed? How do careworkers experience the influence of local politicians? These are the questions we address in our empirical study.

Working in Swedish elder care: a case study

In this section, we present a case study that aims to deepen understanding of the recent changes in the organisation and political regulation of Swedish elder care. The empirical base is a mail questionnaire carried out in the autumn of 2003, which surveyed all categories of care personnel and local politicians in eight Swedish municipalities. We received just over 5,800 responses to questions about working conditions, internal organisational relationships, and views of elder care. The response rate was 66 per cent among careworkers and 72 per cent among politicians (for further information, see Gustafsson & Szebehely 2005). In this chapter, we analyse only the answers from the largest group of personnel, those involved in elder care services (n=3,522). This group includes skilled and unskilled careworkers in home-based and residential elder care. We refer to these personnel throughout as *careworkers*.

The choice of eight municipalities was mainly dictated by our ambition to include both those municipalities where all elder care was still in public hands, and those with a relatively large share of outsourced elder care (none, however, had adopted a consumer-choice model). Of the careworkers in our study, 14 per cent had private employers; the share varied from 0 per cent in four municipalities to between 10 and 50 per cent in the other four municipalities. Almost the entire group of the privately employed careworkers worked in for-profit companies; only a few were employed by non-profit organisations. The eight municipalities in the study are, taken together, representative of elder care services in Sweden in terms of the occupational distribution, forms of employment, part-time/full-time, age and gender (see Gustafsson & Szebehely 2005).

In what follows, we compare the views of publicly and privately employed careworkers on their work environments, the role of local politicians, and the outsourcing of elder care.

Private and public employment and the psychosocial work environment

Previous studies of elder care have shown that, generally, the work environment has deteriorated since outsourcing was introduced. Above all, the workload has grown (Bäckman 2001; Gustafsson & Szebehely 2005). However, these studies do not allow us to ascertain the extent to which deteriorating working conditions are caused by outsourcing alone, or by simultaneous cutbacks in financing and other (possible) interacting factors. In contrast, our survey allows us to analyse possible differences between the work experiences of publicly employed careworkers and the experiences of privately employed (outsourced) careworkers, in tax-financed Swedish elder care today.

Earlier research has found that elder careworkers experience their work as meaningful and rewarding, but also as physically and mentally demanding. Given the complexity of the work, it is important to capture both positive and negative dimensions of the work environment. We designed questionnaire items to assess:

1) *Relations with management* ('Do you have a good working relationship with your supervisor(s)?');
2) *Control* ('Can you affect your working conditions so that, for example, you can work at your own pace?');

3) *Job content* ('Are your work tasks varied enough?' and 'Do you find your work interesting and stimulating?');

4) *Workload* ('Do you feel you have too much to do at work?');

5) *Relations with care recipients* ('Do you feel inadequate because the care recipients do not get the help they need?').[5]

All these dimensions seem to be important for health and wellbeing according to previous research on the work environment in general and in elder care in particular (Dellve 2003).

Along with these indicators of the careworkers' evaluations of their work environment, we were also interested in their experiences of physical and mental fatigue. These feelings are clearly related to the work environment, even if exhaustion may have causes other than working conditions. Questions were formulated as follows: 'Do you feel mentally exhausted after your working day?' and 'Do you feel physically exhausted after your working day?'[6]

It is obvious from our own research and from other studies that the work environments in residential and home-based care services are rather different. The two care settings differ in terms of workload and relations with both supervisors and care recipients. In most respects, work in residential care is more arduous than work in home-based care (Gustafsson & Szebehely 2005; Trydegård 2005). To take these differences into account, therefore, we analyse the two care settings separately.[7]

Table 4.1 shows the percentages of publicly and privately employed careworkers in the two care settings who answered 'Yes, most often' to each of the eight indicators. The data show that there are only

---

5 Each item has four response alternatives: 'Yes, most often'; 'Yes, sometimes'; 'No, seldom'; and 'No, never'.

6 The response categories for both questions on fatigue were: 'Yes, most often'; 'Yes, quite often'; 'Yes, sometimes'; 'No, seldom'; and 'No, almost never'.

7 Residential care in this context includes both traditional institutions such as nursing homes and old people's homes, and different forms of sheltered accommodation.

Table 4.1: Careworkers' assessment of their work environment and experience of fatigue[8]

	Residential care		Home-based care	
Shares answering 'Yes, most often' (%)	Publicly run (n≥2142)	Privately run (n≥362)	Publicly run (n≥860)	Privately run (n≥101)
Can affect working conditions, e.g. pace of work	31.7	31.9	26.5	25.7
Have good contact with supervisors	50.1	60.1 ***	54.9	43.6 *
Find work sufficiently varied	36.8	36.9	46.4	43.6
Find work interesting and stimulating	52.4	57.0	60.3	50.5
Have too much to do	37.0	39.8	29.5	26.7
Feel inadequate because recipients do not get the help they need	33.1	26.5 *	23.8	26.7
Physically exhausted after a working day	29.4	27.2	20.6	26.5
Mentally exhausted after a working day	17.8	14.7	10.6	18.6 *

* $p<0.05$; *** $p<0.001$

minor differences between the perceptions of publicly and privately

---

[8] Note that a higher percentage in the four questions above the dotted line in Table 4.1 indicates a better work environment, while a higher percentage in the four questions below the line indicates that the work environment is worse.

employed careworkers on most dimensions of their working conditions. We also see that the few statistically significant differences between public and private employment in residential care and home-based care point in opposite directions. In some respects the work environment is perceived to be slightly better among privately employed careworkers in residential care (compared to careworkers in publicly run residential care). In home-based care, by contrast, publicly employed careworkers find their work environment to be slightly better in some respects, compared with careworkers in privately run home-based care.

To check whether the pattern found is related to the form of operation (public vs. private employment), or to possible differences in the composition of the care workforce in the two settings, we used multivariate analysis (logistic regression). In that analysis, we controlled for differences between the privately and the publicly employed careworkers in five respects: age, gender, part-time/full-time, length of employment, and locality (that is, the municipality where the careworker is working), see Appendix. This analysis shows that when we take into account variations in age, gender, work time, length of employment and locality, there remain even fewer differences between the privately and the publicly employed careworkers' evaluations of their work environment. The public employees working in residential elder care run a 41 per cent higher 'risk' (odds) of feeling inadequate in relation to the needs of the care receivers. In home-based care, on the other hand, the public employees have almost twice the 'chance' (odds) of having good relations with their supervisors.

Our results suggest, then, that outsourcing has had different consequences for careworkers in home-based and residential care services. At the same time, it is important to note that differences between public and private employees' experiences turn out to be small (and often less than the differences between home-based and residential care, see Table 4.1). We find only marginal differences on such important work environment issues as workload, control over working conditions, and how varied the work is. To sum up, the results indicate that there are no systematic or substantial differences between publicly and privately employed careworkers' evaluations of their work environments that can be linked to the form of operations (public or private).

However, there are differences between the *municipalities* in the study. These are far greater than any differences between public and private employment. A clear—if simplified—conclusion, therefore, is that careworkers looking to improve their lot would be better served by seeking employment in the right municipality than by considering the pros and cons of publicly versus privately run elder care.

Perceptions of local politicians in purchaser-provider systems

A fundamental and explicit idea behind the outsourcing of care services in Sweden is that politicians should have less to say about the details of how things should be run, in order to be free to concentrate on overall policy, prioritise resources, and focus on their role as consumers' advocates (Montin & Elander 1995). With the introduction of purchaser-provider models in elder care, local politicians' direct control over private employees' work environment has been deliberately reduced (Gustafsson & Szebehely 2002). The question now is how the careworkers view this reduced political control.

Figure 4.1 shows the careworkers' responses to the question 'how do you assess your local politicians' influence on the organisation and working environment in elder care?' A clear pattern emerges: within *publicly managed* elder care the dominant response is that politicians have substantial influence over working conditions (53 per cent compared with 30 per cent of the privately employed). A reasonable interpretation is that this is a reflection of the true nature of things, namely that local politicians, having relinquished

Figure 4.1: Careworkers' assessment of local politicians' influence on organisation/work environment in elder care[9]

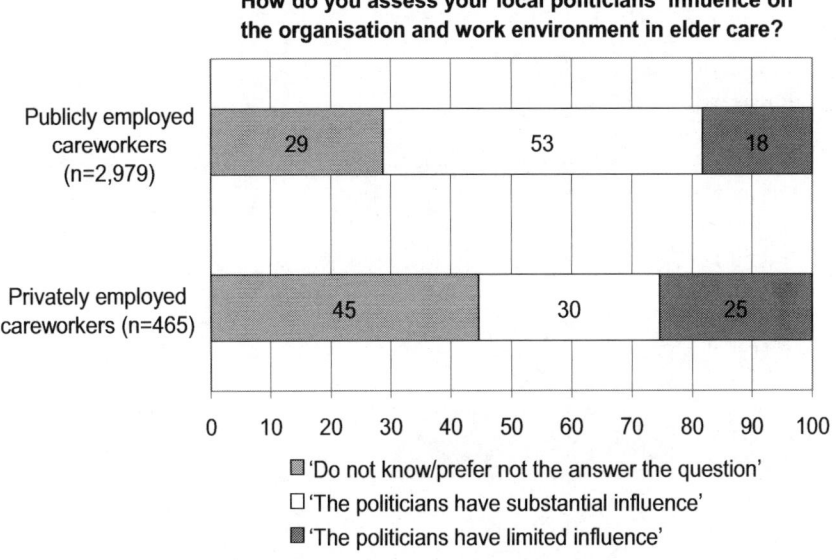

control of services to private companies, no longer have employer responsibility for those privately employed. The figure also shows that the most common response among the *privately employed* is 'do not know/prefer not to answer the question'. The significantly higher share of uncertainty among the privately employed (45 per

---

9 A χ^2 test shows the difference to be significant: p=0.000. Concerning the issues discussed in Figure 4.1 and the rest of the article, there were only marginal differences found between home-based careworkers and those working with residential care. We do not, therefore, make any separation in the following. We have consistently conducted analyses (multinominal logistic regressions) where we have controlled for differences between public and private employees regarding age, gender, work time, length of employment, locality and home-based or residential workplace. The difference between public and private employees in their assessment of local politicians' influence over work environment/organisation in Figure 4.1 is statistically significant (p=0.000) even after controlling for these factors.

Figure 4.2: Careworkers' assessment of local politicians' influence on economic and quality issues in elder care[10]

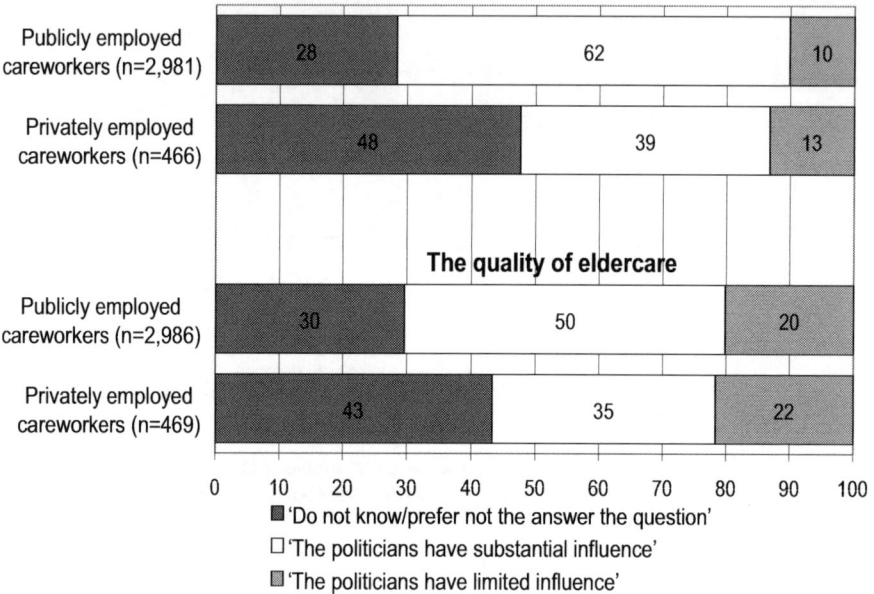

cent compared with 29 per cent among public employees) can be interpreted to mean that private employees experience the role of local politicians as more diffuse and the relations as more 'distant'. This interpretation is supported by the response pattern shown in Figure 4.2.

Figure 4.2 shows careworkers' responses to the questions 'how do you assess your local politicians' influence on the utilisation of the municipality's economic resources' and on 'the quality of elder care'.

---

10 A χ^2 test shows the difference to be significant: p=0.000. Multinominal logistic regression (see note 9) shows that the difference between public and private employees' opinions of local politicians' influence over economic resources (p=0.028) and elder care quality (p=0.003) is statistically significant.

We can see that a significantly larger share of the private employees (compared with public employees) is uncertain even in the matter of local politicians' influence over the economy and quality of elder care.

We can also see that private employees are much less inclined to attribute any degree of influence to local politicians.[11] This pattern applies even to areas where—according to the advocates of purchaser-provider models—outsourcing is not intended to reduce political influence. All in all, this suggests that careworkers' relations with local politicians tend to be experienced as more diffuse when mediated by a private entrepreneur, as is the case with outsourced elder care.

Who wants more outsourced elder care?

One important factor for the future development of elder care that has been largely ignored in research and public debate is careworkers' opinions for or against a market orientation in elder care. Our study has been able to ascertain that local politicians and senior civil servants have much more positive views towards outsourcing than the average careworker (Gustafsson & Szebehely 2002; 2005). In the following, we analyse opinions for and against outsourcing of elder care services in relation to the careworkers' assessments of their own work environments and in relation to their estimations of the local politicians' influence over the work environment. We begin with an overall description of the state of opinion.

Our point of departure is the following question in the survey: 'The

---

11 It is important to note that it is only in their relation to politicians that the 'don't know' response is higher among the privately than the publicly employed. While 51 per cent of public employees and 64 per cent of private employees stated they did not know whether their work was appreciated by local politicians, on the questions of whether they felt appreciated by supervisors and by workmates, the percentage of 'don't know' responses did not vary with public vs. private employment—6 per cent and 7 per cent respectively (supervisors) and 3 per cent and 4 per cent (workmates). The percentages were also significantly less. Therefore, this is not about a general tendency towards more uncertain responses among the privately employed.

following proposals have appeared in the political debate. What is your opinion of each proposal?' Here we analyse the proposal: 'More elder care should be run under private management'.[12] Of the *publicly employed* careworkers, 21 per cent considered this to be a very good or good idea, 52 per cent that it was a bad or very bad idea, while 28 per cent were neither for nor against. Thus among the public employees there were significantly more who were negative than positive towards expanding privately run elder care. Their balance of opinion can thus be stated as –31 (the percentage of those positive minus the percentage of those against). Of the privately employed careworkers, 38 per cent pronounced this a very good or good idea, 33 per cent a bad or very bad idea, while 30 per cent were neither for nor against, giving a balance of opinion of +5. In summary, the dominant attitude among the public employees was clearly sceptical, while among the private employees there was a weak tendency towards support for the proposal.

We shall now consider a possible connection between careworkers' opinions about market orientation and their assessments of the extent of political influence over the work environment (that is, the item that produced the response pattern shown in Figure 4.1). Figure 4.3 clearly shows that the dominant attitude to further outsourcing is negative among public employees, irrespective of how they assess local politicians' influence over their work environment (balance of opinion between –37 and –24), while the privately employed have a neutral to slightly positive balance of opinion (between –2 and +10).[13]

---

12 Response alternatives were as follows: 'A very good idea'; 'A good idea'; 'Neither good nor bad'; 'A bad idea' and 'A very bad idea'.

13 Bivariate analysis (χ^2) shows that the difference in attitudes to further outsourcing between groups with different views of politicians' influence is significant (p=0.000) among the publicly employed but not among the privately employed. Separate multinominal logistic regressions for both public and private employees (controlled for the variables listed in note 9) show the pattern to be constant: among private employees there is no statistically significant correlation between view of politicians' influence and view of market orientation, while the correlation is significant among public employees (p=0.000).

Figure 4.3: Attitudes to further outsourcing of elder care (balance of opinion) among careworkers with different assessments of local politicians' influence over work environment and the organisation of elder care

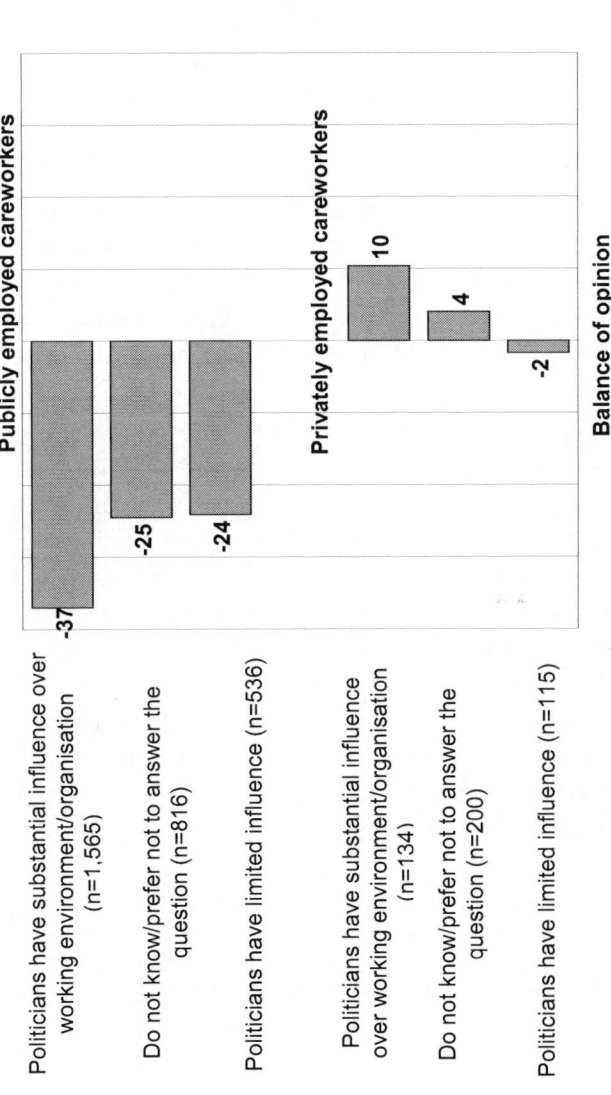

Among the *public employees*, however, we also see that the most negative attitudes are held by those who judge the local politicians to have a considerable influence over their work environment (balance of opinion –37). According to Figure 4.3, even *private employees* have different attitudes to further outsourcing depending on their views of political influence over the work environment. These differences— which point in the opposite direction—are not, however, statistically significant.

These findings indicate that the perception of the local politicians' role is of differing importance for publicly and privately employed careworkers' views on outsourcing. We draw the conclusion that for public employees, there is a connection between scepticism towards outsourcing and perceived political influence over the work environment, while this connection does not exist among the private employees.

How important, then, are evaluations of the work environment for attitudes to market orientation? Figure 4.4a depicts a predominantly negative attitude to market orientation among the *public employees*, irrespective of their views on their own work environment (balance of opinion from –26 to –36).[14] It also shows that differences in the balance of opinion are small between those who gave a positive evaluation (lighter bars) compared to those who gave a negative evaluation (darker bars) of their work environment. There is only *one* statistically significant correlation between work environment and balance of opinion on outsourcing: public employees who most often have good contact with their supervisors are more negative towards outsourcing (balance

---

14 This note refers to both figures 4.4a and 4.4b. χ^2 test: ** $p<0.01$; * $p<0.05$. Multivariate analysis (see note 9) shows that among the public employees *no* work environment indicators have any statistically significant correlations with view of outsourcing when controlled for differences in group make-up with regard to age, gender, locality, et cetera, while among the private employees the three correlations between own work environment and view of outsourcing that are significant in Figure 4.4b remain; ($p=0.005$, $p=0.016$ and $p=0.001$ respectively).

Figure 4.4a: Attitudes to outsourcing of elder care (balance of opinion) among public careworkers by evaluation of work environment, per cent

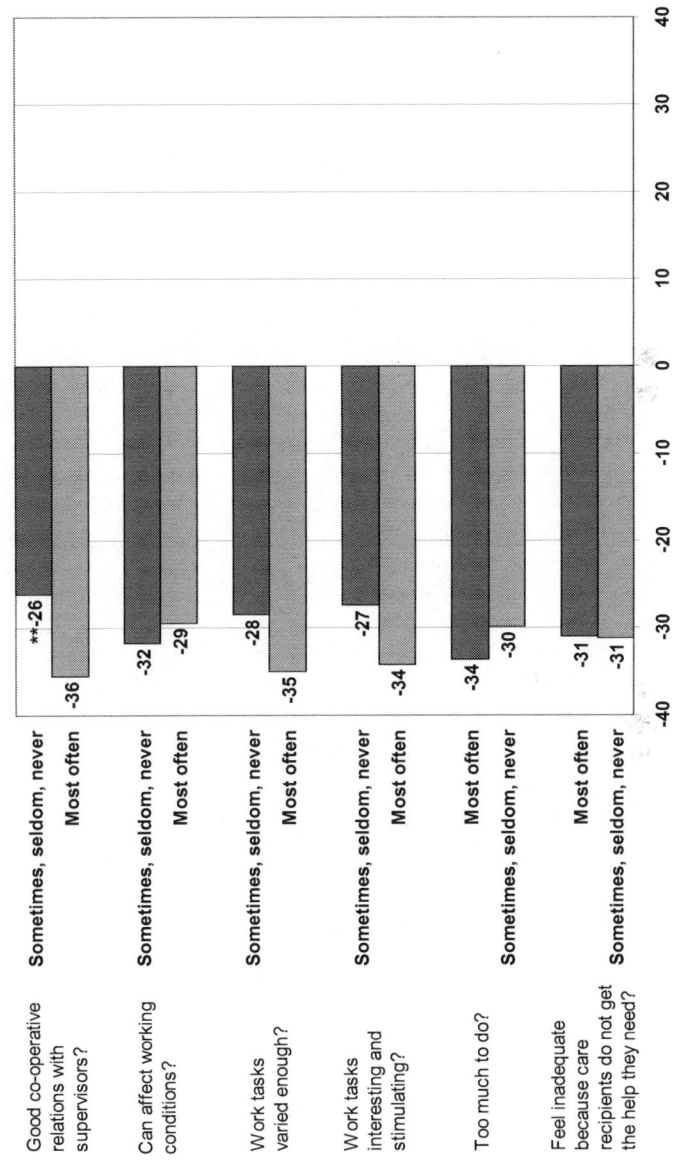

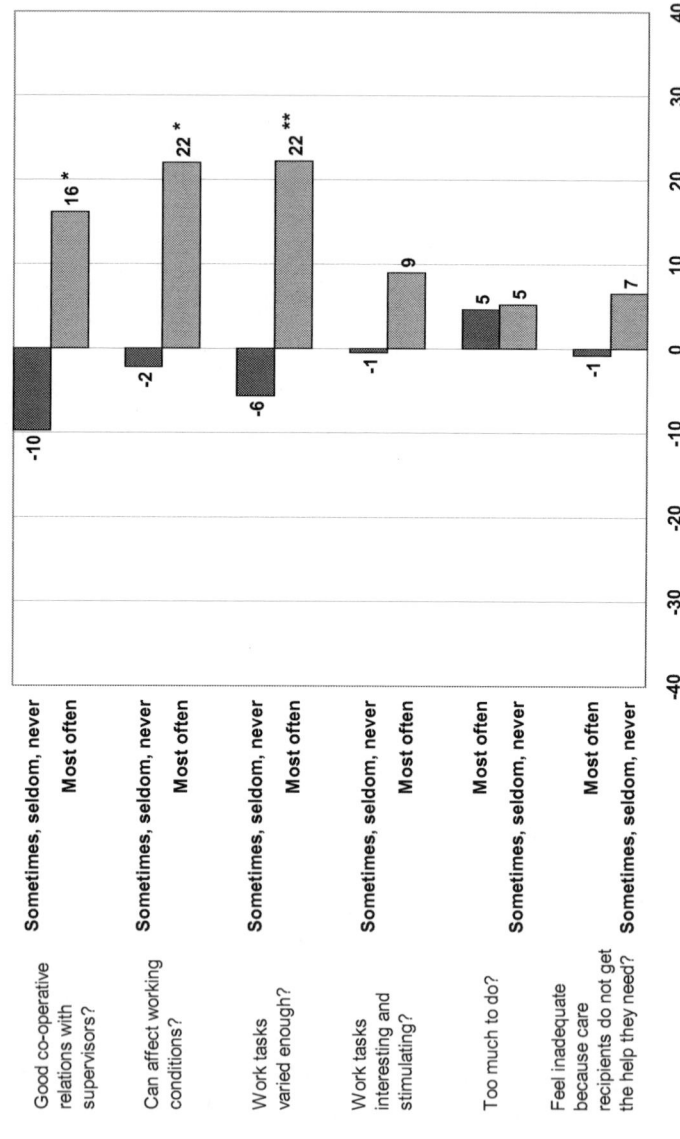

Figure 4.4b: Attitudes to outsourcing of elder care (balance of opinion) among private careworkers by evaluation of work environment, per cent

of opinion −36) than those who 'sometimes', 'seldom' or 'never' experience good relations (balance of opinion −26). However, when controlled for other differences between the groups, this correlation is *not* significant (see note 14). There are, then, no statistically significant correlations between public employees' evaluations of their work environments and their attitudes to outsourcing. To stress the point, one can say that publicly employed careworkers tend to be sceptical of the market approach, even when they report a bad work environment in their own non-outsourced elder care. Later we discuss how this somewhat surprising result can be interpreted.

Figure 4.4b shows that there are greater differences in the balance of opinion towards outsourcing between the *private employees* who consider themselves to have a 'good' work environment and those who report a 'bad' work environment. The most positive towards market orientation are those who 'most often' can affect their own working conditions (balance of opinion +22), who experience the work as varied (balance of opinion +22) and who experience their relations with supervisors as good (balance of opinion +16). The most negative (balance of opinion −2 to −10) are those who responded 'sometimes', 'seldom', or 'never' to these three work environment questions. The difference in response pattern between the private employees with 'good' and 'bad' work environment respectively is statistically significant, and remains so even when controlled for other differences in group make-up (see note 14). Other work environment indicators have no correlation with the view of market orientation, however.

Is there an underlying logic that explains these response patterns? At first sight, it might seem natural to point to the work environment itself. Even if there are no clear, large or systematic differences between privately and publicly run elder care in how careworkers overall evaluate their work environments, there are workplaces with 'good' or 'bad' work environments within both forms of operation.

An anomaly in the results is that the public employees seem to apply a different logic from that of private employees, since public employees make no specific connections between their own work environments and the outsourcing of elder care. Among the private employees, by contrast, there is such a connection; a good work environment is coupled with a positive view on outsourcing, while those with less satisfactory work environments tend to have negative views. Both the private and the public employees' response patterns become comprehensible, however, if the ongoing outsourcing trend is seen as a process affecting careworkers' *relations to local politicians.*

Within publicly managed elder care we have established a strong negative balance of opinion against outsourcing, especially among those careworkers who estimate that the politicians have an extensive influence over the work environment (Figure 4.3). Since these careworkers' assessments of their own work environments have little impact on their views of market orientation in the publicly run elder care, it seems reasonable to conclude that few publicly employed careworkers see outsourcing as a way to improve their work environments; not even among those with negative work environment experiences do we find a positive balance of opinion for outsourcing (Figure 4.4a). Our tentative conclusion, therefore, is that publicly employed careworkers see local politicians' influence over their work environment as—at least partly—a positive force, or in any case as a protective factor.

On the other hand, within outsourced elder care—that is, in a context where careworkers estimate that political influence over the work environment is limited—we have established several connections between assessment of the work environment and attitude to outsourcing. Our interpretation here is that private employees who have a positive evaluation of their own work environment attribute this, at least partly, to outsourcing.

Summary and conclusions

In this article we have attempted to give a broad empirical analysis of the experience of, and attitudes to, outsourcing of elder care in Sweden among careworkers. The main results—which build on more than 3,500 careworkers' questionnaire responses in eight Swedish municipalities in 2003—can be summarised as follows.

Work environment

When we isolated the differences in the work environment that could be directly connected to the form of operation (that is, public or private), only a few statistically significant correlations could be established. We have not found any systematic, unequivocal, or large differences between public and private employees' evaluations of their work environments. All in all, the results must be interpreted to mean that the 'public-private management' variable cannot be coupled with work environment as a decisive factor.

Variations between municipalities play a far more important role in this connection. Exactly what, in turn, determines these municipal differences we have not been able to establish, but we surmise that local variation is shaped by the interplay of contextual factors such as personnel policy, the level and allocation of economic resources for elder care, and the way competitive tendering is handled. Different municipalities and companies operate under different conditions and policies. Thus, to estimate the specific and probably minor importance of forms of operation for the work environment, further research is needed, mainly in the form of case studies. Further studies are also needed to ascertain whether outsourcing has different effects on the work environment in home-based and residential care, respectively. This is also true of other possible 'outcome variables' that have emerged in the Swedish debate, not least the quality of elder care and its cost effectiveness.

Political control

Our study directs attention to previously unresearched differences between private and public elder care employees in terms of their perceptions of local political control. For private employees, the local politicians' role appears substantially more diffuse and of less importance than for public employees. In this area, it turns out, there are systematic and large differences that can be linked to the public-private employment variable: private employees are far less inclined than public employees to attribute a significant degree of influence to local politicians over the organisation/work environment, the quality of care and even the use of taxpayers' economic resources.

Opinions for and against outsourcing

Most public employees have negative attitudes towards outsourcing (irrespective of how they assess their own work environment), while the private employees are in general more positive towards continued outsourcing (especially if they perceive their own work environment in positive terms).

Since we have established that outsourcing has no clear 'winners' or 'losers' on the aggregate level, we suggest that opinion for or against outsourcing is conditioned by different perceptions of the role of the local politicians. Private employees who, by their own evaluation, have a relatively good work environment—those who may consider themselves 'the work environment winners of outsourcing'—see no danger in 'freeing' their work environment from local political influence. And vice versa: those publicly employed careworkers who can be considered 'the work environment losers of public management', and who generally appear to be more interested in local politics than the private employees, seem to be hanging on to a hope that the local politicians will come to take more responsibility for work environments.

The private elder care employees' response pattern might be interpreted as an expression of a more individualistic stance, where one's own work environment experiences laid the ground for opinion on outsourcing. The public employees, on the other hand, can be seen as more publicly or collectively oriented. Public elder care employees are usually more negative towards outsourcing—and more knowledgeable about and positive towards political influence over the work environment—even when they assess their own work environment as unsatisfactory.

Considered together, our results indicate that outsourcing is a process that severely weakens careworkers' relations to local politicians, which in turn colours their general attitude to political control, rather than a process that improves quality of care, reduces costs or, for that matter, changes working conditions for the better or for the worse. In our interpretation the outsourcing trend signifies a crucial change concerning the internal legitimacy of the political steering of the elder care services. Outsourcing is connected to a diminishing visibility of, interest in, and possibly belief in the positive role of local government among privately employed careworkers, especially those who happen to be 'work-environment winners'. This more diffuse view on political influence through locally elected representatives applies, somewhat surprisingly, even to matters that are formally kept under political influence in outsourced elder care, that is, 'the utilisation of the municipality's economic resources for elder care' and the local politician's influence on 'the quality of elder care'.

Internal legitimacy and social infrastructure

Our article should be seen as an empirically based attempt to expand welfare policy analysis: elder care personnel and managements do not only produce help for the elderly. Elder care is also a part of society's social infrastructure. Opinions and attitudes of relevance for the long-run democratic development of society are created in the interaction between politics, management and care work.

If the tendencies we have demonstrated among the private elder care employees in our study were to become a general trend in Swedish elder care—and we can see no reason why this should not be the case in the wake of a continued expansion of outsourcing—this may erode the legitimacy of the welfare state as a part of the social infrastructure of a political democracy. Local politicians who pursue a market policy—because they believe in competition, because they hope to reduce costs, because they wish to promote individual choice, or because they believe and hope that the quality of care and possibly the work environment will improve—risk undermining careworkers' belief in a positive role of politics and its accountability.

References

Antman, P. 1994, 'Vägen till systemskiftet—den offentliga sektorn i politiken 1970–1992' [The road to the system shift: the public sector in politics 1970–1992] in *Köp och sälj, var god och svälj? Vårdens nya ekonomistyrningssystem i ett arbetsmiljöperspektiv [A Work Environment Perspective on New Economic Management in Care Services]*, ed. R. Å. Gustafsson. Arbetsmiljöfonden, Stockholm, pp. 19–66.

Anttonen, A. 2002, 'Universalism and social policy: A Nordic-feminist revaluation', *NORA: Nordic Journal of Women's Studies*, vol. 10, no. 2, pp. 71–80.

Blomqvist, P. 2005, 'Privatisering av sjukvård: politisk lösning eller komplikation?' [Privatisation of health care: A political solution or complication?] *Socialvetenskaplig Tidskrift*, no. 2–3, pp. 169–89.

Bäckman, O. 2001, 'Med välfärdsstaten som arbetsgivare' [The welfare state as employer], in *Välfärdstjänster i omvandling [Welfare Services in Transition]*, ed. M. Szebehely, SOU 2001:52, Research Volume, Government Report, The Welfare Commission, Stockholm, pp. 189–238.

Dellve, L. 2003, Explaining Occupational Disorders and Work Ability among Home Care Workers (PhD thesis), The Sahlgrenska Academy, Göteborg University.

du Gay, P. 2000, *In Praise of Bureaucracy*, Sage, London.

Gustafsson, R. Å. 1996, 'Freedom of choice and competition in the public sector—A conceptual analysis', in *Health Care in Europe: Competition or*

Solidarity? eds S. Iliffe & H.U. Deppe, Verlag für Akademische Schriften, Frankfurt-Bockenheim.

Gustafsson, R. Å. 2000, *Välfärdstjänstearbetet: Dragkampen mellan offentligt och privat i ett historie-sociologiskt perspektiv.* [*Welfare Work: Struggles for Public and Private from the Perspective of Historical Sociology*], Daidalos, Göteborg.

Gustafsson, R. Å. 2005, 'The welfare of the welfare services', in *Worklife and Health in Sweden 2004*, eds R. Å. Gustafsson & I. Lundberg, National Institute for Working Life, Stockholm.

Gustafsson, R. Å. & Szebehely, M. 2002, 'Skilda perspektiv på politikerrollen inom äldreomsorgen—om beställar-utförarmodeller i praktiken' [Differing perspectives on the role of politicians in elder care: the purchaser-provider split in practice], *Tidskrift for Velferdsforskning*, vol. 5, no. 2, pp. 68–84.

Gustafsson, R. Å. & Szebehely, M. 2005, Arbetsvillkor och styrning i äldreomsorgens hierarki—en enkätstudie bland personal och politiker [Working Conditions and Steering in the Hierarchy of Elder Care. A Survey Study among Employees and Politicians], Department of Social Work, Stockholm University.

Gustafsson, R. Å. & Szebehely, M. 2007, 'Privat och offentlig äldreomsorg—svenska omsorgsarbetares syn på arbetsmiljö och politisk styrning' [Private and public elder care: Swedish careworkers' opinions on their work environment and local government], *Socialvetenskaplig Tidskrift*, vol. 14, no. 1, pp. 47–66.

Hood, C. 1998, *The Art of the State—Culture, Rhetoric and Public Management*, Oxford University Press, Oxford.

Kolberg, J. E. (ed.) 1991, *The Welfare State as Employer*, Sharpe, Armonk, N.Y.

Kröger, T. 1997, 'The dilemma of municipalities: Scandinavian approaches to child day-care provision', *Journal of Social Policy*, vol. 26, no. 4, pp. 485–508.

Mann, M. 2006 [1993], *The Sources of Social Power. The Rise of Classes and Nation-States 1760–1914*, Cambridge University Press, Cambridge.

Millar, J. & Warman, A. 1996, *Family Obligations in Europe*, Family Policy Studies Centre, London.

Ministry of Health and Social Affairs 2007, 'Care of the Elderly in Sweden', Fact Sheet, September, Government Offices of Sweden.

Montin, S. & Elander, I. 1995, 'Citizenship, consumerism and local government in Sweden', *Scandinavian Political Studies*, vol. 18, no. 1, pp. 25–51.

National Board of Health and Welfare 2004a, *Konkurrensutsättningen inom äldreomsorgen*. [*Competitive Tendering in Care of the Elderly*], National Board of Health and Welfare (Socialstyrelsen), Stockholm.

National Board of Health and Welfare 2004b, *Konkurrensutsättning och entreprenader inom äldreomsorgen. Utvecklingsläget 2003* [*Competitive Tendering and Outsourcing in Care of the Elderly. Report of the Situtation 2003*], National Board of Health and Welfare (Socialstyrelsen), Stockholm.

National Board of Health and Welfare 2007a, *Current Developments in Care of the Elderly in Sweden*, National Board of Health and Welfare (Socialstyrelsen), Stockholm.

National Board of Health and Welfare 2007b, *Lika olika socialtjänst? Kommunala skillnader i prioritering, kostnader och verksamhet* [*Similar or Different Social Services? Municipal Differences in Priorities, Expenditure and Services*], National Board of Health and Welfare (Socialstyrelsen), Stockholm.

Organisation for Economic Co-operation and Development 2005, *Long Term Care for Older People*, Organisation for Economic Co-operation and Development, Paris.

Palme, J., Bergmark, Å., Bäckman, O., Estrada, F., Fritzell, J., Lundberg, O., Sjöberg, O., Sommestad, L. & Szebehely, M. 2003, 'A welfare balance sheet for the 1990s. Final report of the Swedish Welfare Commission', *Scandinavian Journal of Public Health*, Supplement 60, pp. 7–143.

Pollitt, C. 1995, 'Justification by works or by faith: Evaluating New Public Management', *Evaluation*, vol. 1, no. 2, pp. 133–54.

Pollitt, C. & Boucaert, G. 2000, *Public Management Reform—A Comparative Analysis*, Oxford University Press, Oxford.

Rosenau, P. & Linder, S. H. 2003, 'Two decades of research comparing for-profit and non-profit health provider performance in the United States', *Social Science Quarterly*, vol. 84, no. 2, pp. 219–41.

Sipilä, J. (ed.) 1997, *Social Care Services: The Key to the Scandinavian Welfare Model*, Avebury, Aldershot.

SOU, 2004:68 *Sammanhållen hemvård* [Integrated home care], Government Report, Stockholm.

Svallfors, S. 2003, 'Welfare regimes and welfare opinions: a comparison of eight Western countries', *Social Indicators Research*, vol. 64, no. 3, pp. 495–520.

Szebehely, M. 2009, 'Are there lessons to learn from Sweden?', in *A Place to Call Home: Long-term Care in Canada*, eds P. Armstrong, M. Boscoe, B. Clow, K. Grant, M. Haworth-Brockman, B. Jackson, A. Pederson, M. Seeley & J. Springer, Fernwood Books, Toronto.

Szebehely, M. & Trydegård, G.-B. 2007, 'Omsorgstjänster för äldre och funktionshindrade: skilda villkor, skilda trender?' [Services for elderly and for disabled persons: different trends, different conditions?], *Socialvetenskaplig Tidskrift*, vol. 14, nos. 2–3, 197–219.

Trydegård, G.-B. 2000, Tradition, Change and Variation. Past and Present Trends in Public Old Age Care (PhD Thesis). Department of Social Work, Stockholm University.

Trydegård, G.-B. 2005, 'Äldreomsorgspersonalens arbetsvillkor i Norden—en forskningsöversikt' [The working conditions of elder care staff in the Nordic countries: A research overview], in *Äldreomsorgsforskning i Norden. En kunskapsöversikt* [*Nordic Elder Care Research. An Overview*], ed. M. Szebehely, Nordic Council of Ministers, Copenhagen, pp. 143–95.

Vabø, M. 2005, 'New Public Management i nordisk eldreomsorg—hva forskes det på?' [New Public Management in Nordic elder care: what do researchers focus on?] in *Äldreomsorgsforskning i Norden. En kunskapsöversikt* [*Nordic Elder Care Research. An Overview*], ed. M. Szebehely, Nordic Council of Ministers, Copenhagen, pp. 73–111.

Vabø, M. 2006, 'Caring for people or caring for proxy consumers?' *European Societies*, vol. 8, no. 3, pp. 403–22.

Appendix

Careworkers' assessments of their work environments and experience of fatigue. Logistic regression. Odds ratios comparing publicly and privately employed careworkers controlling for age, gender, full-time/part-time, length of employment with present employer and municipality.

	Residential care (n≥2367)		Home-based care (n≥915)	
	Publicly run	Privately run	Publicly run	Privately run
Have good contact with supervisors (most often)	1	1.14	1	0.51 ***
Can affect working conditions, e.g. working pace (most often)	1	0.92	1	1.08
Find work sufficiently varied (most often)	1	1.29	1	0.82
Find work interesting and stimulating (most often)	1	1.26	1	0.66
Have too much to do (most often)	1	0.93	1	0.76
Feel inadequate because care receivers do not get the help they should (most often)	1	0.71 *	1	1.08
Physically exhausted after a working day (most often)	1	0.83	1	1.17
Mentally exhausted after a working day (most often)	1	0.71	1	1.31

*** $p<0.001$; * $p<0.05$

5

Caring for profit? The impact of for-profit providers on the quality of employment in paid care

Debra King and Bill Martin

Nursing homes and hostels are active partners in the delivery of care services in Australia and there is no doubt that the ways these organisations operate can either help or hinder the provision of good care (Meagher 2006, p. 48; Scott et al. 1995, p. 78). One of the central ways in which aged care organisations influence the quality of care is through the recruitment and management of the care workforce. Indeed, in a detailed multivariate analysis of the supply of careworkers, Martin (2007, p. 194) argued that 'all of the most important predictors of aged care workers' job satisfaction are determined primarily by how work is organised in aged care facilities, and are therefore largely under the control of facility managers'. But facility managers do not have absolute autonomy. They are embedded in a particular organisational setting, with specific administrative procedures, access to technology, funding and accountability processes, and overarching values—all of which influence their capacity to organise careworkers in ways which would maximise the quality of care that can be provided to residents.

One of the most obvious differences between aged care organisations is the form of ownership. Analysts argue that for-profit organisations prioritise the needs of shareholders/owners to maximise profit over the needs of either those in receipt of care, or the careworkers who provide it (Knijn 2004, p. 234; Cancian 2000), In contrast, government and non-profit organisations are viewed as somewhat less market oriented and capable of prioritising professional and welfare state objectives over those focused on maximising returns (Knijn 2004). In particular, proponents of non-profits argue that they derive superior performance and productivity from shared values and commitment to common goals that overrides a narrow focus on profits and costs (for example, Cheverton 2007, p. 432). The corollary of this argument is the belief that the quality of care provided within for-profit organisations is likely to be inferior.

More broadly an influential line of thought has seen an inherent tension between care and money (England 2005; Folbre 2006; Ungerson 1997). This tension is said to be particularly problematic when money is the *primary* reason that care is provided: hence the suspicion of for-profit ownership of care organisations. The money versus care argument is typically applied at the level of careworkers—that is, the extent to which paying careworkers compromises the quality of care that they will provide. This debate often focuses on the difference between the qualities and values of familial care, which is mostly unpaid, and those of contracted care which is undertaken only because of the payment that ensues. More recently, the debate has expanded to include the moral and political dimensions of care which places the payment associated with the contractual arrangement within a broader context. Meagher (2006), for example, argues that taking this broader approach facilitates a perspective that views paid carers as capable of providing 'good enough' care. The focus in this debate has been on the relationship between careworker and care recipient. However the relationship between careworkers and the organisations that pay them is equally important, since this relationship frames the way careworkers can actually provide care to care recipients.

This paper examines whether differences in the form of ownership of residential aged care facilities has any influence on the experience of work for aged care workers. Do for-profit facilities organise staffing and work differently from others? Do workers providing care in for-profit organisations have different work experiences than others? To address these questions, we examine the perception that the market approach to the provision of aged care services is inappropriate or deficient. We then draw upon data collected by the National Institute of Labour Studies (NILS) for the Commonwealth Department of Health and Ageing to test the argument that for-profit provision makes a difference. Two data-sets are analysed: a census of all residential aged care facilities across Australia, and a random survey of employees in these facilities. The evidence suggests that, despite there being some differences in the aged care workforce according to the form of facility ownership, there was little support for the argument that for-profit residential aged care facilities are worse employers or that their workforce is less satisfied with the level of care they are allowed to provide. The paper concludes with a discussion about why the form of ownership may not matter to careworkers as much as some arguments suggest.

Caring for-profit? Or caring for *profit*?

For-profit providers have been an important component in Australian residential aged care since at least the 1960s. Their concentration today in providing 'high care' places reflects their historic focus on nursing home, rather than hostel ('low care'), provision. In contrast to some other areas of care provision, notably child care, the proportion of residential aged care beds provided by for-profits has not changed markedly over the past three decades (see Healy 2002; Howe & Healy 2005; Kendig & Duckett 2001). However, governments have moved to progressively increase the role of market mechanisms in the provision and allocation of residential aged care places (Howe & Healy 2005). At the same time, government funding arrangements and regulation, particularly through licensing requirements, mean that all residential aged care providers must conform to a range of key constraints imposed by government (see Hogan 2004, Ch. 2; Stack 2003). In this complex environment, the question of whether for-profit facilities should be expected to differ in their staffing practices and characteristics as workplaces is especially difficult.

One possibility is that for-profit organisation produces greater efficiency and lower costs (Bishop 1988). Here, for-profits are taken as a paradigm for best practice because market principles, based on the commodification of care, price sensitivity and rational economic behaviour, are best able to meet demand, manage supply and distribute services efficiently. Although the operation of such a mechanism will be limited in Australian aged care because there is little or no price competition, for-profit facilities may still represent best practice. In seeking profits, they may maximise the most important forms of efficiency by focusing on the provision of quality care at minimum cost. In relation to staffing, they might make optimal arrangements to hire and retain workers and organise their work. For-profit aged care organisations may be far less likely than non-profit or government organisations to exhibit internal conflict between market principles and other principles such as charity, benevolence, welfare or professional duty that may guide their operations.

Of course, many analysts have argued that 'market failure' is much more likely than successful competition in areas like aged care. Placing a feminist slant on this view, Nancy Folbre has argued that paid care services cannot be 'bought and sold like any other commodity, simply relying on the forces of demand and supply' (2006, p. 12). She points out that for the market to operate efficiently in the field of aged care it would need to ensure that both workers and consumers have perfect information upon which to make a rational choice; and that price changes would induce efficient adjustments. She demonstrates that, given the nature of aged care, neither of these has occurred or is likely to occur in the future. Folbre's analysis is focused on the United States, where price competition is much more important than in Australia. Indeed, a plausible view might be that Folbre's concerns are not particularly relevant to Australia because government subsidies and regulation will minimise market failure. Nevertheless, a focus on profits in for-profit facilities may lead to a kind of secondary market failure, through a tendency to exploit workers and provide lower quality care. Indeed, the consistent reporting of abuse of residents and low standards of care within the aged care sector suggest that cost cutting and quality of care issues still affect the lives of at least some residents in aged care (Choice 2006; Owen 2007).

Thus, both proponents and critics of market-based provision of care might expect differences in staffing arrangements and the experience of work in for-profit and other aged care facilities. However, while proponents expect more efficient staffing, more focused (and, possibly, positive) work experiences, and overall higher quality care, critics expect the opposite. In contrast to both these views, other interpretations suggest that ownership type should make little difference to these outcomes.

One body of research suggests that market relations need not undermine the provision of care, as long as certain conditions are met. These conditions include: restricting profit-making or cost-cutting; having structures of authority that provide caregivers and care receivers with considerable power; having values, incentives and training that promote the emotional/relational as well as physical/technical aspects of care (Cancian 2000); and providing caregivers with a degree of role flexibility, and time to engage with care recipients and allow continuity of care over time (Scott et al. 1995). This work may accept the view that the market imperfections in aged care and the moral paradox of caring for profit result in a possible tension between care, profit and quality. However, it also implies this tension may be resolved without negative effects. The empirical question is whether the relevant arrangements are effective in achieving this end.

The literature on organisational 'isomorphism' suggests another perspective on why there may be little difference between for-profit and other aged care facilities. Aged care facilities face a range of pressures that might be expected to produce what DiMaggio and Powell (1983) famously referred to as 'institutional isomorphism'—a tendency for organisations in a given 'field' to look very similar, irrespective of differences such as those of ownership. Certainly, all aged care facilities face strong 'coercive' pressures through government funding and regulatory arrangements (see Braithwaite et al. 2007; Hogan 2004, Ch. 2; Stack 2003), and these may lead to similar cost constraints and work arrangements irrespective of ownership type.[1] Moreover, the professional background of most facility managers in nursing, and their continued professional networks, may lead to 'normative' processes that produce otherwise unexpected similarities in how facilities arrange staff and their work.

One of the few pieces of empirical research conducted on the organisation of aged care in Australia and its impact on careworkers focused on the trend toward accountability, continuous improvement and flexibility within aged care (Stack 2003; Stack and Provis 2000a; 2000b). This case-study research focused on four facilities operated by a non-profit body in Adelaide, South Australia. It involved semi-structured interviews with careworkers and managers, observation, and a survey of about 70 careworkers in the facilities. While this study was not differentiated by ownership type, it nevertheless points to a range of issues relevant to our research. The researchers were particularly concerned to find that when the provision of care was dominated by economic imperatives, the labour process became depersonalised 'in the interest of speeding it up and making

---

1 All Australian residential aged care facilities are heavily subsidised by the Commonwealth government. Funding is provided primarily on a per bed basis (at differing rates depending on the care level provided), with additional capital and other funding available through various programs. Facilities are licensed to provide a specific number of beds, and funding is not provided beyond the licensed beds. Facilities are not permitted to charge costs for care beyond the levels of funding provided by government, though they can make charges for additional so-called 'hotel' services (for example, larger rooms, higher quality food). Regulation is primarily through a system of inspections and accreditation; it is illegal for unaccredited facilities to continue to operate. To maintain accredited status, facilities must meet certain standards when inspected. These standards are focused around the care provided to residents (including the maintenance of physical infrastructure, the provision of competent caring, and management systems), but do not include prescriptive standards on staffing levels or training.

it cheaper' (Stack 2003, p. 8). When analysing the organisational response to 'flexibility', for example, Stack and Provis (2000a) found tensions in the organisation and delivery of care work between:

- performance of emotional labour and the increased controls over the performance of work;
- requirements for effective caring and other attempts by organisations to seek efficiency;
- workers' emotional commitment to individual clients and workers' inability to provide effective assistance;
- flexible performance of caring work and the control of quality or management of risk;
- use of staff committed to professional values, and numeric flexibility, standardised procedures and detailed control of work;
- workers' commitments to their own wellbeing and to standards of care, and attempts to gain 'attitudinal' flexibility from workers.

Similarly, they found that desirable elements of care work were devalued on the basis of efficiency: the time allowed with patients was decreased; rosters were introduced which limited the levels of continuity staff had with aged clients; investment in training and development was undervalued; and the scope for collegial interaction and effective team communication was diminished (Stack & Provis 2000b, p. 6–7). Subsequently, Stack (2003, p. 8) argued that cost-efficiency and the marketisation of aged care has meant that the structure of work in residential aged care is increasingly unable to deliver the vision of a 'community of care' that aged care is supposed to be.

Within this research, tensions around care and quality appeared to be as much about definitions as they were about accountability. Quality care meant something quite different to the organisation, where it was an issue of accountability and accreditation, than it did to the workers for whom it was an issue of alleviating distress and tending to the vulnerable. As Stack and Provis (2000a, p. 13) claimed in their conclusion, 'where cost is the only consideration, quality as a social outcome appears to be devalued'.

This brings us back to the tension between profit and care in aged care facilities, and the impact on workers. The review of current thinking indicates one line of analysis suggesting that workers may be worse off working in organisations that are primarily organised around profit-making principles, as for-profit aged care facilities ostensibly are. In contrast, other arguments suggest that there are strong forces homogenising the organisation of aged care work. In the following sections these contrasting possibilities are examined in more detail by comparing the work conditions and work experiences of direct care staff in for-profit aged care facilities to those working in non-profit and government facilities. In particular the analysis focuses on whether for-profit organisations:

- are more likely to have a smaller, more flexible, less qualified workforce;
- minimise the continuity in, and amount of time that workers have to care for aged residents;
- have lower levels of job satisfaction among their workers.

The data

In 2003, a census of residential aged care facilities and survey of workers from each facility was conducted by NILS on behalf of the Commonwealth Department of Health and Ageing. This resulted in data relating to the workforce profile of each facility, and to the workplace experience of direct careworkers (nurses, personal care attendants and allied health workers).[2] Once de-identified, these data were merged to enable analysis of the experience of carework-

---

2 The survey of workers was carried out by asking each facility to distribute questionnaires to a random sample of their direct care employees. For further details of the census and survey see Richardson and Martin (2004).

ers in relation to the facility where they worked. For the purpose of this paper, facilities have been differentiated according to ownership type: for-profit, non-profit and government.

Of the 2881 facilities included in the census, 1737 responded (covering 1801 facilities due to some facilities being co-located), producing a 62.5 per cent response rate. For-profit facilities made up 24 per cent of all facilities, with non-profits comprising 66 per cent (N=1155) and government facilities 10 per cent (N=167).[3] For-profit facilities showed some systematic differences from others.

Table 5.1: Ownership type by state

State	Non-profit %	For-profit %	Govt %	Total
NT	100.0	-	-	100
NSW	75.4	22.1	2.5	100
VIC	46.4	30.7	22.8	100
QLD	72.8	20.4	6.8	100
SA	72.9	20.0	7.1	100
WA	75.7	23.7	0.7	100
TAS	80.9	10.6	8.5	100
ACT	83.3	16.7	-	100
Total N=	1,155	415	167	1,737

As Table 5.1 indicates, the state with the highest proportion of for-

---

3 For-profits were, on average, slightly larger than other facilities. They contained about 25.7 per cent of all beds in responding facilities, compared to official figures indicating that 28.5 per cent of beds were in high care facilities at the time of the census. Thus, respondents to the census were quite closely representative of all facilities, and there is no evidence of significant non-response bias.

profit facilities was Victoria (which also had the highest proportion of government facilities), with fairly similar distributions in each of the other mainland states. Reflecting their historical development as nursing homes (rather than hostels), for-profit facilities are much more likely than the other ownership types to have only high care beds (Table 5.2). Consistent with this pattern, for-profits are also much more likely to be located in metropolitan areas, especially compared to government-owned facilities. These features of for-profits are likely to influence their workforce profiles, given that facilities with only high care beds may require a different mix of staff than others. Moreover, the availability and recruitment of staff may be easier in metropolitan areas than in regional and remote areas.

Table 5.2: Ownership type by location, and levels of care

Location	For-profit %	Non-profit %	Govt %	Total N=
Metropolitan	70.1	49.1	14.4	879
Regional	17.1	21.1	19.8	347
Rural	12.8	29.8	65.8	505
Total	100	100	100	1,731
Level of Care				
Low care	13.2	41.9	21.8	568
High care	69.0	18.9	50.9	587
High and low care	17.8	39.2	27.3	566
Total	100	100	100	1,721

A representative sample of workers was taken from each facility (response rate = 41.2 per cent). Four categories of worker were surveyed: registered nurses (RN), enrolled nurses (EN), personal care attendants (PCA) and allied health workers. This chapter focuses on the experiences of nurses and personal care attendants. Responses were received from 1093 workers (nurses and PCAs) in for-profit facilities, 3336 workers in non-profit facilities, and 485 workers in government facilities. Just over 93 per cent of aged care workers are women, with for-profit facilities having a slightly higher (two percentage points) proportion of men than non-profit facilities. For-profit facilities also employed younger workers as PCAs than other ownership types. The average age of 39.8 years for PCAs in for-profit facilities was five years younger than those in other facilities. An indication of the proportion of migrants working in aged care is the level of employment of workers with fluency in a language other than English. For-profit facilities employ higher proportions of workers with fluency in another language—28.4 per cent compared to 20.8 per cent in non-profit facilities and just 13.7 per cent in government facilities. However, for-profit facilities are no more likely than others to ask their workers to use these language skills in their job. While 48 per cent of workers in for-profit facilities who spoke a language other than English used it in their work, 50 per cent of those in non-profit and 52 per cent of those in government facilities used their language skills at work.

Working in aged care

In comparing the workplace for nurses and PCAs in for-profit facilities to those in other forms of ownership, there are two levels of analysis: the facility and the workers. As outlined above, there are a number of competing hypotheses about likely differences in the organisation of staffing and the experience of workers in for-profit facilities compared to others. These are the focus of our analysis. The first is the hypothesis that for-profit facilities would have worse work conditions, exemplified here by whether they employ fewer staff on a more casualised (flexible) basis and are less concerned with qualifications (especially for PCAs). Secondly, given that part of the motivation and reward of care work are related to a worker's relationship with residents, the hypothesis that the profit imperative will lead to work conditions that decrease contact with residents can be examined in relation to staff: bed ratios, the time workers actually spend in direct care, and the capacity for continuity of care vis-à-vis use of agency staff and staff turnover. Finally, the argument that working in for-profit facilities is likely to be less satisfying will be explored through an analysis of employee opinions about and satisfaction with their work.

The workplace: flexibility and the staffing mix

Over the past 15–20 years there has been a general shift in Australian workplaces towards increasing casualisation and enhancing flexibility (Watson et al. 2003). These trends have been particularly noticeable in jobs with high proportions of women (Watson et al. 2003). With its high proportion of female workers, it would be expected that the aged care workplace would exemplify this trend. The question here, though, is whether for-profit facilities have gone further than other ownership types in paring back work conditions to maximise financial returns.

The level of casualisation can be gauged by the extent to which facilities employ casual workers. As illustrated in Table 5.3, the majority of employees are *not* on casual contracts, although PCAs are more likely to be than nurses. In comparing the facility type, for-profit facilities have a higher proportion of ENs on casual contracts than do either non-profit or government facilities.

Having a flexible workforce is important in an industry where resident numbers and levels of care fluctuate. In addition, there are also 'peak' periods, such as showering, that require more staff than at others. However, flexibility can become a problem when it works to disadvantage employees by splitting shifts or not offering them enough

Table 5.3: Proportion employees who are casual and part-time by employment category by ownership of facility*

Casual	For-profit %	Non-profit %	Govt %
Registered nurse	15.4	16.1	14.8
Enrolled nurse	26.2	16.2	13.8
PCAs	32.4	34.9	36.0
Total N=	1404	3066	479
Part-time*			
Registered nurse	53.0	60.5	61.3
Enrolled nurse	70.9	67.1	65.4
PCAs	69.2	77.2	79.5
Total N=	1393	3022	478

*Part-time workers are those working less than 35 hours per week.

hours. As illustrated above (Table 5.3), most employees in aged care work part-time, and this may well be their preference. To examine whether organisational flexibility is meeting the needs of employees or the needs of the organisation, we have measured the extent to which employees are working their preferred number of hours. As demonstrated in Table 5.4, it appears that over a quarter of workers in aged care are underemployed. This differs by ownership type, but in this case it is non-profit facilities that have the lowest proportion of employees satisfied with their working hours. That similar majorities of employees in all facility types are working their preferred hours indicates that for-profits are no more likely than others to be achieving flexibility by circumventing workers' preferred hours.

Table 5.4: Hours employees would like to work by ownership of facility

	For-profit %	Non-profit %	Govt %
Want to work MORE hours	27.0	30.4	20.3
Want to work SAME hours	60.0	55.3	63.8
Want to work LESS hours	12.9	14.3	15.9
Total N =	703	1541	271

Table 5.5: Proportion of effective full-time equivalent employees by employment category by ownership of facility

	For-profit %	Non-profit %	Govt %	Total N=
Registered nurse	35.8	38.4	37.2	3,079
Enrolled nurse	25.8	25.9	34.1	2,252
PCAs	38.4	35.7	28.7	3,083
Total N=	1,922	5,499	993	8,414

Nevertheless, having a good workplace is about more than job security and getting the desired number of hours of work each week. It is also about whether the staffing mix is right. This influences whether there are enough supervisors to ensure that staff are not taking responsibility for tasks they are not trained for or, alternatively, whether workers get the opportunity to use their skills in their work. The staffing mix is influenced by a number of factors, one of the most important being the level of care the facility offers—the numbers of high and low care beds. As discussed earlier, for-profit facilities are predominantly high care facilities and it would be expected that their staffing mix would reflect this by having a higher proportion of nurses and qualified staff.

Yet, as Table 5.5 illustrates, for-profit facilities employ a slightly lower proportion of nurses and higher proportion of PCAs than either of the other ownership categories. This is especially so at the RN level. RNs in for-profit facilities comprise 35.8 per cent of the direct care workforce, compared to being 37.2 per cent of the workforce in government facilities and 38.4 per cent in non-profit facilities. As will be demonstrated in the next section of the paper, this has a flow-on effect regarding workload.

This disparity in staffing mix might be off-set by for-profit facilities employing qualified PCAs, especially those with a Certificate IV in Aged Care which reflects similar levels of skill as a Diploma in Nursing. Tables 5.6 and 5.7 show that for-profit facilities certainly employ more qualified PCAs than government facilities, but they are very similar to the profile of non-profit facilities. In addition, the proposition that they might employ more PCAs with a Certificate IV is not borne out by the evidence. However, as there is no 'wage premium' associated with Certificate III or IV qualifications (Martin 2005), and while facilities may well desire more qualified PCAs, there is little financial incentive for employees to undertake this level of training.

Overall, the for-profit workplace is slightly better than that of non-profit workplaces for offering preferred hours of work; and is much better than government facilities for employing qualified PCAs. Where the for-profit workplace may fall down, comparatively speaking, is in the staffing mix. Despite being much more likely to have only high care beds, for-profits have no higher proportions of nursing staff than other ownership types. The next section examines the affect of this on the level of care that workers can give to residents.

Table 5.6: Proportion of facilities with more than half or less than half of PCAs with Certificate III in Aged Care, by ownership of facility

	For-profit %	Non-profit %	Govt %
Less than half with Cert III	41.2	37.6	56.6
Half or more with Cert III	58.9	62.5	43.3
Total N =	389	1062	150

Table 5.7: Proportion of facilities with some or no PCAs with Certificate IV in Aged Care, by ownership of facility

	For-profit %	Non-profit %	Govt %
No PCAs have Cert IV	61.5	59.0	75.3
Some PCAs have Cert IV	38.5	40.9	24.6
Total N =	408	1129	162

The work: caring for residents

One of the key issues in 'caring for profit' debates is whether paying for care will result in the decreasing quality of care for care recipients. The provision of quality care is a concern at all levels of the care chain. At the organisational level, indicators of quality care are built into accreditation processes, though some analysts doubt that they are valid measures of whether residents actually receive quality care (Stack 2003). At another level, being able to provide quality care is an important aspect of care work and contributes to the intrinsic motivations and job satisfaction of employees within the aged care industry (Martin 2007). Previous studies on care work have found that careworkers receive non-monetary rewards from their work if they are permitted to meet the emotional and social needs of residents as well as their physical/medical needs—that is, when they see their work as contributing to the wellbeing and quality of life of another person (King 2007).

Two factors contribute to the capacity of careworkers to provide levels of care that incorporate both the physical/medical dimension and the emotional/relational dimension: time and continuity. The amount of time that carers spend in direct care work, as opposed to doing paperwork and other administrative tasks, provides an indication of a facility's priorities, for example, whether it is overly bureaucratised or whether it focuses on resident care. Direct care staff are employed specifically to tend to residents' needs, but their capacity to do this is affected by the ways in which their work is scheduled, including the allocation of tasks and the intensity of work. Aged care workers and residents also recognise the value of providing continuity of care. The ability of careworkers to build long-term relationships with residents facilitates both social wellbeing and physical wellbeing as changes in health status are more easily picked up when a resident is 'known' to a carer. The question for this section, then, is whether working in a for-profit organisation diminishes the capacity to fulfil the caring role that employees seek in their care work.

Differences in the amount of time employees say they spend actually caring for residents can be seen in Table 5.8. A higher proportion of workers (44 per cent) in for-profit facilities spend at least two-thirds of their time in direct care work than do workers in other kinds of facilities. When this is broken down to the different levels of staff, PCAs in for-profit facilities are much more likely to spend the majority of their work time performing direct care tasks. The story is somewhat different for nurses, who are more likely to perform direct care tasks in government facilities. Nevertheless, even nurses in for-profit facilities spend more time in direct care than those in non-profit facilities.[4]

---

[4] The pattern in government facilities arises because more of their nurses are ENs, and ENs do more direct care than RNs. Although government facilities, mostly located in Victoria, have fewer PCAs than others, it is striking the their PCAs are much less likely than those in other facilities to spend more than two-thirds of their time in direct care work.

Table 5.8: Proportion of staff who spend more than two-thirds of their time in direct care work by employment category by ownership of facility

	For-profit %	Non-profit %	Govt %
Nurses	22.9	17.9	37.7
PCAs	58.0	48.3	35.5
All staff	44.0	39.7	37.0

While for-profit facilities certainly appear to prioritise the performance of direct care tasks (rather than paperwork, for example) by their careworkers, the capacity to spend sufficient time with residents is also influenced by the number of beds each person has to look after. As Table 5.9 makes clear, for-profit facilities have more beds per EFT-equivalent staff member than either of the other ownership types. In some areas the differences are very large. For example, in the 13.2 per cent of for-profit facilities which offer only low care places, there is an average of one full-time registered nurse to work on 91.4 beds—this is nearly double the workload that registered nurses have in either of the other ownership types. It is not just that for-profits give nurses greater caring workloads, since even PCAs in low care for-profit facilities have a 30 per cent higher staff/bed ratio than in other types of facilities. Workload differences are also evident in the high care facilities. Here, all three categories of staff in for-profit facilities have a higher staff/bed ratio than in other ownership types. However, while still markedly above the ratio in government facilities, these are more in line with the ratios in non-profit facilities.

This evidence suggests that work is organised somewhat differently in for-profit, non-profit and government-owned facilities. For-profit facilities somehow are able to have their staff spend more time on direct care, possibly by using the higher level organisational skills of RNs to undertake non-caring tasks. This may explain the greater

Table 5.9: Average ratio of beds per employed EFT-equivalent staff by employment category in each type of facility by ownership of facility

Type of facility	Employee level	For-profit	Non-profit	Govt	Total N=
Low care places only	RN	91.4	42.1	48.5	230
	EN	34.0	42.4	27.2	137
	PCA	8.9	6.3	5.1	303
High care places only	RN	9.6	8.0	5.3	393
	EN	29.0	25.1	4.2	314
	PCA	4.3	3.7	2.6	337

use of full-time RNs in for-profits noted earlier. As a result, they may operate with somewhat fewer staff per resident than other facilities. Our data cannot tell us whether the net result is that staff in for-profit facilities spend more or less time with each resident than those in other facilities.

In examining whether employees in for-profit facilities had more continuity with residents, indicators such as the numbers of shifts worked by agency staff and the tenure of employees were analysed. The capacity to give continuity of care to residents is important for developing the kinds of caring relationships that are recognised as contributing to the overall quality of care (Stone 2000; James 1992). Where there is a dependence on agency or temporary staff, it is less likely that such continuity of care would be possible. As Table 5.10 illustrates, only a very small proportion of shifts in residential facilities is worked by agency staff, irrespective of ownership type. However, for-profit facilities did cover a greater proportion of shifts with agency staff compared to other types of facilities. This is particularly so for RNs, with an average of 3.3 per cent of shifts worked by RNs in

Table 5.10: Average proportion of shifts worked by agency staff in each employment category by ownership of facility

	For-profit %	Non-profit %	Govt %	Total N=
Registered Nurse	3.3	1.6	1.3	1601
Enrolled nurse	0.6	0.6	1.5	1684
PCAs	2.8	1.4	2.0	1545

for-profit facilities being done by an agency RN. This is more than double the proportion worked in other ownership types, however the percentages are quite low. Somewhat greater reliance on agency staff by for-profit facilities is also evident at the level of PCAs. While reliance on agency staff can be institutionalised, with 'regular' staff being sourced from agencies, it does point to a certain level of temporariness among staff that could affect the continuity of care of residents. These figures may also indicate difficulties in finding replacements when vacancies arise. If so, then it seems that for-profit facilities may well have higher vacancy rates than other ownership types.

Indeed, as Table 5.11 shows, for-profit facilities have a somewhat higher turnover than others, particularly among ENs and PCAs. On average, for-profit facilities have 31 per cent of PCAs who have been in their jobs less than one year, compared to 23 per cent in government facilities and 24 per cent in non-profits. In a similar vein, for-profit facilities have an average of 25 per cent of ENs with less than a year's tenure, compared to 18 per cent in government and non-profit facilities. With regard to RNs, there is little difference between for-profit and non-profit facilities, but government facilities have significantly lower RN turnover.

The evidence from this section indicates that employees in for-profit facilities care for more residents than other employees. The impact of

Table 5.11: Proportion of employees with tenure of less than one year by employment category by ownership of facility

	For-profit %	Non-profit %	Govt %	Total N=
Registered nurse	26.6	25.6	17.1	1523
Enrolled nurse	25.0	17.5	18.4	1130
PCA	31.0	23.5	23.3	1634

this apparent higher workload on workers' capacity to provide care could be moderated by the fact that they spend a higher proportion of their time on direct care tasks. However, if the higher staff/resident ratios in for-profits reflect higher workloads in these facilities, then we might expect effects on worker motivation and job satisfaction, which in turn could explain the slightly higher turnover that we observe in for-profits. In the next section we turn to how workers view their jobs, including their job satisfaction, to see whether the apparently different staffing and work organisation of for-profits does produce differences in the subjective experience of work.

The workers: attitudes, opinions and job satisfaction

The previous sections have focused on the more objective measures relating to the experience of work for direct care employees. This section draws on employees' subjective assessment of what it is like to work in aged care facilities. Three groups of questions were asked to assess what employees thought about their work. The first asked employees to rank their level of agreement or disagreement with statements about their work along a seven-point scale. These statements were identified from discussions of current issues affecting careworkers in the literature and within aged care industry forums. The second group of questions asked employees their satisfaction with various aspects of their work: pay, job security, the work itself, ability to balance paid work and other commitments, hours of work, and overall

Table 5.12: Proportion of employees agreeing with the following statements, by ownership of facility

	For-profit %	Non-profit %	Govt %
I feel under pressure to work harder in my job	41	42	44
I am able to spend enough time with each resident	23	22	24
I have a lot of freedom to decide how I do my work	51	51	48
I use many of my skills in my current job	85	87	81

job satisfaction. The questions asked respondents to rate their satisfaction in each area on an eleven-point scale with higher values representing greater satisfaction. The third group were open-ended questions asking respondents to identify the best and worst things about their job. The responses, received from 764 careworkers, were subsequently coded and the top responses for each question analysed in relation to the ownership type of the facility.[5]

From the analysis of the data so far, it would be reasonable to expect employees in for-profit facilities to be experiencing greater pressure to work harder in their job and have less time to spend with residents than employees in other types of facilities. However, Table 5.12 shows how little variation there is between the types of facilities on these two questions. If anything, it is employees at government facilities who appear to be under more pressure at work, despite having a better staff/bed ratio. Furthermore fewer than a quarter of employees, irrespective of their workplace, claimed to have enough time to spend with each resident. For the remaining two issues—work autonomy and usage of skills—responses from employees are virtually

---

5 See Moskos and Martin (2005) for the full report on this aspect of the research.

Table 5.13: Average job satisfaction of employees by ownership of facility

	For-profit	Non-profit	Govt	Total
Total pay	3.4	3.7	5.3	3.8
Job security	7.1	7.2	6.7	7.1
Work itself	7.1	7.0	6.8	7.0
Hours worked	7.5	7.1	7.5	7.2
Work-life balance	7.0	6.7	6.8	6.8
Overall job satisfaction	7.2	7.1	7.1	7.1

Source: Adapted from Martin 2005.[6]

identical in all ownership types. In short, there is no indication from these figures that for-profit employees feel disadvantaged compared to their counterparts in other facilities.

Turning to employees' levels of satisfaction with their work, it is interesting to note a similar phenomenon. Overall, employees in for-profit facilities are just as—even slightly more—satisfied with their jobs than employees in either non-profit or government facilities. Table 5.13 depicts the mean rating given by employees for each item relating to job satisfaction, with the maximum score for any item being 10. As is evident from the table, levels of satisfaction with the amount of pay in aged care were very low. While employees in for-profit facilities were even less satisfied with their pay than employees in other facilities, they were not markedly different from employees in non-profit organisations. In addition, the higher than average mean score for satisfaction with hours worked (7.5 against an average of 7.2) and work-life balance (7.0 against an average of 6.8) reflect the

---

[6] Note that figures in Tables 5.13 and 5.14 represent *all* staff: nurses, PCAs and allied health workers.

Table 5.14: Proportion of employees nominating the worst things about work, by ownership category*

	For-profit %	Non-profit %	Govt %	Total %
Pay	29.0	19.7	14.8	21.7
Too much paperwork	12.6	19.1	21.9	17.5
Staff shortages	17.0	14.7	10.9	14.7
Time constraints	13.4	15.6	8.7	13.4
Not enough time to care for residents	11.8	14.8	10.0	12.8

* Respondents often mentioned more than one area, therefore columns do not add up to 100 per cent.

higher levels at which employees in for-profit facilities are able to work their desired hours (discussed earlier). Perhaps more surprisingly, given the access to full-time work and stability in employment in government facilities, is the fact that employees in for-profit facilities have higher levels of satisfaction (7.1) than their government counterparts (6.7) about job security. These data suggest that for-profit facilities could compensate for dissatisfaction with pay by being more accommodating of employees' preferences in the hours worked and therefore in their ability to manage their work-life responsibilities.

The third set of data, obtained from two open-ended questions, reinforce issues identified earlier. On the one hand, the worst aspects of the job were identified by employees as the pay and those aspects of work that prevented them from feeling as though they could provide adequate care for the residents (Table 5.14).

Employees in for-profit facilities were far more likely to mention pay than those in other facilities, at 29.0 per cent compared to 19.7 per cent of employees in non-profit facilities and 14.8 per cent of government

Table 5.15: Proportion of employees nominating the best things about work, by ownership category*

	For profit %	Non-profit %	Govt %	Total %
Care for residents	51.9	49.3	38.4	47.9
Supportive coworkers	34.8	42.3	46.7	40.7
Flexibility in hours	17.6	13.5	18.5	15.9
Social environment	10.0	16.3	20.1	15.0

* Respondents often mentioned more than one area, therefore columns do not add up to 100 per cent.

employees. Other research has noted the very low pay satisfaction of aged care workers, and found that it cannot be explained by objectively low pay rates (see Martin 2007).[7] All of the other issues in the top five worst things about their job had consequences for the amount of time employees could spend with residents (this was also identified as a separate issue by some people). Overall, the patterns across facilities of different ownership type were consistent with the finding that workers in for-profit, non-profit and government facilities had almost identical levels of job satisfaction.

While it is not surprising that care for residents is high on the list of the best things employees nominated about their work, the differences between facilities is interesting (Table 5.15). Employees from government facilities mentioned care less often than they mentioned having supportive coworkers. Employees in for-profit facilities, however, were less likely than their counterparts in other facility types to mention their coworkers or having a good social environment as positive aspects of their work. This could be due to the younger co-

---

[7] Accounting for the apparently greater concern about pay among private facility employees must remain a topic for further research, as the data used here cannot further illuminate it.

hort of PCAs in for-profit facilities who would be more likely to be combining child-rearing with their aged care work. In contrast, the older workers in government and non-profit facilities seem to place a high value on their workplace as a social environment, rather than simply being a place where they earn money or provide care to the aged.

Does ownership type really matter?

Our results show that, contrary to many expectations, the small differences between for-profit facilities and others in staffing patterns do not translate into differences in the subjective experience of work. Though for-profit facilities have fewer staff per bed, younger PCAs, somewhat greater use of agency staff and higher staff turnover, the mode of ownership had little impact on workers' perceptions of their job and experiences of work. Furthermore, the data suggest that the impact of cost pressures on care provision occurred across all three modes of ownership. For employees, then, there was not a lot of difference whether their employers were caring 'for profit' or not. The question is, why not?

Some have argued that market values are now so pervasive in the aged care industry that the differences between ownership types have become negligible (Stack 2003; Stack & Provis 2000a; 2000b). This seems to point towards facilities experiencing a kind of 'normative' pressure that leads to similar organisational structures and practices—DiMaggio and Powell's 'institutional isomorphism' (1983). However, 'coercive' pressures in the form of regulatory and subsidy regimes seem at least as likely to produce this effect as simple 'market values'. In other words, the demands placed on facilities as conditions of receiving subsidies and remaining accredited are directly coercive, so that adherence to them does not require belief in the intrinsic value of the market model (see Braithwaite et al. 2007). Although our results lend support to this interpretation, there is one area in which facilities arrange their staffing differently depending on ownership type. It appears that for-profit facilities operate with somewhat leaner resident/staff ratios than others, but that they compensate for this by having staff spend more of their time providing direct care. However, this does not translate into significant differences in employees' subjective experience of work. This result suggests that facilities face another set of constraints too, ones that produce further pressures towards institutional isomorphism. In order to retain staff, employers—irrespective of ownership type—need to respond to a variety of their employees' needs and values.

Notwithstanding their concerns about pay, what mattered to employees was that they be given the opportunity to care. That careworkers express a moral orientation to their work is not a new insight. Being able to care for and care about residents has long been recognised as one of the motivations and intrinsic rewards of being a careworker (Meagher 2006; King 2007). What this research pointed to, however, was that the employees' commitment to providing care was not restricted to caring for residents. It also extended to caring for their families and caring for their coworkers.

The importance of having their preferred work hours and being able to achieve work-life balance is well recognised for workers with family responsibilities. While this is mostly thought of in terms of being able to balance work with caring for children, it is also relevant to those workers who have older relatives to care for. The skills involved in this kind of familial care work would be valued in the aged care sector, and family carers would be an obvious source of workers, especially as PCAs. It is therefore of benefit for both employers and employees for workers to be provided with the opportunity for achieving their desired work-life balance.

The value that many aged care workers placed on their relationships with coworkers also reinforces the overall care orientation of careworkers. The capacity to use workplace relationships to generate and sustain emotional wellbeing in the workplace is particularly important in care work where employees engage in high levels of emotional labour (James 1992). If they are not provided with opportunities to replenish their emotional needs, this can lead to burnout and withdrawal from the labour market. At the same time, having good emotional connections with colleagues is important for developing skills related to emotional intelligence—also used extensively in care work. Although Stack and Provis (2000a) found that organisational concerns regarding efficiency were decreasing the likelihood of collegiality developing within the workplace, it is obviously an aspect of work that many employees value and which is likely to have flow-on benefits for clients and the levels of morale within an organisation.

It could well be, then, that the differences between for-profit and other ownership types in the organisation of work are being masked by the extent to which employers are providing their workers with equal opportunities to care: whether that be for clients, family or colleagues. Perhaps, as Martin (2007) suggests, it is the facility managers in their role of recruitment and rostering, rather than the ownership type per se, that has the most influence over workers' experience of work. Nevertheless, it is interesting to note slight differences between the ownership types on how the relationship between the care orientations—and pay—is played out. Employees within all ownership types were dissatisfied with their pay, none more so than those in for-profit facilities. The majority of employees were also dissatisfied with the amount of time they had to spend with residents, though the actual work of caring for residents was rated highly by employees in all facilities except for government facilities.

The implications of such an argument are double-edged for workers. On one side, it seems that employees are able to weave their aged care work into their lives in ways that are highly satisfying. On the other side, employers can use careworkers' 'care orientation' to offset the need for decent pay and work conditions. Perhaps, as Folbre (2006) argues, there is a need to develop more powerful political coalitions to bring about change, but the kind of change needed goes beyond the high pay/high quality strategy she suggests. It needs to addresses the four dimensions identified by our research: pay, quality care, work-life balance and collegiality.

References

Bishop, C. E. 1988, 'Competition in the market for nursing home care', *Journal of Health Politics, Policy and Law*, vol. 13, no. 2, pp. 341–61.

Braithwaite, J., Makkai, T. & Braithwaite, V. 2007, *Regulating Aged Care: Ritualism and the New Pyramid*, Cheltenham: Edward Elgar.

Cancian, F. 2000, 'Paid emotional care: Organizational forms that encourage nurturance', in *Care Work: Gender, Class and the Welfare State*, ed. M. Harrington Meyer, Routledge, New York, pp. 136–48.

Cheverton, J. 2007, 'Holding our own: Values and performance in non-profit organisations', *Australian Journal of Social Issues*, vol. 42, no. 3, pp. 427–36.

Choice 2006, 'Regarding nursing homes', *Choice: Journal of the Australian Consumers' Association*, September, pp. 18–22.

DiMaggio, P. J. & Powell, W. J. 1983, 'The iron cage revisited: Institutional isomorphism and collective rationality in organizational fields', *American Journal of Sociology*, vol. 48, no. 2, pp. 147–60.

England, P. 2005, 'Emerging theories of care work', *Annual Review of Sociology*, vol. 31, pp. 381–99.

Folbre, N. 2006, 'Demanding quality: Worker/consumer coalitions and "high road" strategies in the care sector', *Politics and Society*, vol. 34, no. 1, pp. 11–31.

Healy, J. 2002, 'The care of older people: Australia and the United Kingdom', *Social Policy and Administration*, vol. 36, no. 1, pp. 1–19.

Hogan, W. 2004, *Review of Pricing Arrangements in Residential Aged Care—Final Report*, Department of Health, Canberra.

Howe, A. & Healy, J. 2005, 'Generational justice in aged care policy in Australia and the United Kingdom', *Australasian Journal on Ageing*, vol. 24, Supplement, pp. S12–S18.

James, N. 1992, 'Care = organisation + physical labour + emotional labour', *Sociology of Health and Illness*, vol. 14, no. 4, pp. 488–509.

Kendig, H. & Duckett, S. 2001, Australian directions in aged care: the generation of policies for generations of older people, *Australian Health Policy Institute Commissioned Paper Series, 2001/05*, The Australian Health Policy Institute, University of Sydney, Sydney.

King, D. 2007, 'Rethinking the care-market relationship in care provider organisations', *Australian Journal of Social Issues*, vol. 42, no. 2, pp. 199–212.

Knijn, T. 2004, Commodifying care: New risks and opportunities, paper presented at the Conference of Europeanists, Chicago, 11–13 March.

Martin, B. 2005, *Residential Aged Care Facilities and Their Workers: How Staffing Patterns and Work Experience Vary with Facility Characteristics*, Commonwealth Department of Health and Ageing, Canberra.

Martin, B. 2007, 'Good jobs, bad jobs? Understanding the quality of aged care jobs and why it matters', *Australian Journal of Social Issues*, vol. 42, no. 2, pp. 183–97.

Meagher, G. 2006, 'What can we expect from paid carers?' *Politics and Society*, vol. 34, no. 1, pp. 33–53.

Moskos, M. & Martin, B. 2005, *What's Best, What's Worst? Direct Carers' Work in Their Own Words*, Commonwealth Department of Health and Ageing, Canberra.

Owen, M. 2007, 'Aged home penalised', *The Advertiser*, 16 May.

Richardson, S. & Martin, B. 2004, *The Care of Older Australians: A Picture of the Residential Aged Care Workforce*, Commonwealth Department of Health and Ageing, Canberra.

Scott, R. A., Aiken, L. H., Mechanic, D. & Moravcsik, J. 1995, 'Organizational aspects of caring', *The Milbank Quarterly*, vol. 73, no. 1, pp. 77–95.

Stack, S. 2003, Beyond performance indicators: A case study in aged care, paper presented at the Association of Industrial Relations Academics of Australia and New Zealand Conference, Melbourne, 4–7 February.

Stack, S. & Provis, C. 2000a, 'Tensions in flexible employment arrangements for caring labour', in *Proceedings of 14th AIRAANZ Conference* (Newcastle), eds J. Burgess and G. Strachan, vol. 2, pp. 162–71.

Stack, S. & Provis, C. 2000b, The slide from public sector to private sector in-home care: Some ethical concerns, paper presented at the conference of the International Institute for Public Ethics, Ottawa, 24–28 September.

Stone, D. 2000, 'Caring by the book', in *Care Work: Gender, Class and the Welfare State*, ed. M. Harrington Meyer, New York, Routledge.

Ungerson, C. 1997, 'Social politics and the commodification of care', *Social Politics*, vol. 4, no. 3, pp. 362–81.

Watson, I., Buchanan, J, Campbell, I. & Briggs, C. 2003, *Fragmented Futures—New Challenges in Australian Working Life*, Federation Press, Sydney.

6

Blurred boundaries: how paid careworkers and care managers negotiate work relationships

Jane Mears

The Australian population is ageing. In 2006 an estimated 2.7 million Australian residents were aged 65 and over, 13 per cent of the population (Australian Institute of Health and Welfare 2007, p. 82). The Australian Bureau of Statistics (2004) predicts this proportion will double by 2051 when those aged 65 and over will make up 26–28 per cent of the total population. As the population ages, increasing numbers of older Australians will need support to stay at home.

Since the 1980s government policy has focused on enabling people to live more independently in the community rather than in residential care, resulting in 'the growing provision of community care options to support people in their homes for as long as is reasonable' (Australian Institute of Health and Welfare 2007, p. 78). We have witnessed a shift from an era where family care for older people was the norm, with state support for some residential care, to the present where the state supports a comprehensive range of home and community services to support older people and their families.

Growth in home and community services has been matched by growth in the workforce providing these services. The community services workforce is one of the fastest growing sectors of the workforce in Australia. Employment in non-residential care services (which includes home care services) expanded faster than any other community services industry between 1996 and 2001 (Meagher & Healy 2005).

This chapter reports some findings from a project that collected and analysed the views of those at the frontline of community aged care work: the paid careworkers themselves. The project aimed to investigate the experiences of agency managers in managing careworkers, and to document and analyse the careworkers' descriptions of their work.

Paid careworkers in Australia

What do we know of the workforce that provides social care (or community services) in Australia? The care workforce overall is predominately female and is ageing.[1] In 2006, 87 per cent of workers in community service industries were female, similar to 2001 (88 per cent), but much higher than in the total workforce (45 per cent). In 2006, 14 per cent were aged 55 and over, up from 10 per cent in 2001, and the ageing of the care workforce was most evident in those sectors of community services that deliver aged care (Australian Institute of Health and Welfare 2007, p. 334).

Careworkers earn lower hourly incomes, on average, than those they work beside in non-caring occupations in community service industries. Further, male careworkers receive, on average, a higher hourly rate of pay than female careworkers (Meagher & Healy 2006, p. 92). A relatively high proportion of careworkers work part-time. In 2001 well over half (54.6 per cent) of all careworkers in community service industries were working part-time, compared with 30 per cent of workers in similar occupations in the labour market overall (Meagher & Healy 2006, p. 62).

---

[1] Data on the home care workforce is not able to be separated out from data on the workforce in non-residential care services overall, which includes a wide range of welfare activities from drug and alcohol rehabilitation to adoption and child welfare services. Further, data about workers in non-residential care services are often combined with data on other community service industries, such as child care and residential aged care. Thus, the figures presented in this section give a summary overview of social care or community service workers, and so approximates rather than specifies the profile of the home care workforce.

In addition, there are few opportunities for promotion, a paucity of training opportunities, no formal training or educational level required in many jobs, and little formal recognition of prior knowledge or experience, paid or unpaid. In 1996 a significant minority (44.3 per cent) of all careworkers reported having no qualification at all; this rate fell to 38.5 per cent in 2001. Overall in 2001, 13,871 or 7.3 per cent of careworkers in the community services industries held a bachelor degree or higher, but worked in an occupation classified as an associate profession or as intermediate service work. Thus, some workers are formally overqualified for their jobs, indicating a lack of employment opportunities in higher-skilled job categories in caring occupations (Meagher & Healy 2006, pp. 36–37).

What do we know of the experiences of careworkers?

What does research tell us about the experiences of careworkers working at the frontline of care? And more specifically, what have careworkers told researchers about their work?

When careworkers are asked what makes for good care, it is the centrality of relationships with those for whom they care that is singled out (Aronson & Neysmith 1996; Piercy 2000; Twigg 2000). Careworkers enjoy their work and consistently report very high levels of job satisfaction (McLean 1999; Szebehely 2005; Twigg 2000). The most satisfaction comes from the aspects of their work over which they have the most control, activities that produce rewards for their efforts, such as improving their clients' quality of life, making people happy and helping them feel part of the community, keeping older people comfortable, and seeing them make progress (McLean 1999; Fleming & Taylor 2006). What careworkers like most about their jobs is the autonomy and freedom of working alone and the opportunity to exercise judgements in relation to how they can best meet the individualised needs of the older person (Szebehely 2005; Twigg 2000). Careworkers' sense of themselves as caring individuals, committed to their elderly clients' wellbeing, was found for many careworkers to be a central feature of their personal and work identities (Rasmussen 2004).

Wærness found that although the careworkers she studied enjoyed their work and were committed to those they were caring for, they also realised that the values they bring to their work and the skills they draw upon were devalued in the public sphere (Wærness 1987). Several later studies confirmed these findings, and researchers have expressed concern that the frontline knowledge that carers possess regarding the centrality of relationships in supportive home care is devalued by employers, and that instrumental tasks are given priority (Aronson & Neysmith 2006; Szebehely 2005).

What careworkers like least about their work is those aspects over which they have little control, for instance, working under conditions where there is little flexibility to change the care they are providing, where there is not enough time to complete tasks, and where there are insufficient resources for them to provide the care they would like to provide. Under these conditions careworkers will do all that they can to provide what they judge to be good care, including 'breaking the rules' and working unpaid overtime. Job satisfaction and enjoyment decline when careworkers have less time to spend with older people and as tasks become more instrumental (Aronson & Neysmith 2006; McLean 1999; Szebehely 2005). Careworkers express legitimate concerns at how this is reflected in the poor rates of pay and the generally held views of care work as a low status profession (Fleming & Taylor 2006; McLean 1999; Szebehely 2005).

The relational and emotional labour central to care work has been further sidelined with moves to managerialism and market models of care, which has increased the standardisation of services. Careworkers report increasing difficulties in meeting the varying needs of the care recipients (Aronson & Neysmith 2006). Home care workers themselves bear the costs as they strive to respect relationships while attempting to offset the impact of efficiency-driven care (Aronson & Neysmith 2006; Rasmussen 2004; Szebehely 2005).

In the remainder of the chapter, I examine the findings from a research project that explored the endeavours of careworkers and managers to organise and provide care to elderly people in their own homes. The managers and careworkers sought to provide care based on 'caring' principles, which privilege the formation of relationships with those receiving the service over instrumental, task-oriented, managerialist principles.

The research project: method and participants

The study reported here was conducted with careworkers and care managers employed by the Benevolent Society of New South Wales. The Benevolent Society is a non-profit provider of home care services for the aged and those with disabilities, and for their carers.[2] The Benevolent Society has been involved in aged care since the 1950s and has managed a number of large aged care residential facilities in Sydney. In more recent times, the aged care section of the organisation has expanded and, paralleling the trends in aged care policy described above, the majority of the aged care budget of the Benevolent Society now goes toward providing home care for older people.

Prior to the commencement of the study, ethics clearance was given by the Human Research Ethics Committee of the University of Sydney. Initial approaches were then made to the Chief Executive Officer of the Benevolent Society. She was very supportive of the research and invited the researcher to the monthly meeting of the senior managers of the aged care section to talk about the research. There were eight managers at this meeting. Detailed descriptions of the proposed research, with draft focus questions, were distributed, and comments and feedback were sought. Permission was sought to interview the managers at the meeting and to have them assist in recruiting careworkers for the study. The researcher promised to

---

2 The Benevolent Society also provides a range of other social care and welfare services, including child and family welfare services, alongside its aged care work.

provide a draft report to inform all participants of the main findings, and to organise focus groups to discuss the findings, check for accuracy and enable feedback and further input from all those who had participated.

All eight managers agreed to be interviewed and to assist in recruiting careworkers. It was also agreed that the Benevolent Society would pay the careworkers for the time they spent on the research, out of the budgets from the branch offices. The researcher addressed several large gatherings of home care workers, explained what the research was about and recruited volunteers who were willing to be interviewed. The participants who volunteered to be part of the study were those who were interested in the research and willing to talk about their work, so were a self-selected rather than a representative sample.

Between July 2004 and February 2006, 34 people were interviewed, 22 careworkers and twelve managers and care coordinators. Two interview schedules were developed, one for careworkers and one for care coordinators and managers. These questions had been developed early in the planning stages of the project and were modified in response to feedback from the managers. A number of focus questions were devised to use as 'discussion starters'. The questions were further modified over the course of the study as the participants introduced issues of interest and concern to them that had not been initially considered. Questions for managers focused on how they organised the provision of care, whereas the questions for careworkers were more oriented to their day-to-day work with older people. The researcher conducted all the interviews. Each interview lasted approximately one hour. The interviews were conducted at four Benevolent Society offices located throughout metropolitan Sydney. The interviews were audio-taped and transcribed and the data was coded utilising QSR International's NVivo software.

In October 2005 a draft report was distributed to all those who had participated in the research. Four focus groups were organised. Two focus groups were conducted with the care managers (one with six and one with three participants), and two with careworkers (one with seven and one with eight participants). Focus group participants were asked to comment on the draft report and to discuss some questions that the researcher devised from the themes documented in the draft report. These sessions were also tape-recorded and their feedback was incorporated into the final report. The final report was submitted to the Benevolent Society in March 2006 (Mears 2006).

The careworkers and care managers who participated in the study fitted the profile of careworkers outlined earlier. They were mostly women aged from 30 to 60, the average age being the mid-50s. They had worked for the Benevolent Society for periods ranging from three months to ten years, most for at least five years. The majority of the careworkers were employed as permanent part-time workers, working up to twenty hours per week. A few were employed as casuals called to 'fill in' when the permanent part-time careworkers were sick or unable to work. All the care coordinators and managers were employed full-time. The participants were based in four offices in metropolitan Sydney.

For most of the participants, home care was a job they had come to later in life. A significant proportion of the careworkers were 'older workers', that is, they were over 45 when first appointed. This was not a 'first job' for any of the people interviewed. They came with a wide range of previous work experience, both paid and unpaid. Those interviewed were highly skilled, with long careers and varied paid work experience in a wide range of jobs. About a quarter had worked in white-collar jobs, for instance, in banks and building societies or as teachers, and one had been a pathologist. The majority had worked in a range of blue- and pink-collar jobs, in offices, as hairdressers, running small businesses, in shops and in clubs and hotels. Approximately one-third of the careworkers in this study had some past work experience in human services, mostly as nurses or nurse aides. Some had previously worked in nursing homes. The wide range of past paid work experience was an unexpected finding. In some instances there were continuities between their past work experience and their present work, for example, from working in hospitals and nursing homes to working as careworkers. However, for the majority of the participants in this study taking on care work was a major change from their previous paid work.

One of the most striking findings of this research was that all the women who were interviewed, both the care managers and the careworkers, had extensive experience as informal, unpaid carers for elderly and disabled relatives. A significant number were still caring for family members, and so combining paid and unpaid care work. The only exception was the one man who participated in the study.

There are no Australian statistics tracking the informal caring responsibilities or the past caring histories of paid careworkers, so it not possible to determine whether this finding applies across the sector or is unique to participants in this particular study. For several of the careworkers, it was their experience of informal care that had influenced their decision to take on paid care work. This was work they understood and were confident they could do well. As one participant expressed it:

> I cared for my mother-in-law when she was dying, seven or eight years ago. And when she passed away, I thought, 'That is a job I think I might like to do' (Ann, careworker, aged 52).

The research project: results

Providing good care

What did the care managers and careworkers see as making a good careworker? There was a high level of agreement between the two groups in their answers to this question. The careworkers possessed the 'way of thinking' Wærness describes as the 'rationality of caring':

> In order to solve specific problems in the everyday world of care, we require a way of thinking, which is contextual and descriptive, rather than formal and abstract. The concept of

the "rationality of caring" suggests that personal knowledge and a certain ability and opportunity to understand what is specific in each situation where help is required, are important prerequisites to be able to provide good care (Wærness 2007, p. 4).

When listing the skills, knowledge and qualities that made for a good careworker, they drew heavily on their experience and knowledge accumulated as informal carers. Indeed, they frequently referred to family care as the model for good care. For example, one careworker explained,

I care for these people as I would care for my own Mum (Pat, careworker, aged 40).

They all spoke at length of the ability to form good working relationships with people as being central to the provision of good care. Their responses add to existing empirical evidence that 'both the providers and recipients of paid care agree that the characteristics and quality of the relationship between the carer and the careworker is both an expression and means of good care' (Meagher 2006, p. 35).

The practice of participants in the study was underpinned by principles of social justice. They spoke of respecting human rights, listening carefully to people, providing individualised care, and responding in ways that enhanced quality of life and empowered the older person. Particular personal qualities that they believed were required of a good careworker were kindness, patience, tolerance and empathy, with an affinity for, and an interest in, older people. Specific skills were good communication skills, being adaptable and flexible, and being able to work alone, unsupervised. Both the careworkers and the care managers used the term 'professional careworker' to describe a careworker who held the principles and possessed the personal qualities and skills described above. They also used this term frequently to describe a careworker who could successfully negotiate boundaries (as discussed in the next section).

Care managers and careworkers all spoke of being strongly motivated by a desire to work with older people in an industry where personal relationships were valued and where they could make a difference to people's lives. Several spoke of experiencing the effects of managerialism on the organisations they had been working for and said that they had deliberately chosen care work because it involved working with people in a satisfying way. As one participant put it:

> I worked for a bank for a long time and I got sick of being told to sell fries with that, to sell more and more services, when people came in for their withdrawals. I just got tired of that. I wasn't interested anymore. I wanted to work with older people (Carol, careworker, aged 54).

All the participants reported high levels of job satisfaction. The high levels of job satisfaction and commitment were further reflected in their plans for their future working lives. The majority of the participants in this study wanted to stay working for the Benevolent Society into the foreseeable future, as the following quote illustrates:

> I love this type of work. At this stage I haven't got any plans to do anything different (Bernadette, careworker, aged 45).

Both the care managers' and the careworkers' accounts of their practice were underpinned with what Tronto talks of as an ethics of care. She suggests a fourfold conceptualisation of care that encompasses: attentiveness, responsibility, competence and responsiveness (Tronto 1993, pp. 127–34).

Transcending boundaries

Deborah Stone has argued that:

> when care 'goes public' worlds clash, the values, feelings and interactions that make up the relational essence of care in the private sphere are sometimes devalued, discouraged and even forbidden in the public world. Caregivers and the people they care for are pressured by the norms, rules and policies of the public world to make care conform to the image of work that predominates in the public world. At the same time, they strug-

gle to sustain the meaning and value of care as they know it in their more intimate relations (2000, p. 90).

Careworkers inevitably become very close to the older people they are caring for. Julia Twigg found that, as a consequence,

> workers attempt to put boundaries on the extent of this closeness; and this applies both to the physical aspects of carework and the emotional ones. Care, with its unbounded ethic of love and its powerful undertow of emotional connectedness, contains the potential to engulf the worker. Setting limits on this is a necessary part of surviving the job (2000, p. 212).

Care managers and careworkers are constantly negotiating the boundaries between work relationships and personal relationships or friendships. These are fraught negotiations with constant merging, clashes and overlaps of personal/private lives with work/public lives. The boundaries are indeed far from clear. The care managers and the careworkers in this study had put a lot of time and thought into developing caring relationships. Much of the time in all the interviews was spent discussing these issues.

Care managers were concerned that the careworkers would breach boundaries and 'break the rules' in ways that may lead to abuse and exploitation of the careworker or the older person. The careworkers acknowledged the managers' concerns. However they were confident they could successfully negotiate these boundaries and provide, in their judgement, good care, with some guidance from care managers and with clear and transparent policies and guidelines.

Care managers' perspectives

Where is the dividing line between a friendship and a work relationship? The care managers expressed the dilemmas succinctly, the careworkers are employed because they care, but they don't want the careworkers to care too much. They seemed to recognised that, as Twigg puts it, 'care work is intrinsically about emotions ... the cold careworker, even if super efficient, can never be a good carer.

Getting attached to clients was an occupational hazard as well as a source of pleasure. Strong feelings were inevitable' (2000, p. 166).

A large part of the care managers' work involved ensuring that the careworkers were able to separate their work lives from their private lives, as illustrated by the following quote from a care manager:

> Everybody struggles with this in this field because you are going in every single day of the week and of course you develop a relationship. We are looking for people who have this ability to be able to be empathetic, understanding, be warm in what they do without actually giving completely of themselves. That is a very difficult balance. I probably have three staff members who do that amazingly well and if I could bottle it I would because you see the others will struggle with it. And that is how we sell ourselves as a relationship-based service (Sandra, care manager, aged 37).

They spoke of how important it was that careworkers possess the skills and ability to negotiate the complex boundaries between personal and professional relationships.

> So it is a huge skill to professionally care for someone in a way that is loving and compassionate and then extricate yourself. And that is what we are asking people to do (Barbara, care manager, aged 58).

The danger, from the care managers' perspective, was that the closer the relationship between older person and the careworker, the greater the chance that the worker would be exploited by the older person. One way to prevent this was for care managers to visit the older person regularly, monitor the situation closely, and ensure the careworkers were not taking on caring loads that were too heavy. Also, the needs of the clients may change and the careworkers simply may not realise that they are taking on too much.

> We visit them regularly. We see what problems the careworkers have with them. Just generally as the clients deteriorate as they do. They can go for periods where they are stable. And if it is a

> good relationship with the careworker and the client, either that remains stable or the careworker is taking on more and more work and because they like the clients and they don't realise they have taken on too much until they get very tired and very worn out (Ruth, care manager, aged 60).

The care managers spoke of the possibility of careworkers burning out because they were too involved with the clients. Caring about one's clients made a good careworker and if you advised people not to become involved with their clients then they were not going to be very good careworkers.

> There seems to be this dilemma that is not settled. How can you actually be human and be emotional, but still cut people off at a certain point without burning out? People are either throwing themselves completely into it or doing an unnatural thing where they are not feeling for people because they are too scared that they are going to cross those boundaries (Sandra, care manager, aged 37).

Care managers found they were constantly advising careworkers to keep a distance between themselves and the client. Careworkers are not paid to be on duty all the time.

> We always tell the careworkers you have to keep your distance. You give a lot of emotional commitment but you've got your life and it is not good to try and live their lives all the time. So I try to get the girls to always keep it professional (Elizabeth, care manager, aged 56).

The care managers' accounts illustrated a high degree of respect for the careworkers and their ability to deal with these dilemmas. They were relying on the careworker to behave appropriately. There was general agreement among the care managers that most careworkers will learn through experience how to deal appropriately with these issues.

> It depends on the careworker. I've seen some careworkers that learn pretty quickly. You will usually find within the first three months they will struggle with these issues and you

> need to talk to them about it. And they will understand. They usually won't understand until they are actually in a situation (Effie, care manager, aged 53).

As one care manager observed, most of the careworkers were mature women with extensive past experience to draw on. Her view was that careworkers draw on past experience and learn quickly to deal with these dilemmas.

> Most of our careworkers are middle aged. They are sensible. I give them the benefit of the doubt. They usually find the first time they've given a phone number and they have a client who is calling them in the middle of the night. They learn. It is the best way to learn. You are never going to stop them anyway (Anita, care manager, aged 50).

A consistent theme that emerged here was the importance of transparent supervision of the careworkers, with good lines of communication between care managers and careworkers to enable discussion and resolution of any problems in regard to these dilemmas.

Careworkers' perspectives

Caregivers who participated in Stone's study said that 'their training, their employers and their professional norms all discourage "getting too close," "getting too attached," or "getting too emotionally involved" with the people they care for' (2000, p. 99). Twigg also found that the 'emotional reward of helping, the warmth of interpersonal exchanges and freedom and autonomy of the job [conflicted with] the emotional strain and the need to set limits' (2000, p. 129). Careworkers who participated in the Benevolent Society study reported similar experiences and conflicts. They found themselves negotiating and renegotiating professional and personal boundaries every time they were at work. Over time, and with experience, they had learnt to impose, negotiate and maintain boundaries that enabled them to do their work and provide good care.

Central to their struggles and negotiations was the clash of values between care as understood in the private sphere, as personal, warm, compassionate, flexible and emotional, and the values of a professional in the public sphere, expected to 'create' distance and work to consistently applied rules. One careworker described her struggle in the following terms:

> When I first started I wanted to do everything for everybody. But now, four years later, I've learnt that boundaries are very important. You've got to stop somewhere. I've learnt the hard way. When I first started I thought about the job all the time but you realise that you can't take care of everybody or solve everyone's problems (Fiona, careworker, aged 46).

Some of the careworkers, like the workers in Stone's study (2000), spoke of 'caring by the book', that is, closely following the rules to prevent any problems arising:

> Sometimes you tend to go very much by the book, follow the rule. The guidelines that we've been given strongly emphasise the problems that could be caused if you go outside the boundaries, outside the guidelines. So I do everything I can within the boundaries. I don't want to step outside them (Jennifer, careworker, aged 34).

However, they all spoke of breaking the rules at some time or other:

> We are never supposed to give our home numbers out to people. But of course we all break the rules and there are certain people we will give the number to and there are certain people you won't. The genuine people will never ring you unless they have to. It is awful really when you are told not to give your phone number out to anybody. And then as I've said to one coordinator, "You've got my home number. You ring me on my home number. What is the difference?" Because it may only be, "Could you pick me up a bottle of milk or something?" And how much easier and time saving is that? (Meg, careworker, aged 53).

The following story is an interesting case study in negotiating these boundaries with different care managers. In this case, the boundaries and rules were changed when the care manager changed. The situation and the ways the careworker broke the rules are almost identical, except that there was a different care manager supervising the careworker in the second instance.

> I had a lady in hospital last year and she was in for six weeks. No family at all. There was another lady in the ward with her that I also know. She told me that this lady was turning her underwear inside out to wear, because the hospital doesn't do washing. She was bed-bound. She couldn't get up and rinse her underwear herself, so I went there and I took them home and washed them. And I got in so much trouble. I said, "Well, I'm sorry but I've done it" (Brenda, careworker, aged 50).

She continues with the story and describes a similar situation and making similar decisions, but running the scenario by a different care manager:

> I had the same situation this morning. The coordinator rang me this morning and asked me if I'd been to see this lady in hospital. I said "No, I'm going to go this afternoon". And I thought, "Oh well, I'll try it, while she's on the phone". I said "Have you got a problem with me taking home any clothing that she's got to wash?" And she said to me, "No, and if you haven't got time to do it, drop them into the office this afternoon and I'll take them home and do them". So it was a completely different story (Brenda, careworker, aged 50).

Brenda had no difficulty justifying her behaviour in providing good care to her client. She was quite comfortable with her transgressions and felt she had behaved responsibly and looked after her client's best interests.

> That is my duty of care as the careworker to this person. That's the way I looked at it. If I had to I would have stayed in the hospital and washed them in the basin in the hospital, but it was just easier for me to take them home, dry them and take them back the next day (Brenda, careworker, aged 50).

She clearly felt far more comfortable with the way the second care manager had handled the situation and felt her own judgment and decisions were vindicated and supported. This was a far more satisfactory resolution from her perspective:

> It just makes you feel so much better. I mean you're not worried about ringing the coordinator. I'm not going behind her back doing things. Before I was doing things on my own and thinking, "I'll just take the consequences when they come". But now I'm not frightened to do that. I find it very easy (Brenda, careworker, aged 50).

Points of tension between managers and careworkers

Care managers and careworkers had different views about how one drew the boundaries between personal and work lives and about how one built and maintained professional relationships between careworkers and the person being cared for. The care managers spoke of having to be constantly vigilant, putting a lot of time and energy into explaining the nature of the desired professional working relationship. By contrast, the careworkers stated that they understood where the managers were coming from, found their guidance useful, but spoke of learning through their own experiences. They felt they were able to negotiate this difficult terrain, learn from their experiences and become better at negotiating professional relationships over time.

> You do learn to put up barriers … as you lose a client the next one that comes in you try and just keep that little tiny tissue paper between you. Not a wall, but just a little tissue paper there. You do have to draw a line in certain things (Jan, careworker, aged 57).

The role of policies and guidelines

The care managers and careworkers interviewed for this research were experienced and knowledgeable providers of care. In formulating policy they took on board frontline knowledge of the centrality of relationships and the secondary importance of tasks in supportive home care (Twigg 2000). Over time, the care managers have developed a range of detailed and transparent policies to cover most contingencies. The policies were pivotal in providing guidance to careworkers, while at the same time enabling careworkers to make professional judgments based on their ethic of care. The care managers saw the development and refinement of policies as a continually evolving process. Once the policies are developed they are 'tweaked' as needed to cover contingencies as they arise. They emphasised that all staff needed to be involved and made aware and continually updated on current policies:

> We have a whole range of policies that cover the whole range of care areas that basically fit the job descriptions. Policies include anything from how to pay for shopping, to what to do when the client isn't home. There is a whole range of policies that we are quite strict about adhering to and we use the team meeting process to make sure the policies are understood (Mary, care manager, aged 52).

They were continually explaining the underlying rationale and stressing the importance of adhering to these policies. One example, as outlined below, is ensuring older people are given receipts for any money they give the careworker. The care managers were aware that this can be time-consuming and inconvenient for the careworker, but ultimately the process ensures that all money is accounted for so there can be no confusion or accusations of exploitation.

> I make a point of adhering to the policy. The policies are there to protect the careworker from being compromised or put into a position where they are doing more than they are paid for. I think careworkers are resistant because it is a hassle sometimes. It is a hassle. It is easier to say, "I'll bring the change back", and not get the clients to sign, and the clients will say, "I trust you". And you've got to go through this rigmarole, "This is the policy. I have to give you a receipt". Sometimes you have to go over things a million times and it

> seems laborious and eats into your time. Sometimes you are pressed for time. You are rushing. The coordinator tells you to fill out the log as you go. But when you are on a rush, as a careworker you haven't got time. So there are all those bits of paperwork that are necessary (Eva, care manager, aged 45).

One of the rules that the care managers expect the careworkers to follow very closely is the rule that all changes to the care plan must be passed by the care managers. The care managers stressed, over and again, the importance of the careworkers running any changes by them, or at the very least, ensuring the care managers are kept updated and informed if changes are made.

> I maintain and review the care plans every three months to make sure that things are working well. I make sure that the clients really know me, so that they have the confidence to ring me in case anything goes wrong. Often they tell their problems to the girls, and then the girls come in and tell me. I would like to minimise that (Maria, care manager, 45).

A major preoccupation of the care managers was putting in place a framework that would protect and enhance the rights of both the workers and the recipients of care, and protect both groups from violence, abuse and exploitation, while providing good care where relationships were central and consistent with the overall aims of the Benevolent Society, an organisation where care managers and careworkers aimed to provide a relationship-based service.

Conclusion

Care managers and careworkers had different views on how relationships should be formed and negotiated day-by-day. The managers felt they were continually reiterating rules about appropriate boundaries, and spending a substantial amount of time supervising and scrutinising relationships between careworkers and older people. The majority of the careworkers were well aware of the managers' concerns, and spoke of numerous ways they negotiated working relationships with older people, day-by-day, not infrequently breaking the rules to provide what they judged to be good care. This took them into a realm of potential conflict with the care managers, and reflects what Twigg calls 'an unbounded element in carework':

> that derives from the importation into it of an ethic of love that derives primarily from the bonds of the family. This is something that workers find hard to resist and they find themselves caught between the personalised demands of this ethic of care—reinforced by emotional bonds that develop over time, particularly in response to personal dependence—and the conditions of waged labour in an increasingly hard nosed and cost pressured sector (Twigg 2000, p. 178).

This study demonstrates that, although it is not easy to negotiate these blurred boundaries, it is clearly possible. There were points of tension in this negotiation for both care managers and careworkers. Negotiating the boundaries between personal and work lives, and forming working relationships with the older people they were caring for, was not straightforward. All the participants acknowledged the importance, to both the careworker and the older person, of building and sustaining these relationships. However, as the careworkers and the care managers were continually emphasising, this is a working relationship and one which requires that boundaries be put in place to limit the nature and extent of the caring work and the degree of emotional involvement.

What made the work satisfying for the careworkers was that they enjoyed forming ongoing, productive, working relationships with their clients. They reported high levels of job satisfaction and were committed to working in the sector for as long as they could. As well, support that is based on strong relationships between worker and client, relationships that are respectful and positive, has been demonstrated to be beneficial in decreasing vulnerability in community care clients. Marsh reports that:

research demonstrates that positive relationships which mirror everyday social relationships are highly desired between elderly people and formal care providers and result in fewer physical symptoms and increased longevity. Consequently strong professional relationships between workers and clients should be viewed as a strength to be harnessed, not a weakness to be avoided (2007, p. 38).

This study found that, rather than advising the careworkers to remove any emotion or personal relationships from their care work and be totally task-oriented, the care managers in this organisation acknowledged the centrality of relationships in care provision and set in place mechanisms to enable these relationships to flourish, while protecting the rights and wellbeing of both the careworker and the person receiving care. As Joan Tronto has argued: 'Care is a central concern of human life. It is time we began to change our political and social institutions to reflect this truth' (1993, p. 180).

References

Aronson, J. & Neysmith, S. 1996, '"You're not just in there to do the work": Depersonalizing policies and the exploitation of home care workers' labor', *Gender & Society*, vol. 10, no. 1, pp. 59–77.

Aronson, J. & Neysmith, S. 2006, 'Obscuring the costs of home care: Restructuring at work', *Work, Employment and Society*, vol. 20, no. 1. pp. 27–45.

Australian Bureau of Statistics 2004, *Disability, Ageing and Carers, 2003*, Cat. No. 4430.0, Australian Bureau of Statistics, Canberra.

Australian Institute of Health and Welfare 2007, *Australia's Welfare 2007*, AIHW Cat. No. AUS 93, Australian Institute of Health and Welfare, Canberra.

Fleming, G. & Taylor, B. 2006, 'Battle on the home front: Perceptions of home care workers of factors influencing staff retention in Northern Ireland', *Health and Social Care in the Community*, vol. 15, no. 1, pp. 67–76.

McLean, J. 1999, 'Satisfaction, stress and control over work', in *Social Services Working under Pressure*, eds S. Balloch, J. Mclean & M. Fisher, Policy Press, Bristol.

Marsh, P. 2007, Safe as Houses: Elderly HACC Clients Describe Experiences of Vulnerability, Home and Community Care Consumer Consultation Project Report, TasCOSS, Hobart.

Meagher, G. & Healy, K. 2005, Who Cares? Volume 1: A Profile of Careworkers in Australia's Community Services Industries, *Paper 140*, Australian Council of Social Service, Sydney.

Meagher, G. & Healy, K. 2006, Who Cares? Volume 2 Employment Structure and Incomes in the Australian Care Workforce, *Paper 141*, Australian Council of Social Service, Sydney.

Mears, J. 2006, The World of Care Work, unpublished report submitted to the Benevolent Society.

Piercy, K. 2000, 'When it is more than a job: Close relationships between home health aides and older clients', *Journal of Aging and Health*, vol. 12, no. 3, pp. 362–87.

Rasmussen, B. 2004, 'Between endless needs and limited resources: The gendered construction of a greedy organization', *Gender, Work and Organization*, vol. 11, no. 5, pp. 506–25.

Stone, D. 2000, 'Caring by the book', in *Care Work: Gender, Labor and the Welfare State*, ed. M. H. Meyer, Routledge, New York.

Szebehely, M. 2005, 'Care as employment and welfare provision—child care and elder care in Sweden at the dawn of the 21st century', in *Dilemmas of Care in the Nordic Welfare State*, eds H. Dahl & T. Rask Eriksen, Ashgate, Aldershot.

Tronto, J. 1993, *Moral Boundaries: A Political Argument for the Ethic of Care*, Routledge, New York.

Twigg, J. 2000, *Bathing: The Body and Community Care*, Routledge, London.

Wærness, K. 1987, 'On the rationality of caring', in *Women and the State*, ed. A. S. Sassoon Hutchinson, London.

Wærness, K. 2007, 'Care in a global perspective', in *Social Omsorg i Socialt Arbete*, ed. S. Johansson, Gleerups, Malmö.

7

Parents as consumers of early childhood education and care: the feasibility of demand-led improvements to quality

Jennifer Sumsion and Joy Goodfellow

The quality of early childhood education and care (ECEC) is important for children, their parents and society more broadly. Positive outcomes for children in centre-based ECEC, particularly those from socially and economically disadvantaged backgrounds, are largely dependent on centre quality (NICHD Early Child Care Research Network 2002; Sylva et al. 2003). Parents' decisions about labour force participation are influenced by the quality of available care, and this is especially the case for mothers (Duncan et al. 2004; Hand 2005). Moreover, high quality ECEC contributes to the development of social capital by enhancing family and community networks (Press 2006).

Yet, in Australia, over the last decade and a half, the policy emphasis on ECEC, particularly long day care, as a competitive service best provided by the market (Organisation for Economic Co-operation and Development 2006), has led to a greater focus on availability rather than sustained attention to quality. With the notable exception of the introduction of a national accreditation system for long day care centres in 1994, quality, for the most part, has been framed as a natural outcome of the efficient operation of market forces. Faith in market rationality as a basis for quality ECEC provision is, at best, naïve given well-rehearsed arguments concerning the market's limitations in providing universally high quality ECEC (see, for example, Cleveland & Krashinsky 2002; Folbre 2006; Helburn & Howes 1996).

Since its election in November 2007, the Rudd Labor Government has consistently reiterated its commitment to the provision of high quality ECEC (Gillard 2008a). At the same time, it has indicated that market competition will continue to play an important role in ECEC policy, while foreshadowing the possible introduction of strategies to deter 'unfair profiteering' by for-profit providers (Gillard 2008b). To what extent and in what ways market forces will play out under the Rudd Government remains unclear. This chapter is premised on the assumption, however, that market forces will continue to play a significant role in Australian ECEC policy and provision. Accordingly, we appropriate the market discourses of supply and demand as a framework for analysis and speculation.

The intent of the chapter is to canvass the feasibility of parents, as consumers of ECEC services, driving demand-led improvements to quality. Our investigation is conceptual and tentative, rather than empirical and conclusive, and focuses primarily on parent knowledge, agency and motives, as well as power relations between parents, service providers and government. In using the term 'parents' instead of 'family', our intent is not to exclude families with diverse structures and caring arrangements, but rather to remain consistent with the terminology used in much of the literature and most of the websites upon which we have drawn. The chapter consists of two main sections. In the first section, we briefly discuss the constructs of market rationality, market imperfections and intervention mechanisms as they apply to the Australian market-oriented system of ECEC provision, in part to identify challenges Australian parents may face as consumers of ECEC services. In the second and larger section, we draw on research focusing on parents as ECEC consumers, and on websites aimed at assisting them to make informed choices, to develop a preliminary typology of perspectives on parents as ECEC consumers. We see the typology as a tool for differentiating ways in which parents are positioned as consumers and for considering possible consequences of these positionings. We also envisage that it may provide a useful springboard for subsequent empirical investigations of parent capacity to drive demand-led improvements to ECEC quality.

Market rationality, imperfections and intervention mechanisms

Proponents of competition argue that it leads to high quality and cost-efficient ECEC because, in theory, 'parents can shop around' and punish providers that do not deliver high-quality services at a competitive price by taking their children elsewhere (Cleveland & Krashinsky 2002, p. 39). Moreover, in a rational market that operates according to the laws of supply and demand, ECEC providers are assumed to have inbuilt incentives to continually monitor quality and efficiency, or risk financial collapse. Government intervention, market proponents argue, can be justified only when the market fails to function as it should. Yet in the Australian ECEC market, where market malfunctions and imperfections abound, intervention mechanisms designed to address the consequent imbalances of demand and supply have been of questionable effectiveness. In a context such as this, there are substantial barriers to parent-led demand for quality improvement. We highlight these below.

We focus first on barriers related to demand-side imperfections (associated with consumer demand for ECEC) and second, on supply-side imperfections (associated with the provision of ECEC). We then outline limitations of current market interventions designed to counter the negative effects of these imperfections. In doing so, we foreshadow three dimensions for conceptualising parents' capacity to bring about demand-led improvements to quality. These dimensions relate to how knowledgeable and perceptive (or informed and discerning) parents might be about quality; their focus on, and/or motivations for, improving quality; and the agency or power they are able to bring to their efforts to realise their goals in relation to quality.

Demand- and supply-side imperfections

Demand-side imperfections arise when consumers have difficulty judging and monitoring the quality of what they are purchasing (Cleveland & Krashinsky 2002; Helburn & Howes 1996; Stanley et al. 2006), perhaps because they are uninformed or undiscerning about the product or service. Conversely, they may be quite knowledgeable and discerning about the quality of the product or service but, for a variety of reasons, not in a position to act on that knowledge. Parents can find it difficult to evaluate the quality of long day care centres for a range of well-documented reasons (Cleveland & Krashinsky 2002; Meyers & Jordan 2006). In brief, they may not have purchased long day care before and may not be knowledgeable about what constitutes high quality. By the time they become experienced—and possibly more informed and discerning—consumers of long day care, their children are likely to be beyond the age where they require care, thus making it difficult to put their experience to good use. Because parents generally spend relatively little time in centres and because many aspects of quality provision are not readily observable, parents who are informed and discerning consumers may still struggle to monitor quality on an ongoing basis. A further complication is that parents are not direct consumers; they purchase long day care on behalf of their children, who are likely to 'have difficulty evaluating the quality of what they are consuming and communicating that evaluation' to their parents (Cleveland & Krashinsky 2005, p. 4). Moreover, the quality of a centre can also be unstable, and may vary markedly with staff turnover and even from day to day, with events on one day not necessarily indicative of those on other days.

The difficulties of evaluating and monitoring quality can be compounded by the emotional nature of the long day care transaction for many parents. Gendered social expectations about parenthood and paid employment, competing family and work demands, and concern for their children's wellbeing can create an array of antipathies and tensions for parents that can further 'distort' their consumer decisions (Vincent & Ball 2006). For example, in convincing themselves that they have acted in their child's best interests, parents may overestimate the quality of the long day care they purchase. Or having settled their child into a centre and formed relationships with staff, they may be reluctant to face the upheaval of moving to a different centre in search of higher quality, if indeed a place were available elsewhere. They might also refrain from raising concerns about quality because of fears that they or their child may be marginalised by centre staff (Cleveland & Krashinsky 2002).

Even in those arguably rare circumstances where parents are able to evaluate and monitor quality, choose their provider, and make decisions unencumbered by emotional constraints, quality may not be their overriding criterion. Given the high relative cost of child care, parents may opt for a lower quality, lower cost centre in preference to one of higher quality and higher cost, for even low or mediocre quality long day care has high utility value to parents if it permits them to work (Cleveland & Krashinsky 2005). Moreover, lack of awareness by many parents of the long-term benefits of high quality long day care (Sylva et al. 2003) may lead them to underestimate the importance of quality, and thus to 'under-invest' in quality in their purchasing decisions (Stanley et al. 2006, p. 27). The effect can be to perpetuate and exacerbate market imperfections.

Demand-side imperfections in the ECEC market such as those outlined above are compounded by supply-side imperfections. Despite growing pockets of oversupply, the overall shortfall of long day care places in Australia, in conjunction with significant levels of market concentration achieved by former corporate giant ABC Learning (see Press & Woodrow 2009) puts providers in a more powerful position than consumers, particularly in locations where parents, in effect, have no real choice of service. Even where parents have choices, supply-side imperfections are endemic. Currently, in Australia, for example, providers have no financial incentive to further improve quality after accreditation has been achieved. Opportunistic providers, therefore, may have an incentive to provide 'superficial evidence' of quality, such as new furnishings or staff uniforms, while engaging in practices that undermine it (Cleveland & Krashinsky 2005, p. 2). They may be able to cut costs, for instance, through dubious staffing practices and hence under-price, and eventually drive out of business, more principled providers that have a stronger commitment to quality.

Additional supply-side imperfections are created by the absence of safeguards against distortions arising from the differential lobbying strengths of providers; hence the possibility of privileged access for some providers to politicians and policy-makers. During the incumbency of the Howard Government (1996–2007), for example, the appointment by ABC Learning of a former Howard Government minister to its board of directors shortly after his 2004 electoral loss highlighted the potential for privileged access, given that the Minister, while in office, had responsibility for child care and the administration of the Child Care Benefit, which, at the time, constituted approximately 50 per cent of ABC Learning's income (Jokovich 2005). Documents obtained under freedom of information laws revealed that the same former minister met with senior government officials to discuss child care provision less than eight weeks after taking up his directorship with ABC Learning (Walsh 2006). Brennan (2007) documents several other similarly close links between former Liberal and National Party ministers and ABC Learning. It is not our intent to tie the likelihood of events such as these to any particular government. Rather, we suggest that they may well be symptomatic of corporatised provision and of the powerful vested interests that parents may face in any attempt to lobby for changes in ECEC policy directions that, for example, might include a greater focus on non-profit provision as a community and broader social good.

Demand- and supply-side intervention mechanisms

In attempting to address the demand- and supply-side imperfections described above, the Hawke-Keating (1983–1996) and the Howard (1996-2007) governments implemented a range of measures. Individually and collectively, these measures have been less than optimally effective in countering distortions in the ECEC market. Demand-side interventions include the Child Care Benefit fee subsidy, a progressive benefit that favours low-income families, and the Child Care Tax Rebate, a regressive benefit favouring high-income families (Brennan 2007). Given the tendency for some providers to increase their fees in line with increases in the Child Care Benefit and the Child Care Tax rebate (Mayne 2008), these interventions appear unlikely to allow parents the scope for nuanced consumer decisions of the kind presumably required to support demand-led improvements to quality. Less direct demand-side interventions include government-funded parent education initiatives to improve parent knowledge about quality long day care and to inform decisions concerning parents' choice of service.[1] The potential effectiveness of such initiatives is discussed later in the chapter.

Perhaps the most significant supply-side intervention with respect to quality has been the establishment in 1994 of the national accreditation system administered by the National Childcare Accreditation Council (NCAC) to complement state-based licensing regulations. This two-tiered regulatory framework is tied to government funding, and as Brennan (2007) points out, has been widely credited with guaranteeing an acceptable level of quality. Yet very few centres that seek accreditation fail to gain it. An analysis of the NCAC's Quality Trends reports for long day care services for the three years from July 2004–July 2007 indicates that the failure rate averaged less than 5 per cent (National Childcare Accreditation Council 2008). Anecdotal evidence suggests similarly low failure rates for state-based licensing. The consistently and implausibly low failure rate has attracted considerable scepticism about the rigour of accreditation and licensing processes (Pryor 2006), and contrary to original intentions, so far appears to have offered limited traction for demand-

---

[1] See, for example, the Raising Children Network (2008).

led improvements to quality. The Rudd Government's initial plans were to replace the satisfactory/unsatisfactory rating currently used in the NCAC's accreditation process with a five-point rating scale (ranging from A for 'excellence' to E for 'unsatisfactory') (Gillard 2008a). These plans have since been shelved, but the proposed five-point scale may have enhanced parent's knowledge of centre quality and thus assisted parent-led demand for quality improvement.

Other supply-side interventions introduced by the former Howard Government included the implementation of several targeted policy initiatives[2] aimed at extending long day care provision for communities with high levels of socioeconomic disadvantage that are unlikely to attract for-profit providers. While each initiative targets different kinds of programs and organisational structures, they all reflect a focus on addressing disadvantage and facilitating community capacity building. Whether parents in the communities served by these initiatives have sufficient cultural and political capital to drive demands for improved quality is, as yet, for the most part unknown.

Apart from some tightening of the national accreditation system, the Howard Government appeared to have no plans to retreat from its strong market orientation. Prior to its electoral defeat it had ruled out further supply-side interventions, such as re-introducing operational funding for services, investing in publicly-funded long day care infrastructure, regulating ownership of long day care centres, engaging in service provision planning, or reducing the funding that goes directly to parents, despite well-reasoned arguments (for example, Cox 2007) in favour of such measures. In contrast, the Rudd Government's plans to boost the ECEC workforce by creating additional university places in early childhood teacher education programs and abolishing fees for diploma-level ECEC, and to increase available long day care places by establishing 260 additional ECEC centres (Gillard 2008a) suggest that it intends to make more use than the

---

2 See, for example, the Stronger Families and Communities Strategy (Department of Families, Housing, Community Services and Indigenous Affairs 2008).

previous government of supply-side interventions. The implementation of these plans, and particularly decisions about whether the 260 new centres, to be located on school sites and community land, will operate on a non-profit basis, will provide insight into whether new possibilities are likely to emerge for demand-led improvements to quality, despite the continuing presence of demand- and supply-side imperfections outlined in this section.

The feasibility of demand-led improvements to quality

Among researchers and policy analysts, there is little consensus about the feasibility of demand-led improvements to quality. In their analysis of the impact of privatisation and corporatisation in Australian ECEC provision, Press and Woodrow (2005) conclude that consumers are unlikely to manage to 'exert an upward pressure' on the quality of child care provided by market forces, because of 'the complex interplay of factors associated with availability, affordability, quality and the imperfect information upon which parents base their decisions' (p. 282). In the United States of America, Emlen (1998) is considerably more optimistic. He contends that debates about how to achieve consistently high-quality child care have been limited by their bias towards improving supply-side interventions. Possibilities for addressing quality through improving demand-side factors, he argues, have been either prematurely overlooked or dismissed.

Canadian researchers Cleveland and Krashinsky (2005) are more circumspect than either Press and Woodrow (2005) or Emlen (1998). They differentiate between 'thick' markets with many potential long day care consumers, including those in middle- and higher-income levels; and 'thin' markets with relatively few potential consumers and a higher proportion of lower-income families.[3] Demand-led

---

3 Cleveland and Krashinsky (2005) designated Canadian communities with at least 25,000 children aged from birth to four years, and with average annual earnings per employed person in 2001 of $31,500 or more, as 'thick' markets. 'Thin' markets comprised communities with fewer than 15,000 children aged birth to four years, and annual average earnings of less than $31,500.

improvements to quality are more feasible in thick markets, they argue, because higher-income consumers are more able and likely than lower-income consumers to demand and obtain quality care. They leave unanswered, however, some key questions. For example, do consumers in thick markets who are relatively well-placed to use their consumer power to demand quality long day care, seek the kind of child care that is commensurate with experts' views of quality? Do they tend to act primarily on the basis of self-interest; and if they do, does their self-interest serve to improve quality across the board to the benefit of the community and of the wider society?

In the remainder of this section, we draw eclectically from research in early childhood education, social policy, educational policy, and feminist economics, as well as parent information and related websites, to develop a conceptual typology of five perspectives on the possibilities of parent-led demands for improved quality in ECEC. Our intent is to identify possible associations between ways in which parents as ECEC consumers are positioned in the literature and the feasibility of demand-led improvements to quality. Before proceeding, however, we outline the processes used to develop the typology.

Developing the typology: an explanatory note

We began by examining a collection of early childhood education research studies reporting on parents' reasons for choosing child care, their perspectives/views on child care, their perceptions of child care quality, and/or their experiences of/satisfaction with child care. Reports of these studies were sourced from four peer-reviewed journals[4] that have a wide readership amongst early childhood education researchers (from issues published between 1997 and 2007). From the references cited in the articles sourced through these journals

---

4 We searched the North American-based journals *Early Childhood Research Quarterly*, the United Kingdom-based *Early Child Development and Care*, the *European Early Childhood Education Research Journal*, and the *Australian Journal of Early Childhood*.

we located a further four relevant studies, making a total of thirteen studies. We then turned to parent education materials, identified by the Google search engine, from Australian websites providing advice to parents on 'choosing long day care centres'. Ten relevant and reputable websites were identified. In addition, we referred to publicly available online summary reports of high-profile studies[5] of the quality and impact of ECEC likely to be of interest to parents seeking research-based information about ECEC. An analysis of Australia's National Childcare Accreditation Council's child care quality assurance system as an example of service user evaluation followed.

Next, we considered recent critiques and empirical studies of ECEC consumer-provider dynamics in market-oriented contexts, taken from early childhood and/or educational research publications identified through our working knowledge of the literature. The critical perspectives underpinning this body of research distinguish this category from the first group of early childhood education research studies outlined above. Finally, we drew on a small sample of research on active citizenship and participatory democracy. Central to this work was an understanding of 'consumer' as a politicised concept that 'may be appropriated at different times for particular purposes' (Henderson & Petersen 2002, p. 5), rather than one with either inherently positive or negative connotations that cause it to 'be either welcomed or resisted depending on one's political persuasion or professional view' (Newman & Vidler 2006, p. 207).

Following processes outlined by Ozga (2000), we inductively analysed the different bodies of literature and web-based materials outlined above to ascertain the language, categories and themes used to construct and position parents as consumers. We also identified emphases, silences and visions of what might be possible concerning parent-led demands for improved quality. From this analysis, we

---

5 These studies include *The Effective Provision of Pre-School Education (EPPE)* study (Sylva et al. 2003), the NICHD study (NICHD 2006) and several Canadian studies (Canadian Centre for Knowledge Mobilization 2006).

developed a typology of perspectives on parents as ECEC consumers. As mentioned previously, we see the typology offering a tentative and partial, rather than a conclusive and comprehensive, categorisation; and for ease of discussion, have used a three-dimensional matrix for conceptualising parents' capacity to bring about demand-led quality improvements to represent categories in the typology (see Figure 7.1). These dimensions were arrived at inductively and are represented by the axes in the matrix. As can be seen in Figure 7.1, the first axis is *parent knowledge/perceptiveness*, the second axis is *parent motivation/focus* and the third axis is *parent agency/power*.

Figure 7.1: Conceptualising parents' capacity to bring about demand-led quality improvements

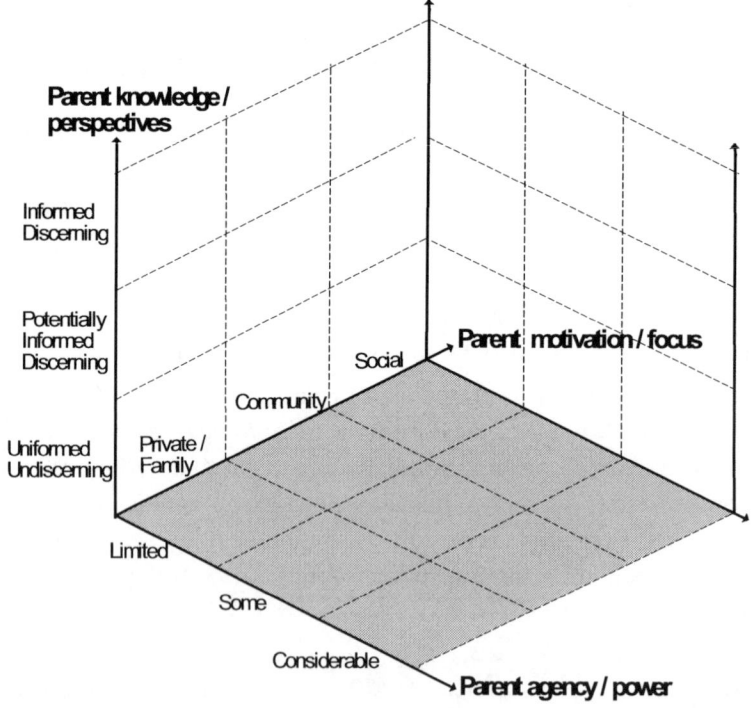

By *parent knowledge/perceptiveness*, we mean parents' familiarity with the determinants of quality ECEC generally agreed upon in the research literature; their understanding of how these determinants can and do play out in practice; their awareness that many aspects of quality are intangible and therefore not readily measurable; and their recognition and appreciation of those less tangible aspects. For the purpose of the matrix, we have identified three variations of this dimension: uninformed and undiscerning; potentially informed and discerning; and well informed and discerning. We acknowledge that we have conflated two scales, knowledge and perceptiveness, and the possibility that some parents may lack formal knowledge but be highly perceptive (discerning), or conversely, have considerable formal knowledge but have difficulty applying it to a child care centre. Given the tentative nature of the matrix, however, we do not address that limitation further.

By *parent motivation/focus*, we mean an amalgam of parents' hopes, desires, interests and concerns in relation to the quality of ECEC, and where they direct their energies in efforts to realise and address them. We distinguish between a family focus concerned with ECEC as a primarily private benefit centred on the wellbeing of one's own children/family; a community focus that may encompass but extends beyond a concern for private benefits to include a commitment to enhancing community wellbeing; and a broader social focus that may include a private/family and a community focus but extends beyond these to an explicit concern for the contribution ECEC might make to society more generally.

By *parent agency/power*, we mean the capacity to bring about the outcomes that one desires and hopes for. This capacity might come primarily from positional advantages and the cultural and economic resources that can assist parents negotiate the complexities and imperfections of ECEC markets, that is, those resources generally associated with middle to high socioeconomic status. Alternatively, the capacity might come from parents, individually or collectively, initiating and using a mix of creative tactics and strategies to secure the best possible outcomes, given their particular circumstances and regardless of their socioeconomic means. At the risk of obscuring and/or conflating different ways in and purposes for which agency and power can be exercised, we have used the terms 'limited', 'some' and 'considerable' to differentiate between varying degrees of agency and power.[6]

In the remainder of the chapter, we identify five categories of ways in which parents are positioned as consumers of ECEC in the bodies of literature and websites outlined above. We use the three-dimensional matrix to represent these categorisations. We also consider the feasibility of parent-led improvements to the quality of ECEC reflected in each of these categorisations.

A. Parents as uninformed, undiscerning consumers, focused on private benefits with limited agency/power

Within the early childhood education research field, there have been many investigations of parents' experiences of ECEC services, their perceptions of the quality of these services and their satisfaction with them (see, for example, Cryer & Burchinal 1997; Cryer et al. 2002; da Silva & Wise 2006; Elliott 2003; Fantuzzo et al. 2006; Knoche et al. 2006; Li-Grining & Coley 2006; Peyton et al. 2001; Ridley-May 2007; Robson 2006; Shlay et al. 2005). Many of these studies dichotomise expert professionals and uninformed, undiscerning service users. For the most part, they emphasise the 'information asymmetry' between parents and service providers arising from the difficulties inherent in monitoring quality in imperfect markets that we referred to above. In general, they also accord professional and scientific knowledge greater legitimacy than parent knowledge

---

[6] Agency and power might be exercised, for example, in selecting a centre, participating in the life and governance of the centre, participating in the community, participating in the community that the centre seeks to serve, and in policy participation at any of the jurisdictional levels concerned with ECEC.

Figure 7.2: Parents as uninformed, undiscerning consumers, focused on private benefits, with limited agency/power

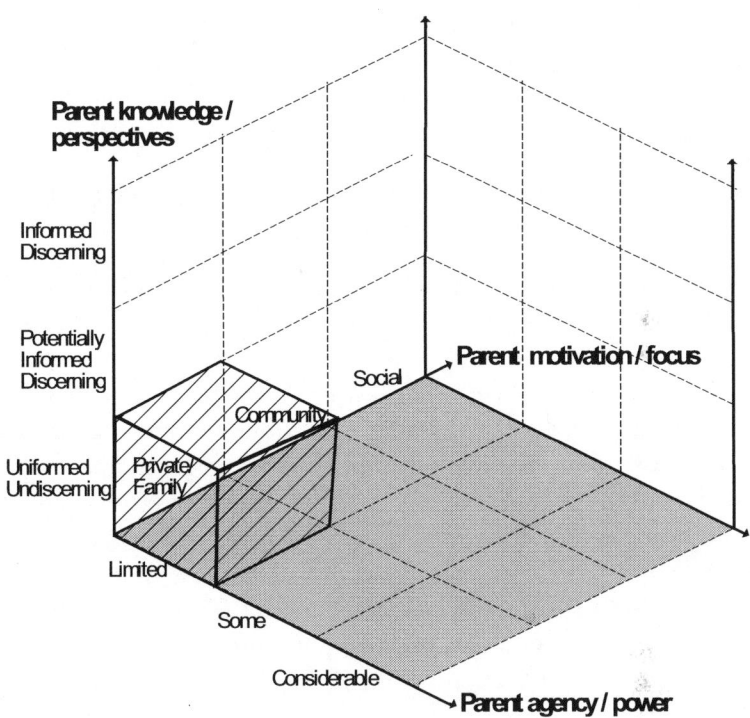

and, for the most part, position parents as naïve consumers with an emotional investment in overestimating, relative to 'objective' researcher assessment, the quality of the service attended by their child. With some notable exceptions (for example, da Silva & Wise 2006; Emlen 1998), researchers have demonstrated relatively little interest in participatory approaches that acknowledge the possibility of parent agency, for example, through joint constructions of quality by professionals, service providers and parents. Nor is there much attention to the possibility that parents may see ECEC as more than a private benefit. Two decades ago, Fuqua and Labensohn (1986, p.

295) concluded that 'parents ... in reality did not have the skills of assistance to them to function as wise consumers of child care', a view echoed in many contemporary studies. For many ECEC researchers, then, the likelihood of demand-led improvements to quality would seem remote. These perspectives of parents, as uninformed and undiscerning consumers who are focused on private benefits but able to exercise little agency or power, are encapsulated in Figure 7.2.

B. Parents as potentially informed and discerning consumers, focused on private benefits with some agency/power

Framed in terms of parents' obligations as consumers to make responsible and appropriate choices, parent education literature aims to counter the information asymmetries that preoccupied researchers in many of the studies referred to above. As Henderson and Petersen (2002) caution, however, consumer education literature—grounded in the naïve and implausible assumptions that consumer behaviour is always fully informed and logical, which underpin rational choice theory—can itself be limited and naïve. The proliferation of parent information websites, for example, reflects assumptions that parents will have the means to readily access internet facilities, which may not necessarily be the case, especially in marginalised communities.

Our analysis of the websites of ten reputable Australian organisations or government-sponsored bodies offering parent education resources leads us to concur with Henderson and Petersen that, with some notable exceptions, much of the available literature seems to take little account of cross-cultural differences, including differences in values or views about what might constitute appropriate choice. Moreover, it rarely engages with the possibility of restricted choice and frequently ignores relations of knowledge and power between service providers and parents. Much of the parent education literature seems more focused on assisting parents to negotiate, rather than to endeavour to change, the current landscape of ECEC provision. It may also inadvertently perpetuate what we suspect is a common

Figure 7.3: Parents as potentially informed and discerning consumers, focused on private benefits with some agency/power

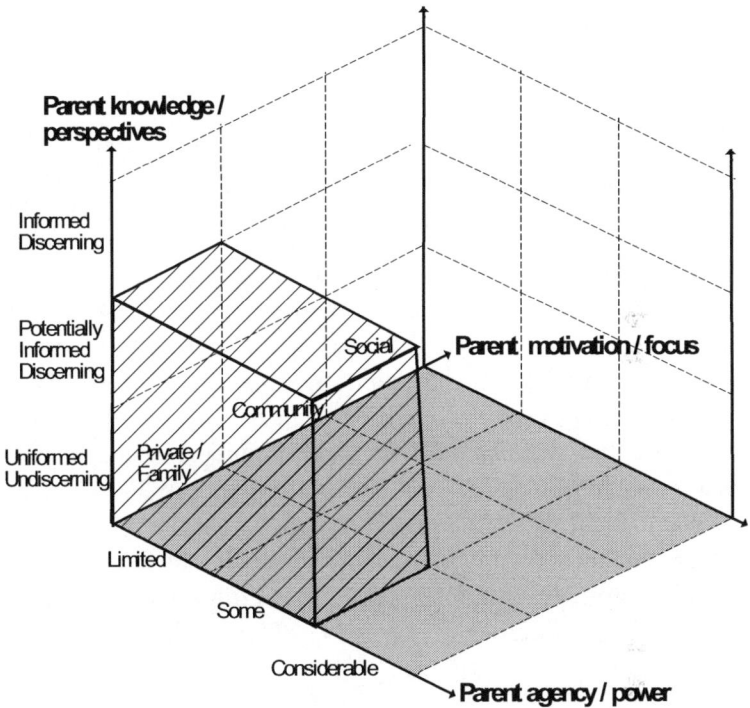

assumption among parents and the broader public—that centres that receive government funding must be of reasonable quality. As represented in Figure 7.3, in general, then, parent education literature seems to position parents as potentially informed and discerning consumers, focused on private benefits and able to exercise some agency/power. We conclude, therefore, that although well-intentioned, this literature may have limited potential to inspire and support demand-led improvements to quality.

A promising development is the recent emergence of freely available, non-specialist, plain language research reports (National Institute of

Child Health and Human Development 2006) and summaries of accumulated research findings (Canadian Centre for Knowledge Mobilisation 2006) of investigations into quality in ECEC. These reports position parents—along with early childhood educators, policy-analysts, and researchers seeking an introduction to ECEC quality—as capable and critical consumers of research who seek empirical evidence as one of the bases for their decision-making. Although some of the criticisms of the more traditional type of parent education literature outlined above could still apply to these reports, they at least refer to the complexities and the contingencies of 'political, social, national and theoretical contexts' in the provision of quality care (Canadian Centre for Knowledge Mobilisation 2006, p. 7). It is feasible, therefore, that they could lead some parents to question the simplistic or superficial notions of quality conveyed by some service providers. These reports are notably silent, however, on key debates associated with market-oriented ECEC provision, including whether a profit motive, and in particular, joint responsibilities to shareholders and parents, are compatible with high-quality services. Their silence on such matters, in keeping with their seemingly apolitical intent, could limit their usefulness to parents seeking politicised strategies to procure high-quality care.

C. Parents as informed, discerning, community-focused consumers with considerable agency/power

Service user evaluation systems position consumers as knowledgeable and discerning, and therefore entitled and equipped to participate in evaluation processes (Newman & Vilder 2006). In Australia, the NCAC aims to encourage active and ongoing parent participation in the life and governance of the service as a means of improving the quality of the service. Accordingly, as part of the NCAC's child care quality assurance (CCQA) systems, parents are asked to complete a survey that requires them to rate the quality of the service their child attends according to seven 'quality areas' and

33 principles (National Childcare Accreditation Council 2005a).[7] Parents' ratings are assigned a weighting of 10 per cent in the overall evaluation of the service, if at least 40 per cent of parents complete the survey (National Childcare Accreditation Council 2005a). By constructing parents as consumers with considerable agency and power, ECEC service user evaluations, at face value, offer hope of differently constructed relationships between government, service provider and consumer to the kinds of relationships implicitly conveyed in much of the early childhood research and parent education literature. In contrast to the two previous categorisations, they position parents as informed, discerning, community-focused consumers who are able to exercise considerable agency and power. This positioning is represented in Figure 7.4.

Recent research findings (Fenech et al. 2008) and the National Childcare Accreditation Council's own evaluations, however, highlight a variety of concerns expressed by ECEC staff about the appropriateness and usefulness of the parent surveys used in the CCQA. They range from staff and parent perceptions of user-unfriendly survey formats that leave parents with no space for comment (National Childcare Accreditation Council 2005b) to ECEC staff concerns that asking parents to rate service quality 'de-professionalises' ECEC staff (Fenech et al. 2008). These concerns appear to reflect deeply entrenched hierarchies that, perhaps unconsciously, privilege the interests of government agencies, such as NCAC, over those of ECEC staff and parents, and the interests of ECEC staff over the interests of parents—in this case presumably enabling NCAC to fulfil its responsibilities to obtain feedback without permitting the type of specific feedback that could necessitate it taking action, and enabling ECEC staff to use the construct of professionalism to shield them from unwanted parent criticism. More broadly, these concerns raise

---

7 There can be a tendency for parent evaluation surveys to become little more than 'one-off' events in each accreditation cycle, rather than simply a component of ongoing parent participation to improve quality, as envisaged by the NCAC.

Figure 7.4: Parents as informed, discerning, community-focused consumers with considerable agency/power

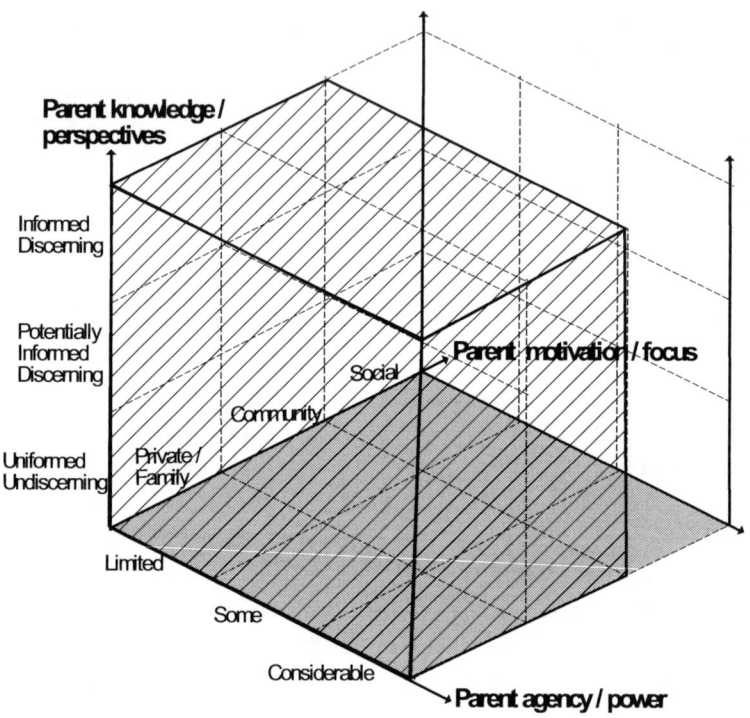

interesting questions about whether service user evaluations are largely symbolic and do little to disrupt traditional power relations between government, service provider and consumer. Indeed, Hodge (2005, p. 164) cautions that ultimately service user evaluations are often 'little more than mechanisms by which state agencies give their decision-making processes legitimacy, in the process failing to address inherently problematic structural issues and excluding voices that are deemed not acceptable'. Service user evaluations may be superficially transparent and democratic. But if, in effect, they maintain 'normative boundaries' that tightly control issues that are allowed on to agendas (Hodge 2005, p. 177), then mechanisms like the NCAC's quality assurance systems may be relatively ineffective vehicles for demand-led improvements to quality. Moreover, by encouraging parents to place their trust in regulatory systems, and thus presumably allaying parents' concerns about quality, service user evaluations could be complicit in depoliticising parents and dissuading them of the need for policy activism in relation to ECEC provision.

D. Parents as informed, discerning consumers, focused on private benefits with considerable agency/power

Critical analyses of ECEC market dynamics, the commodification of ECEC, and implications for power relations between parents and service providers are now emerging (see, for example, Goodfellow 2005; Harris 2008; Vincent & Ball 2006; Woodrow & Press 2007). Some of these analyses (for example, Goodfellow 2005; Vincent & Ball 2006) offer a different way of positioning parents to the three perspectives outlined above—namely (some) parents as informed, discerning, but essentially self-interested consumers for whom ECEC is an 'individualised calculation' (Lupton 1997, p. 374, cited by Salter 2004, p. 45), as implied in Figure 7.5. The stakes in getting these calculations 'right' are high, argue Vincent and Ball (2006, p. 5), for choice of ECEC service plays an important role 'in attaining social advantage and in maintaining social divisions', at least in the largely white, middle-class, inner London context of their study.

Critical perspectives leave open the possibility that information asymmetry, which has featured so strongly in most previous analyses of market-oriented ECEC, does not necessarily equate with power asymmetry. Vincent and Ball contend that to negotiate the child care market successfully, parents need to be 'energetic, inventive, persistent, flexible and resilient' and able 'to deploy the full range of capitals available to them, economic, cultural and social, to achieve their purposes in this market' (2006, p. 162). Conceivably, the capacity of middle-

Figure 7.5: Parents as informed, discerning consumers, focused on private benefits with considerable agency/power

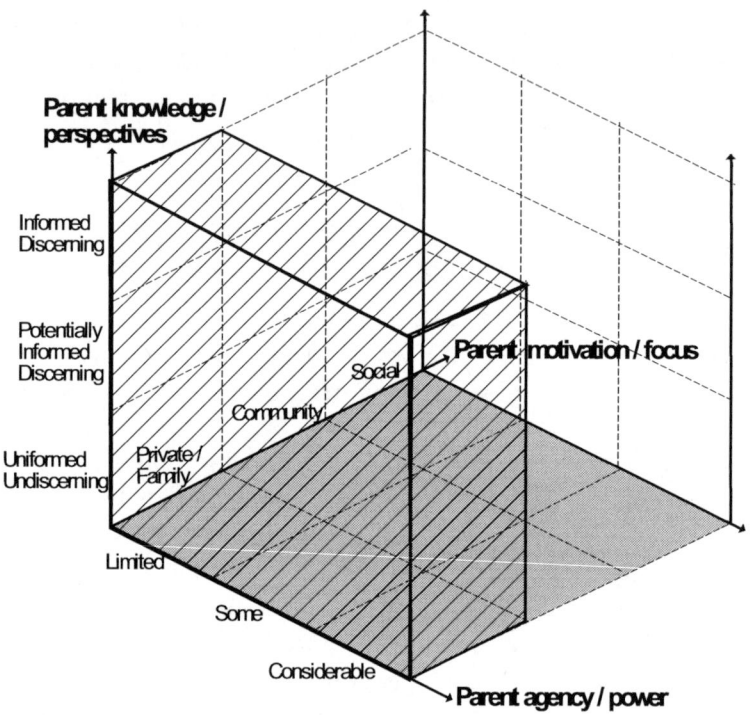

class parents to draw on considerable reserves of capital might enable them to redress information asymmetries, and enable them to be more successful than parents with fewer capital resources in driving demand-led improvements to quality. But if, as Vincent and Ball (2006) argue, ECEC is a mechanism of social reproduction that perpetuates and entrenches middle-class advantage, then middle-class parents' investments in ECEC in a market-oriented context may tend to focus more on personal advantage, than on enhancing social capital and community infrastructure more broadly. The end result of parent demands for quality in this scenario could lead simply to a more stratified system of ECEC provision, with high-quality services for those who can afford them and low-quality services for those who cannot.

Similarly, where self-interest is a primary motivator, there is scope for collusion between service providers that want to attract what they see as 'high value' children, a term used by Kenway and Bullen (2001), and parents who want to avoid services that, in their view, accept 'low value' children. Take, for example, provision for children with special needs, which Cleveland and Krashinsky (2002, p. 40) refer to as a 'little discussed, but potentially important, problem in relation to demand-side subsidies'. As they point out:

> providing ECEC for special-needs children is resource-intensive and may therefore divert resources away from other children. Parents, concerned generally with the welfare of their own children, will tend to avoid centres that divert resources in this way. As parents self-select into centres without special-needs children, centres with them will be driven out of business (p. 40).

A related possibility is that parents may be well-informed about experts' views about quality but, in locations where choice is possible, may actively select a service that is more aligned with parents' own values and goals, perhaps for religious or cultural reasons, or as already discussed, for reasons of social advantage. None of these scenarios is conducive to broadly based demand-led improvements to service quality.

E. Parents as informed, discerning, activist citizen-consumers, focused on social benefits with considerable agency/power

This perspective represents a distinct shift from market discourses of consumerism based on consumption for private gain, to discourses of activist consumerism grounded in participatory democracy and active citizen involvement for the common good (see also Dalton & Wilson 2009). Casting children, and social policy provision for them, as a shared responsibility positions parents as politically astute consumers *and* citizens who, by acting collectively, can exert demand-side pressure to raise the overall quality of services, rather than simply being content to make informed but ultimately self-interested choices for their private benefit or that of their immediate community as represented in Figure 7.6. An underpinning assumption is that a collective sense of responsibility and concern, in this case for children's wellbeing, can be a powerful force for change that goes beyond the level of the service and the community in which it is located through articulating new demands, challenging entrenched provider interests, and ultimately shaping 'the discourses and practices of government' (Herbert-Cheshire 2003, p. 468).

Whether those most affected by particular policies can successfully challenge, negotiate, and ultimately transform those policies (Herbert-Cheshire 2003) is contestable. According to Henderson and Petersen (2002), the selective appropriation of consumerist discourses by activist groups has proven a useful strategy:

> the identity label "the consumer" and the language of consumerism have proved useful to numerous groups in their efforts to make visible their claims … and to protect and advance their interests. The strategic use of identity labels, or so-called "strategic essentialism" where groups assume a cohesive identity for specific political purposes, has been shown to be effective in feminist struggles and in advancing the position of minority groups (p. 4).

Similarly, but with a different focus, Itkonen (2007) analyses successful approaches to political activism by parents of children with special education needs in the United States. She documents in considerable detail specific strategies used by these parent activists to secure much improved provision for their children. The most effective strategies for gaining political traction in policy networks included highly strategic issues-framing and problem definition, and 'sophisticated political storytelling' (Itkonen 2007, p. 600).

Figure 7.6: Parents as informed, discerning, activist citizen-consumers, focused on social benefits with considerable agency/power

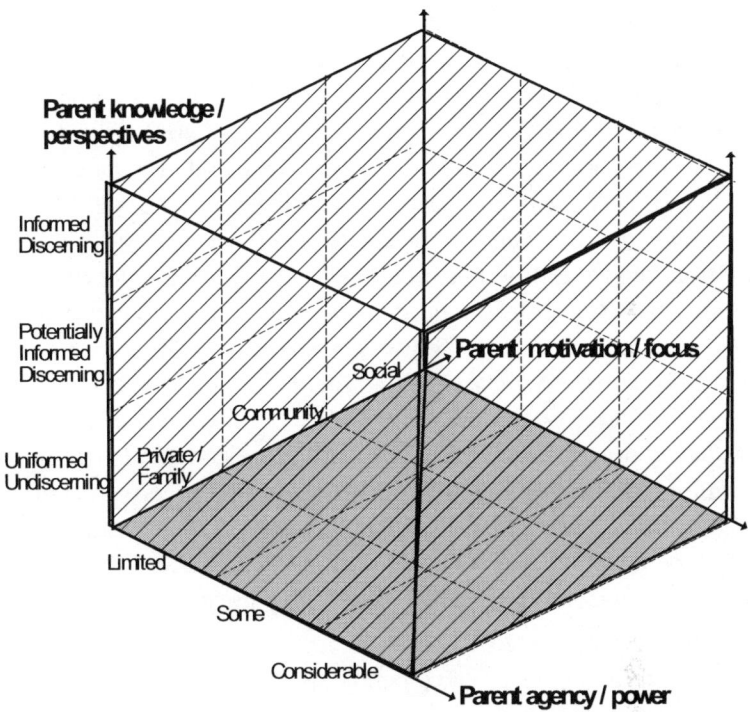

In contrast, Salter (2004, p. 66) counters that government and powerful providers 'know that it is in their best interests to construct a consensus' and hence are 'disinclined to destabilise' the status quo by admitting 'new and unpredictable' activist networks into policy decision-making in any meaningful way. Citing the relatively limited impact of consumer health movements in the United Kingdom, Salter warns that, at most, we might see 'a reformulation of the relationships between the principal actors ... but not a significant redistribution of power between them' (2004, p. 187). Although there are parallels between what Salter sees as the somewhat limited outcomes achieved by United Kingdom consumer health activism movements and the outcomes achieved by Australian ECEC activists to date, contextual differences countenance hope. Unlike the United Kingdom medical establishment, ABC Learning, for example, while an indisputably powerful entity, does not and cannot claim to speak on behalf of the ECEC field. Despite concerns about the former Howard Government's ECEC policy creating a mutual dependency between childcare corporations and the state (Sumsion 2006), ABC Learning particularly since its corporate collapse, remains more dependent on the Australian Government for its survival than the government is on it.[8] Consequently, in terms of power relations between consumers, government and service providers, ABC Learning is comparatively less powerfully positioned than the United Kingdom medical establishment, as portrayed in Salter's analysis, and therefore more vulnerable to shifts in power relations. If, as Salter suggests, these power relations are constantly changing, this vulnerability presumably provides openings for consumer activists to influence Australian ECEC policy decisions. As Salter (2004, p. 65) cautions, however, any 'translation of consumer pressure into significant power shifts' will be an inevitably uncertain and complex process.

To date, there appear to have been few formal, in-depth investigations specifically focused on shifting power relations between consumers, governments and ECEC providers in Australian ECEC policy networks. Notable exceptions include the historical and contemporary analyses undertaken by Brennan—see especially Brennan (1998) for a tracing of parent-led demands for quality improvement in the 1970s and the establishment of long day care services in Australia, through to the 1990s. Nor, indeed, has there been much attention

---

8 This is not to imply that the Rudd Government would readily introduce policies that would disadvantage ABC Learning, but rather to note that a corporate collapse or withdrawal by ABC Learning from the ECEC market would not trigger the collapse of long day care provision. As such, ABC Learning would not have to be propped up by the government regardless of the cost involved in doing so.

to activist consumerism or citizenship as a theoretical lens or basis for empirical investigations of efforts to enhance quality in ECEC. Such investigations would constitute a distinct shift in thinking about the possibility of parents initiating demand-led improvements to quality because they would involve rejecting the commonly arrived at conclusion that, inevitably and necessarily, parents tailor their views about quality to accommodate the 'social and economic realities that limit their range of feasible options' (Meyers & Jordan 2006, p. 60). Rather, they would keep alive the possibility of parents collectively challenging, instead of acquiescing to and accepting, those 'realities', including the problems stemming from market imperfections. Empirical investigations would contribute to developing a much-needed knowledge base about effective citizen activism.

In her economic analysis of the potential of the paid care sector, including ECEC, to build political coalitions, Folbre (2006) emphasises the scope to build powerful strategic alliances between careworkers and care consumers because of the strong emotional and personal valency of their connections. In Australia, ECEC professionals have engaged parents in campaigns to improve quality, including the recently successful '1:4 Make it Law' campaign in New South Wales for improved staff-child ratios for babies and toddlers in long day care. Conceivably, parent-initiated campaigns that engage ECEC professionals, as well as community and business leaders, could ratchet up demand-led pressure for quality improvement. Harris' (2008) qualitative study of women's reflections on choosing long day care in a regional community in Queensland highlights the importance the participants placed on high-quality ECEC; their dissatisfaction with the market model of ECEC provision; the lack of choice they perceived it offered them; and a deep scepticism about the compatibility of the pursuit of high-quality care and corporate profits. We argue that when proponents of market mechanisms ignore the impact of these mechanisms on people's lives and people feel passionately about the aspects of their lives affected, as Harris (2008) maintains is so with ECEC, there is the potential for mobilisation—in this case for demand-led changes to ECEC policy and quality.

Admittedly, it would be easy to romanticise the notion of parents as activist consumers and citizens demanding and procuring universally high-quality ECEC. Prior to the 2007 Australian federal election, it would also have been easy to dismiss the prospect as remote, given the Howard Government's seemingly entrenched market-oriented approach to social policy provision generally and its concomitant, concerted and arguably successful efforts to re-configure its citizens as self-interested and self-absorbed consumers (Pusey 2003). Yet in the light of the emergence of the albeit socially conservative Family First political party[9] at the 2004 Australian federal election, perhaps it would be premature to discount the possibility of parents' commitment to, and investment in, their children's wellbeing providing a catalyst for a groundswell of community-wide repudiation of market-based policies in social services provision, including ECEC. The Rudd Government's 'Community Cabinet' meetings offering citizens the opportunity to register for a chance to meet with a federal minister of their choice (O'Brien & MacDonald 2008) also holds new possibilities for influencing ECEC policy in participatory democratic ways. As an ad hoc political force, in a changing political environment, parents could conceivably bring about what the market has so far failed to deliver.

Concluding thoughts

As we have reiterated throughout, the five perspectives on parents as ECEC consumers outlined in this chapter are neither exhaustive

---

9 The 2004 Australian Federal Election saw the emergence of the newly established, conservative Family First party as a new and influential political force, with sole elected representative, Steve Fielding holding the balance of power in the Senate. Senator Fielding remained in a strong bargaining position when the new Senate took effect in July, 2008. Family First promotes family values and the need for government policies to take account of the interests of families. As a formal political party, it differs from the ad hoc political action envisaged in this paper, but nevertheless demonstrates the potential political power that can come from mobilising parents' interests and broader community support for families.

nor mutually exclusive but simply a starting point for addressing the many 'absences and silences' (Vincent & Ball 2006, p. 134) concerning the feasibility of demand-led improvements to quality in market-oriented ECEC provision. In our view, these perspectives provide a tentative but potentially fruitful framework for conceptualising relations between governments, service providers and parents in the ECEC market place, and for considering how these relations might be reconfigured. They also invite consideration of how different policy contexts, market structures and interventions might create or make possible particular perspectives on, and positionings of, parents as consumers of ECEC, and render other perspectives and positionings irrelevant. For example, in a policy context where major decisions about ECEC policy directions required joint negotiation between government, communities and providers with an emphasis on ongoing collaboration to meet jointly agreed-upon goals, perspectives on parents as actively engaged citizens might become unremarkable. Likewise, if there were universal access to high-quality services, there would appear little need for self-interested pursuit of high-quality places for one's children, and a stratum of self-interested consumers might not emerge. Empirical evidence of any relationships between policy contexts, market structure and interventions and the positioning of parents could add impetus and a new dimension to considerations of the real and opportunity costs and benefits of ECEC policy decisions, especially in relation to opportunities for social engagement and community building, as the marked difference between Figures 7.2 and 7.6 suggests.

Similarly, the perspectives identified in the typology invite consideration of how policy contexts might interact with local ECEC markets to position parents in particular ways. In 'thick' markets (Cleveland & Krashinsky 2005), for example, where parents have a choice of services, a wider range of positionings might be possible than in local contexts where demand for places far outstrips supply. If this were the case, then questions arise about implications of policy-market relations for urban, regional, and rural communities, especially about what might be possible for parent-led demands for improvements to quality.

The dimensions of variation in the typology, and corresponding axes in the matrix, identify some useful directions for further conceptual investigation and highlight areas where empirical evidence is needed. The 'parent agency and power' dimension, for example, raises questions about the kinds of activism and 'parent power' that it might take for the governments to want, or need, to forge new kinds of political alliances with parents that go beyond the somewhat tokenistic parent representation in ECEC policy in Australia, at least in the last decade or so. It also raises questions about what these political alliances might look like, whose interests they might serve, and how the voices of marginalised parents, and not just those of middle-class parents, could be heard. Further questions could focus on the scope for joint activism by parents and ECEC staff, and on processes of activism that tend to be most effective in particular kinds of contexts. Knowing more about processes by which consumer and citizen demands for change could be translated into new policies, at the level of service provider, and beyond, rather than merely accommodated in ways that maintain traditional power relations, would also be useful (Salter 2004); in other words, identifying how to bring about change at service provider and government policy level that goes deeper than rhetoric. Each dimension of variation in the typology has the scope to provide an equivalent set of questions.

Investigations of the kinds suggested here would focus much needed attention on some of the under-addressed dynamics of ECEC market forces and the relations underpinning them. In particular, they would render more complex current conceptualisations of parents as consumers of ECEC and hopefully identify new and alternative stances that parents as participants in ECEC market transactions might take up. Clearly, much work is needed before any conclusions can be drawn concerning the feasibility of parents driving demand-led improvements to quality. We believe, however, that there are grounds for cautious optimism, and that the possibilities raised in this chapter warrant further investigation.

References

Brennan, D. 1998, *The Politics of Australian Child Care: Philanthropy to Feminism and Beyond,* (2nd ed.), Cambridge University Press, Melbourne.

Brennan, D. 2007, 'The ABC of child care politics', *Australian Journal of Social Issues,* vol. 42, no. 2, pp. 213–25.

Canadian Centre for Knowledge Mobilisation 2006, CCKM's Research Guide to Child Care Decision Making [Online], Available: http://www.cckm.ca/ChildCare/home.htm [2006, Oct 11].

Cleveland, G. & Krashinsky, M. 2002, *Financing ECEC Services in OECD Countries: OECD Occasional Papers* [Online], Available: http://www.oecd.org/dataoecd/55/59/28123665.pdf#search=%22Financing%20ECEC%20services%20in%20OECD%20Countries%22 [2005, Mar 3].

Cleveland, G. & Krashinsky, M. 2005, *The Nonprofit Advantage: Producing Quality in Thick and Thin Child Care Markets* [Online], Available: http://childcarepolicy.net/pdf/non-profitadvantage.pdf [2006, Feb 4].

Cox, E. 2007, 'Funding children's services', in *Kids Count: Better Early Childhood Education and Care in Australia,* eds E. Hill, B. Pocock & A. Elliott, Sydney University Press, Sydney.

Cryer, D. & Burchinal, M. 1997, 'Parents as child care consumers', *Early Childhood Research Quarterly,* vol. 12, no. 1, pp. 35–58.

Cryer, D., Tietze, W. & Wessels, H. 2002, 'Parents' perceptions of their children's child care: A cross-national comparison', *Early Childhood Research Quarterly,* vol. 17, no. 2, pp. 259–77.

da Silva, L. & Wise, S. 2006, 'Parent perspectives on childcare quality among a culturally diverse sample', *Australian Journal of Early Childhood,* vol. 31, no. 3, pp. 6–14.

Dalton, B. & Wilson, R. 2009, 'Improving quality in Australian child care: The role of the media and non-profit providers', in *Paid Care in Australia: Politics, Profits, Practices,* eds D. King & G. Meagher, Sydney University Press, Sydney.

Department of Families, Housing, Community Services and Indigenous Affairs 2008, Stronger Families and Communities Strategy [Online], Available: http://www.facsia.gov.au/internet/facsinternet.nsf/aboutfacs/programs/sfsc-sfcs.htm [2008, Aug 14]

Duncan, S., Edwards, R., Reynolds, T. & Alldred, P. 2004, 'Mothers and child care: Policies, values and theories', *Children and Society*, vol. 18, no. 4, pp. 254–65.

Elliott, R. 2003, 'Sharing care and education: Parents' perspectives', *Australian Journal of Early Childhood*, vol. 28, no. 4, pp. 14–22.

Emlen, A. C. 1998, From a Parent's Point of View: Flexibility, Income, and Quality of Child Care: Background Paper [Online], Available: http://www.ssw.pdx.edu/focus/emlen/documents/pdfBethesda1998.pdf#search=%22Emlen%20from%20a%20parent's%20point%20of%20view%22 [2006, Mar 3].

Fantuzzo J., Perry, M. A. & Childs, S. 2006, 'Parent satisfaction with educational experiences scale: A multivariate examination of parent satisfaction with early childhood education programs', *Early Childhood Research Quarterly*, vol. 21, no. 2, pp. 142–52.

Fenech M., Sumsion, J. & Goodfellow, J. 2008, 'Regulation and risk: Early childhood education and care services as sites where "the laugh of Foucault" resounds', *Journal of Education Policy*, vol. 23, no.1, pp. 35–48.

Folbre, N. 2006, 'Demanding quality: Worker/consumer coalitions and "high road" strategies in the care sector', *Politics and Society*, vol. 34, no. 1, pp. 1–21.

Fuqua, R. W. & Labensohn, D. 1986, 'Parents as consumers of child care', *Family Relations*, vol. 35, no. 2. pp. 295–303.

Gillard, J. 2008a, *Budget: The Education Revolution*, Commonwealth of Australia, Canberra.

Gillard, J. 2008b, Radio Interview ABC, 8.45am Wednesday, 4 June 2008 [Online], Available: http://mediacentre.dewr.gov.au/mediacentre/Gillard/Releases/ChildcarefeesFuelWatch.htm [2008, Dec 31].

Goodfellow, J. 2005, 'Market childcare: Preliminary considerations of a "property view" of the child', *Contemporary Issues in Early Childhood*, vol. 6, no. 1, pp. 54–65.

Harris, N. 2008, 'Women's reflections on choosing quality long day care in a regional community', *Australian Journal of Early Childhood*, vol. 33, no. 3, pp. 42–49.

Hand, K. 2005, 'Mothers' views on using formal child care', *Family Matters*, vol. 70, pp. 10–17.

Helburn, S. W. & Howes, C. 1996, 'Child care cost and quality', *The Future of Children*, vol. 6, no. 2, pp. 62–82.

Henderson, S. & Petersen, A. 2002, 'Introduction: Consumerism in health care', in *Consuming Health: The Commodification of Health Care*, eds S. Henderson & A. Petersen, Routledge, London and New York, pp. 1–30.

Herbert-Cheshire, L. 2003, 'Translating policy: Power and action in Australia's country towns', *Sociologia Ruralis*, vol. 43, no. 4, pp. 454–73.

Hodge, S. 2005, 'Participation, discourse and power: A case study in service user involvement', *Critical Social Policy*, vol. 25, no. 2, pp. 164–79.

Itkonen, T. 2007, 'Politics of passion: Collective action from pain and loss', *American Journal of Education*, vol. 113, no. 4, pp. 577–604.

Jokovich, E. 2005, 'Family payment: About face muddies the waters', *Rattler*, vol. 73, pp. 6–7.

Kenway, J. & Bullen, E. 2001, *Consuming Children: Education-Entertainment-Advertising*, Open University Press, Maidenhead and Philadelphia.

Knoche, L., Peterson, C. A., Edwards, C. P. & Hyun-Joo, J. 2006, 'Child care for children with and without disabilities: The provider, observer, and parent perspectives', *Early Childhood Research Quarterly*, vol. 21, no. 1, pp. 93–109.

Li-Grining, C. P. & Coley, R. L. 2006, 'Child care experiences in low-income communities: Developmental quality and maternal views', *Early Childhood Research Quarterly*, vol. 21, no. 2, pp. 125–41.

Mayne, S. 2008, *Time to put ABC Learning out of its misery*, Crikey Business [Online], Available: http://www.crikey.com.au/Business/20080611-Time-to-put-ABC-Learning-out-of-its-misery.html [2008, Dec 31].

Meyers, M. K. & Jordan, L. P. 2006, 'Choice and accommodation in parental child care', *Community Development*, vol. 37, no. 2, pp. 53–70.

National Childcare Accreditation Council 2005a, *Quality Improvement and Accreditation System: Information about the Accreditation Decision* [Online], Available: http://www.ncac.gov.au/support_documents/qias_decision_information.pdf [2006, Apr 4].

National Childcare Accreditation Council 2005b, *Validation Evaluation Form Analysis: Validation visits conducted October/November 2005* [Online], Available: http://www.ncac.gov.au/report_documents/vef_analysis_2005.PDF [2006, Apr 4].

National Childcare Accreditation Council 2008, *Quality Trends Reports* [Online], Available: http://www.ncac.gov.au/reports_statistics/reports_stats_index.html#papers [2008, Jan 21].

Newman, J. & Vidler, E. 2006, 'Discriminating customers, responsible patients, empowered users: Consumerism and the modernisation of health care', *Journal of Social Policy*, vol. 35, no. 2, pp. 193–209.

NICHD (National Institute of Child Health and Development) and Network, Early Child Care Research 2002, 'Early child care and children's development prior to school entry: Results from the NICHD study of early child care', *American Educational Research Journal*, vol. 39, no. 1, pp. 133–64.

National Institute of Child Health and Development and Network 2006, *The NICHD study of early child care and youth development: Findings for children up to age 4½ years* [Online], Available: http://www.nichd.nih.gov/publications/pubs/upload/seccyd_051206.pdf [2006, Oct 10].

O'Brien, A. & MacDonald, J. 2008, 'It's the simple questions that count', *The Australian*, January 21, pp. 1–2.

Organisation for Economic Co-operation and Development 2006, *Starting Strong 11: Early Childhood Education and Care*, OECD, Paris.

Ozga, J. 2000, *Policy Research in Educational Settings*, Open University Press, Buckingham.

Peyton, V. Jacobs, A., O'Brien, M. & Roy, C. 2001, 'Reasons for choosing child care: Associations with family factors, quality, and satisfaction', *Early Childhood Research Quarterly*, vol. 16, no. 2, pp. 191–208.

Press, F. 2006, *What about the kids? Policy directions for improving the experiences of infants and young children in a changing world,*

Commissioned report to the NSW Commission for Children and Young People, Commission for Children and Young People, and Child Guardian, and the National Investment of the Early Years (NIFTeY) NSW Commission for Children and Young People, Sydney.

Press, F. & Woodrow, C. 2005, 'Commodification, corporatisation and children's spaces', *Australian Journal of Education*, vol. 49, no. 3, pp. 278–91.

Press, F. & Woodrow, C. 2009, 'The giant in the playground: Investigating the reach and implications of the corporatisation of childcare provision', in *Paid Care in Australia: Politics, Profits, Practices*, eds D. King & G. Meagher, Sydney University Press, Sydney.

Pryor, L. 2006, 'Child care horrors kept from parents', *The Sydney Morning Herald*, 13 March, p. 1.

Pusey, M. 2003, T*he Experience of Middle Australia: The Dark Side of Economic Reform*, Cambridge University Press, Melbourne.

Raising Children Network 2008, Raising children network: The Australian Parenting Site [Online], Available: http://raisingchildren.net.au/ [2008, Aug 14].

Ridley-May, K. 2007, *Sure Start Children's Centres Parental Satisfaction Survey Report and Annexes 2007. Research Report RW108*, Department for Education and Skills, [Online], Available: http://www.dfes.gov.uk/research/data/uploadfiles/RW108.pdf [2008, Jan 14].

Robson, S. 2006, 'Parent perspectives on services and relationships in two English early years centres', *Early Child Development and Care*, vol. 176, no. 5, pp. 443–60.

Rudd, K. & Macklin, J. 2007, Labor's plan for high quality care: Election 2007 policy document [Online], Available: http://www.alp.org.au/download/now/microsoft_word_071023_quality_child_care_policy_document_final.pdf [2008, Jan 21].

Salter, B. 2004, *The New Politics of Medicine*, Palgrave Macmillan, Basingstoke and New York.

Shlay, A. B., Tran, H., Weinraub, M. & Harmon, M. 2005, 'Teasing apart the child care conundrum: A factorial survey analysis of perceptions of child care quality, fair market price and willingness to pay by low-income, African American parents', *Early Childhood Research Quarterly*, vol. 20, no. 4, pp. 393–416.

Stanley, K., Bellamy, K. & Cooke, G. 2006, Equal access: Appropriate and affordable childcare for every child [Online], Available: http://www.ippr.org/members/download.asp?f=%2Fecomm%2Ffiles%2Fequal%5Faccess%2Epdf [2008, Dec 31].

Sumsion, J. 2006, 'The corporatisation of Australian childcare: Towards an ethical audit and research agenda', *Journal of Early Childhood Research*, vol. 4, no. 2, pp. 99–120.

Sylva, K., Melhuish, E., Simmons, P., Siraj-Blatchford, I., Taggart, B. & Elliot, K. 2003, The effective provision of pre-school education (EPPE) project: Findings from the pre-school period, Summary of findings [Online], Available: http://www.ioe.ac.uk/schools/ecpe/eppe/eppe/eppefindings.htm [2006, Oct 10].

Vincent, C. & Ball, S. *2006, Childcare, Choice and Class Practices: Middle-Class Parents and Their Children*, Routledge, London and New York.

Walsh, L. 2006, 'Job's not as easy as ABC', *Courier Mail* [Online], Available: http://www.couriermail.news.com.au/story/0,20797,19401027-953,00.html [2006, Jun 8].

Woodrow, C. & Press, F. 2007, 'Repositioning the child in the policy politics of early childhood', *Educational Philosophy and Theory*, vol. 39, no. 3, pp. 312–25.

8

Improving quality in Australian child care: the role of the media and non-profit providers

Bronwen Dalton and Rachel Wilson

It is widely acknowledged that the quality of centre-based care for young children is a critical determinant of a range of positive social, education and health-related outcomes (Barnett & Ackerman 2006; Vandell et al. 1988; Schweinhart et al. 1993). Yet in 2001, Australia ranked at near the bottom of an OECD league table measuring how much countries invest in children's earliest years (Organisation for Economic Co-operation and Development 2001). Further, Australia's quality assurance regime for child care has been criticised, particularly for its failure to make reliable or comparable information on the quality of child care services readily available to parents (Radich 2002; Hill, Pocock & Elliott 2007; Rush 2006).

In this relative information vacuum, parental choices about child care can be particularly affected by dominant constructions of what constitutes 'quality child care' in the public sphere. One key component of the public sphere is the mass media. Through its interpretation of events, the media can influence the way an issue is discussed and evaluated and so influence individual perceptions (Krippendorff 2004; Meyrowitz 1985; Gamson 1988). In this chapter we analyse recent media coverage of child care in Australia. We argue that media attention to issues such as the affordability and availability of centre-based child care and the physical environment in child care centres far outweighs the attention given to the quality of care provided. This has provided an opportunity for large corporate players with mass marketing strategies to further shape parents' expectations.

So how can smaller, generally non-profit, child care centres play a role in the establishment of a well-functioning quality assurance regime? The public sphere is not just inhabited by the mass media or dominated by the marketing messages of large companies. There are other important sites where ideas are expressed and contested. In the case of parents forming judgements about child care, a key site is their own local child care centre, and among these centres, non-profit providers are particularly well-placed to play a significant role in shaping how parents understand and interpret child care. Further, through advocacy, non-profits can have an impact on child care policy. Thus, we discuss communication strategies available to non-profit child care providers to become an effective voice for parents and children, and so a legitimate and influential interlocutor in child care debates.

Evaluating child care: quality versus quantity measures

In Australia, child care centres provide a major part of the care given to young children. According to the child care survey undertaken in 2005 by the Australian Bureau of Statistics (ABS), centre-based long day care is the most commonly used type of formal child care among the 21 per cent of Australians aged twelve years and under attending formal child care in any given school week. Formal child care use has increased from 19 per cent in 2002 (Australian Bureau of Statistics 2006, p. 3). According to 2007 figures, Australia has more than 8,500 child care services listed on the Australian Child Care Index and more than 10,000 child care services estimated across the country (The Australian Child Care Index 2007). It is therefore crucial that we understand how centre-based care can deliver positive outcomes for children and, by extension, for the broader community.

There is a growing body of research evidence indicating that positive outcomes for young children in centre-based care, particularly those from socially and economically disadvantaged backgrounds, are largely dependent on the quality of care provided (NICHD Early Child Care Research Network 2002; Sylva et al. 2003; Wylie et al. 2006). As a result, a significant body of research focuses on how quality child care can be evaluated (see Sakai et al. 2003 for an overview). Within the broad quality measures category there are two distinct but related concepts: *structural* quality and *process* quality.

Structural quality measures relate to the child care environment and include variables such as the child-staff ratio, environmental health and safety, classroom size, the average education level of the staff, and staff turnover. The concept of structural quality also includes measures more peripheral to the actual service experience, or at least the child's experience of child care, such as location, affordability, and availability of child care services (Blau & Mocan 2002; Ghazvini & Mullis 2002; Helbum & Howes 1996).

Structural measures of quality are thought to be inputs to the production of 'process quality', which focuses on the nature of the interactions between the care provider and the child, and of the activities to which the child is exposed. Thus, process quality measures are those that relate directly to the nature of service provision and that affect the child's experience of care. According to child development theorists, like Vygotsky and Bronnfenbrenner, the quality of these 'process' interactions within care drives child development. In a similar vein, Howes and colleagues (2008) point out that structural quality measures like the teacher-child ratio and teacher qualifications appear to have a negligible impact upon children's developmental outcomes, whereas process quality is more strongly associated with children's social and academic development (Howes et al. 2008).

The child care quality assurance regime in Australia

Research has clearly established that high quality, particularly process quality, is critically important for a range of positive outcomes in child care. Researchers have also developed robust means of measuring quality and proposed strategies for enhancing it. Despite these developments, Australia is yet to establish an effective quality assurance regime. One reason is that quality assurance measures have not been supported with government resources, as demonstrated by Australia's low ranking in the OECD league table we mentioned in our introduction. In particular, the OECD draws attention to the lack of Australian research in early childhood education and reports that, although early childhood educational professionals implement innovative services, there are considerable gaps between research findings, existing service provision, and the policy directions of government (Organisation for Economic Co-operation and Development 2001; 2006).

As a consequence, Australia has a relatively under-developed and under-resourced quality assessment regime. Despite the fact that structural quality measures, like adult-child ratios, have been shown to be poorly predictive of positive outcomes in children (Howes et al. 2008), all the Australian state regulatory practices are based upon them. Further, state government licensing arrangements and the Child Care Quality Assurance (CCQA) framework of the federal government's Department of Families, Housing, Community Services and Indigenous Affairs rely heavily on self-regulation. They do not represent a consistently monitored and enforceable compliance regime, and tend to rely on spot checks and punitive measures rather than providing operators with incentives to aspire to clearly articulated quality standards. Nor are these regulatory frameworks well integrated. In Hill's (2007) words, they are a 'fragmented mess'. For example, centres can breach aspects of state licensing requirements but still operate and receive federal funding (Rush 2006).

Of particular relevance to this study is that current government controls over child care do not mandate regular and standardised reporting and thus fail to generate statistically reliable and verifiable data sets. In the absence of agreed, evidence-based, and transparent quality measures, and incentives to meet quality standards, parents' interpretations of what constitutes 'quality' care are relatively more open to being shaped by a range of other influences.

Factors influencing parental decisions about child care

Meyers and Jordan argue that discrete choice events of parents are best understood within a social context, because perceptions are 'developed through repeated interactions within a social environment' (2006, p. 61). Other studies have understood child care choices as socially constrained and have identified factors influencing parental decisions around child care (Walzer 1997; Meyers & Jordan 2006; Vincent & Ball 2006; Cleveland & Krashinsky 2002). Within these broad framing ideas about decision-making, a range of material and interpretive factors that affect parents' decisions have been identified by previous researchers.

For many parents cost can become an overriding concern when choosing child care. Some US econometric work finds that research about the influence of child care costs on employment decisions among all mothers underestimates the barriers that fees pose for low income mothers specifically (for a review, see Baum 2002, pp. 140–41). According to the ABS, the cost of child care rose 10 per cent in 2005 and 62 per cent in the four years to 2005 (Australian Bureau of Statistics 2006).

Access can also be an important factor. Gornick and Meyers (2003) compared child care in 14 industrialised countries and found that Australia rated relatively low on scales of availability and affordability for children aged less than three years, and in the middle for older preschool-aged children. These findings are contradicted by a recent Australian government Treasury report. According to this report 'The available evidence indicates that in recent years, the supply of formal child care (which includes long day, family, after school and occasional care) has generally kept pace with demand' (Davidoff 2007, p. 68), although the author also considered evidence on spatial variation in the supply of formal child care places (Davidoff 2007, pp. 72–73). According to the 2005 ABS child care survey, between June 2002 and June 2005 there was a decrease in the number of children for whom additional family day care was required (down from 29,100 to 17,700), and no significant change in demand for other types of formal care (Australian Bureau of Statistics 2006, p. 8).

Research has also found that interpretations of quality can be affected by a range of parent characteristics including education, race/ethnicity, and place of birth. Then there is the significant variation in individual beliefs and tastes. Further, social networks are a source of information for parents, providing normative cues for specific choices which can, over time, crystallise an option into a taken-for-granted pattern of action.

A range of external factors also affects parents' choice sets and behaviour, from the influence of opinions of those in parents' social circle, to the subliminal effects of marketing messages, to the appeal of the physical environment of centres or the way centre staff interact with parents. Meyers and Jordan (2006) describe these factors as decision-making shortcuts upon which parents rely when making their decisions relating to child care. They argue that these shortcuts assist parents to both simplify and rationalise their choices. According to Meyers and Jordan:

> Parents' assessment of the costs and benefits of alternative arrangements will reflect not only the observable features of care, such as price, but also the congruence of the arrangement with socially-constructed norms—from beliefs about gender roles to perceptions of quality in child care (Meyers & Jordan 2006, pp. 59–60).

Indeed, Sylva and colleagues argue that 'quality is not a universal concept but depends on national curricula and cultural priorities' (2003, p. 46).

Research has also found that the appeal of environmental factors in child care centres can shape parent choices. Mocan, who analyses data from a study of 400 centres across three US states, found that

> parents are weakly rational ... parents do not utilise all available information in forming their assessment of quality ...

> There is some limited evidence for moral hazard as non-profit centres with very clean reception areas tend to produce lower level of quality for unobservable items (2007, p. 743).

Cleveland and Krashinsky (2005, p. 2) comment on the use of 'superficial evidence' of quality, such as new furnishings or staff uniforms, and observe that this may be the limit of owners' investment in the absence of financial incentives for child care centres to further improve quality after accreditation has been achieved. In this context there is a clear incentive for centres to invest in attractive buildings and grounds over less observable aspects of quality.

Related to this, marketing messages also play a role in shaping parental choices. The marketing practices of child care providers with well-resourced infrastructure and sophisticated brand management techniques may, at least subliminally, conflate non-quality and quality measures. At worst these practices may promote quantity/market attributes as true signs of quality care that can either distract or in other ways convince parents of the superior quality of their service, without the added expense of having to make any substantial change in service practice.

For various reasons quality can also often be overestimated by parents. Cleveland and Krashinsky (2002) discuss how, in entrusting their small children to others, parents must then manage how they relate to those carers, who have considerable autonomy vis-à-vis their child. Some parents may feel that to question centre staff on the quality of their practice may have negative repercussions for the way those staff treat their child. Cleveland and Krashinsky also point out that in this context many parents convince themselves that they have acted in their child's best interests, which in turn leads them to overestimate the quality of the long day care they select (Cleveland & Krashinsky 2002).

Some parents may not appreciate the importance of quality compared to other factors and 'under-invest' in care services. Blau and Mocan (2002), for example, argue that parents are relatively insensitive to quality differences in their selection of child care, based on estimates of the elasticity of their demand for structural quality features such as group size, adult-child ratios, and provider education. They conclude that, although parents appear willing to pay a little more for higher quality care, their demand for these quality features does not increase with a decrease in price or an increase in maternal wages, and increases only modestly with family income.

In summary, when conceptualising the complexity of decision-making around child care, it is fruitful to adopt a framework that places 'choice' in the context of financial, market, and social constraints. This approach draws on research in economics about the relationship between discrete choice and social interactions (for a review of this literature see Brock & Durlauf 2001). Pescosolido (1992) describes this approach as integrating assumptions about rational choice—including action and utility maximisation—with theories of bounded rationality and attention to the 'the primacy of social interaction' and 'social structures as defining the bounds of the possible' in individual decision making (p. 1098). We argue that, like social networks, a key shortcut to rationalising choice for parents is via the consumption of the mass media.

The role of the media in influencing parental understandings of quality child care

In addition to the factors outlined above, the media plays a crucial role in shaping parental perceptions of child care quality. This is because the media, through its interpretation of events, influences the way an issue is discussed and evaluated in the public arena. Social movement scholar, William Gamson, has stressed how discourse in the mass media reflects wider symbolic struggles over meaning and interpretation. Gamson argues that the mass media plays a central role in modern societies because it is the most generally available forum for debates on meaning and it is the major site in which contests over meaning must succeed. In other words, the mass media not only *indicates* but also *influences* cultural changes (Gamson 1988). By employing a particular discourse, the media can promote certain perspectives while silencing others.

Of course not all parents will be affected by media in the same way, and moderating variables such as gender and family environment are likely to be significant (Krippendorff 2004; Meyrowitz 1985; Malamuth & Impett 2001; Milkie 1994). Nevertheless, given the widespread influence of the media, it is important to be aware of media constructions of child care as a way of understanding both wider discourse and how the media or other groups may distort this discourse in ways that influence individuals' perceptions of their own interests.

Based on our analysis of a sample of media content in Australia, we argue that dominant media constructions of child care centre not on 'quality' but on availability and affordability—on 'who gets it' and 'how much it costs'. The potential effect is that parents will conflate market and quality-related child care measures in ways that give pre-eminence to market issues as a measure of the quality of child care. We therefore argue that we can examine public discourse, and by extension parental perceptions of quality, through the analysis of how child care issues are dealt with by the mass media.

Content analysis of media coverage of child care

To examine the content and themes of Australian media reports relating to child care we undertook a content analysis of individual newspaper reports produced in one newspaper over the course of one year. Each report was coded and classified according to a series of categories relating to child care issues, including categories addressing quality issues (both structural and process), and categories addressing other non-quality issues like the cost of care and access to care.

Method

Our study of media treatment of child care related stories is based on reports in New South Wales' highest circulating broadsheet newspaper, *The Sydney Morning Herald* (*SMH*), over twelve months to September 2007, as identified by the media search engine Factiva™. We used a variety of search words in different combinations to cover a range of topics relating to child care. These included the terms 'child care'; 'child centre', 'long day care', 'child minding', and 'nursery school(s)'. Some 256 articles included the key word terms listed above. Articles were sorted according to relevance by Factiva, based on the number of key word occurrences in each article, and only the first 40 were assessed as having child care as the primary focus of the article. We subjected these articles to inductive content analysis to determine their content and orientation.

Analysis

Inductive coding and refining of codes was conducted by the authors and a group of research methodology students. Inter-coder reliability was examined and met minimum requirements; however, training strategies were developed to further improve inter-coder reliability.

We began by coding articles for surface content at the full article level, because we believed that surface coding was sufficient to extract primary content themes. The framework for analysis and coding sheets was designed around the following:

- The primary focus of the article—did the report focus on market issues, quality issues, or other? This used mutually exclusive coding and forced the coder to determine the dominant focus of the whole article.
- Coding for the article orientation—did the whole article focus predominantly on parent issues or child issues?
- Coding for the type of care discussed—did the article discuss

ABC Learning Ltd,[1] other corporate, government, non-government community, other, or all types? Multiple types of care could be coded for each article.

- More detailed coding on content topics—these codes detailed subcategories relating to the primary focus of the article. For example, quality issues could be coded as structural and/or process. A single article could be coded as addressing several content topics.

Results

The primary focus of the *SMH* newspaper articles is reported in Figure 8.1, which clearly shows the dominance of market issues (including government subsidy arrangements, market demand, growth in the number of new centres, and market supply in general) in the paper's coverage during the year to September 2007. Only 13 per cent of articles had child care quality as a dominant focus.

Figure 8.2 elaborates on the articles' focus and shows topic sub-categories by article orientation. The topic categorisations are not mutually exclusive and a single article can be coded as including several topics. It is apparent that the large majority of articles had a parent orientation and were concerned with issues that did not directly relate to children's day-to-day experience in child care. Rather, the majority of articles commented on market issues relating to finance, supply and demand. Further analysis of articles showed that they focused on: finance and payment (100 per cent of market-focused articles addressed this), market demand (60 per cent), the opening/planning of new centres (55 per cent) and overall market growth (40 per cent).

---

1 ABC Learning Ltd is a large corporate child care provider. For more information about its role and actions see Brennan and colleagues (2007) and Press and Woodrow (2009).

Figure 8.1: Primary focus of *SMH* child care articles

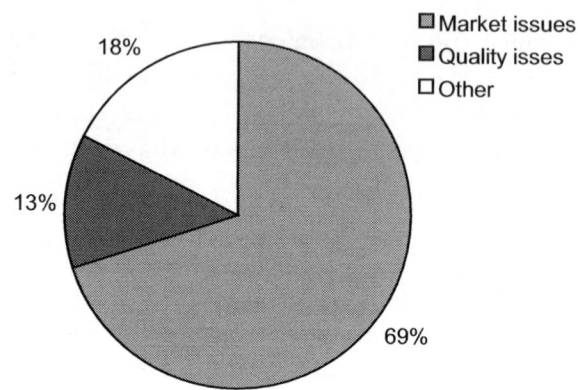

Figure 8.2: *SMH* child care articles' content and orientation

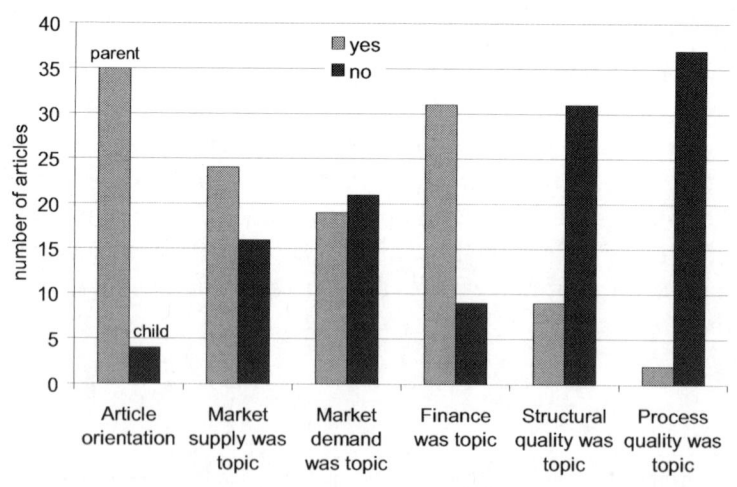

A total of 13 per cent of articles addressed either structural or process quality issues. Of these articles, the majority focused on structural quality elements. Further subcategories for articles focusing on structural quality included: health and safety (100 per cent of quality-focused articles commented on this), staff qualifications and skills (50 per cent), adult-child ratios (25 per cent) and 25 per cent commented on market issues in addition to quality issues. Only two articles commented on process dimensions of quality like staff-child interaction, curriculum issues or learning opportunities.

Finance issues (government subsidies, funds and costs, affordability, payment structure and options, other finance issues) were also coded in more detail as they became a strong emerging category and were analysed separately. Some 78 percent of articles commented on financial issues. Subcategories for these are shown in Figure 8.3. The dominant focus was on government subsidies, with substantial attention also paid to fee pricing, other child care costs and affordability.

Figure 8.3: *SMH* child care articles addressing finance topics

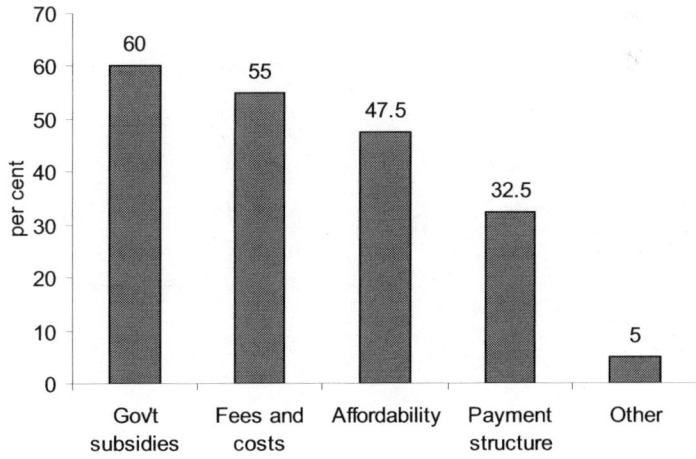

As any individual article could cover several subcategories of topics, it is apparent that some reports focused on market issues also commented on quality issues and vice versa. Table 8.1 shows the percentage of articles addressing different topics under each primary focus. The most frequently addressed topics are, in order: government subsidies, child care fees and costs, affordability and access. Reporting on child care quality tended to focus on health and safety issues, which are addressed in 20 per cent of articles.

Table 8.1: *SMH* child care articles' topics and subcategories

	Topic sub-categories	Count	% articles
Market supply	Market growth	10	25
	New centres	5	13
	Number of centres	12	30
Market demand	Waiting lists	6	15
	Access	15	38
Finance	Child care costs	22	55
	Payment structure	13	33
	Government subsidies	24	60
	Affordability	19	48
Structural quality	Child/staff ratios	3	8
	Health & safety	8	20
	Staff qualifications	2	5
Process quality	Staff skills	2	5
	Staff/child interaction	0	0
	Curricula	1	3
	Learning opportunities	2	5

Discussion of findings

Although this study is based on a limited sample, and further refinement of the content analysis coding procedures is possible with a larger selection of news reports, the set of *SMH* articles shows some interesting and robust trends. First, the reports are dominated by a focus on market issues and few articles focus on child care quality.

Second, and perhaps unsurprisingly, most articles focus on parents as customers and not on children's experience of child care as consumers. Indeed, three out of four articles included comment on financial issues in child care. This imbalance may reflect—or indeed contribute to—the information asymmetry that parents experience in their quest to select and evaluate providers. If media reports do not highlight issues directly related to children's day-to-day experience in child care, it seems unlikely that broad dimensions of child care quality will be scrutinised by either the wider public or, by extension, child care policy-makers.

Third, analysis of reports that do refer to child care quality, whether or not quality is the article's primary focus, reveals that most refer to structural quality dimensions. The quality of a child's experience and interaction—the 'process' quality which is most predictive of children's education progress—is rarely addressed. Health and safety issues relating to physical environment and equipment are a more frequent topic. Although an important part of child care quality, and more readily assessed by parents choosing child care provision, health and safety and structural quality in general form only one dimension of quality. Studies outlined earlier have established the need for high quality care in a wide range of aspects and have shown how quality elements, including process quality, like the quality of child-adult interaction, are predictive of a child's later developmental outcomes (Sylva et al. 2003).

The *SMH* content analysis provides evidence of media trends and reflects public discourse on child care. We conclude that this market dominated discourse, which neglects issues of quality, can serve to reinforce other messages about interpretations of quality in the public sphere. In particular it can reinforce the marketing messages of major corporate players, which make claims to quality but without actually having to invest seriously in quality improvements.

However, the public sphere is not just inhabited by the mass media nor dominated by the marketing messages of large companies. Ideas are expressed and contested in other important sites. In the case of parents forming judgements about child care, a key site is their own local child care centre. Among these centres, non-profit providers are particularly well-placed to play a significant role in influencing not only parental interpretations of quality but also potentially those of child care policy-makers.

Improving quality in Australian child care: the role of non-profit providers

In this section we examine the potential for non-profit providers of child care, not only to shape parental interpretations of quality, but also to garner widespread parental support to become key advocates for improvements to the current quality assurance regime. We argue that non-profits are well placed to realise this potential due to their position within the so-called third sector, their social mission, and their connections to local communities. However, to realise this potential, non-profit child care providers will need to re-examine their capacity to influence parent choices and behaviours and to act more broadly as advocates for the establishment of a more effective quality-assurance regime.

Many child care researchers have acknowledged the significance of activism, in particular feminist activism, where women's organisations have participated in the construction of Australia's welfare policies throughout the 20th century (Sawer & Groves 1994; Brennan 1998; O'Connor et al. 1999). More recently, researchers have begun to explore the role that parents, as consumers of child care services, can play in driving reform (Vincent & Ball 2006; Sumsion & Goodfellow 2009). These 'parent power' models represent an exciting and innovative approach to thinking about the politics of quality enhancement. We seek to build on the work of scholars such as Sumsion and Goodfellow and to link proposed parent-led quality improvements to the potential role and influence of non-profit child care providers as influential players in current child care debates.

The possibility that non-profit centres can readily transform parents into committed activists can seem somewhat remote. Like their decisions about child care, parents' approaches to becoming involved in advocacy will be affected by a range of social interactions and constraints. A key finding of a study of parents and schools by Vincent and Martin (2002) was that 'parental access to and deployment of a number of social resources significantly affected how often, how easily and over what range of issues they approached the school' (p. 108). Schools have traditionally played a much more prominent role in involving and engaging parents.

However, there is scope for non-profit child care centres to further engage parents and mobilise their support. This is largely due to three characteristics non-profits can turn to their advantage, namely that they are legally constrained from distributing profits; that they outwardly endorse a social mission; and that they are embedded in local communities.

The first characteristic that distinguishes non-profit child care providers is that they are constrained from distributing profits and, as some economists have observed, without an apparent profit incentive to cut costs associated with quality, consumers are more likely to consider non-profit providers trustworthy when compared to for-profit providers (Hansmann 1987; Weisbrod 1978; 1988; 1989; Rose-Ackerman 1996). According to Hansmann's 'contract failure' hypothesis, purchasers prefer non-profit service providers over for-profit counterparts in industries where there are high levels of information asymmetry. Hansmann (1980) argues that:

> The nonprofit producer, like its for-profit counterpart, has the capacity to raise prices and cut quality in such cases [of informational asymmetries] without much fear of customer reprisal; however, it lacks the incentive to do so because those in charge are barred from taking home any resulting profits. In other words, the advantage of a nonprofit producer is that the discipline of the market is supplemented by the additional protection given the consumer by another, broader "contract", the organization's legal commitment to devote its entire earning to the production of services (Hansmann 1980, p. 844).

Trust in for-profits can grow if regulation becomes accepted as an adequate means to police producers. In Australia, though, in the absence of a well-functioning quality-assurance regime, non-profit providers may be able to capitalise on this tendency to be considered relatively trustworthy, or at least as less untrustworthy, translating this into relatively greater influence over parent perceptions of, and choice sets in, child care.

A second advantage of non-profit providers relates to their position within the third sector. A wide range of literature has highlighted how third sector organisations (TSOs) can act as vehicles for collective interests and drive social and economic change (Almond & Verba 1989; Lipset 1956; Hall 1995; Keane 1998; Tarrow 1994). One reason is that TSOs have a social mission. Evidence suggests that groups driven by altruistic or idealistic factors can motivate people to commit themselves to founding, funding, and striving to advance the goals of non-profit organisations (DiMaggio & Anheier 1990; Lyons 2001).

Third, non-profit child care centres are embedded within a community. With a grassroots constituency comes a mandate and legitimacy to seek to influence policy. The key is to develop the commitment and activist orientation of that grassroots constituency, and then the leadership to communicate the depth of the organisation's support to decision-makers. That parents and centres are in regular contact and usually live locally are advantages supporting grassroots mobilisation.

Non-profit child care centres, then, can serve as a crucial context for the dissemination of political messages to parents and a place where parents are exposed to opportunities for involvement in advocacy to change policy. Whether they realise this political role depends on whether non-profits themselves have the will and capacity to engage in effective advocacy campaigns.

From service providers to advocates? Strategies for making an impact

Despite their potential advocacy role, to date the success of non-profit child care led campaigns has been mixed. However this patchy performance is not necessarily due to deficiencies of non-profits. It may also be due in part to distortions arising from the differential lobbying strengths of non-profit and for-profit providers. There is already some evidence of privileged access for some providers to politicians and policy-makers. Brennan and colleagues have reported that: 'From the start, ABC Learning has been closely associated with influential Liberal party figures' (2007, p. 6). They note how ABC Learning's board of directors included the former Federal Minister for Children and Youth Affairs, Larry Anthony. Some have argued that this, and other connections and party donations, have influenced the size and flow of government subsidies (Birnbauer 2006).

So how can non-profits address this power differential between themselves and for-profits, and realise their potential as activists for quality improvements? We conclude by briefly discussing some strategies for developing non-profit child care centres' strategic communication skills.

Strategic communication

It is important that non-profits understand the meanings and contestation that surround child care discourse in Australia if they are to respond effectively. They must understand the cultural settings within which they act, the institutional and discursive terrain, and use this understanding to inform their arguments and choice of political strategies. This depends on successfully refocusing/reframing debate to centre on quality by linking interpretations of quality to pre-existing norms and beliefs within society. This refocusing or reframing, in turn, involves strategic use of the media. Non-profits can conduct or sponsor research and then disseminate findings via the media—for example findings from early childhood research, risk assessment analyses, and industry quality audits. Other marketing and communication exercises can also send a message, from advertising campaigns through to public engagement activities. The 'Parent Voices' initiative sponsored by the Child Care Advocacy Association of Canada (2003) has some straightforward tips, such as 'finding statistics and articles on request, providing ways to share community-based campaign strategies, helping with local information flyers and linking different parent groups with one another'.

Critical to success is finding the resources necessary to support this communication-based strategy. This is a major challenge for busy child care centres reliant on limited income from fees. One option is considering founding centre-based fighting funds—perhaps raised from levies or contributions drawn from parents—a fund modelled on that raised by some unions and clubs. Introducing membership dues could also provide another source of untied funds. Non-profits are also well placed to access the legal, financial and public relations expertise (for example) needed for a campaign, by drawing on board members or parents.

Realising advocacy potential effectively also depends on child care centres adopting a more politicised culture. But for some centres assuming this role will require some internal cultural readjustment. To date most non-profits have seen themselves as service providers. Reassessment of their role as advocates and not just service providers will involve a deeper appreciation and internal acceptance of themselves as legitimate actors in the political process, and a change in organisational culture where advocacy is considered core business.

Conclusion

We have attempted to provide insight into what the community, and parents in particular, understand to be 'good' child care and use this to inform a non-profit advocacy strategy to refocus public debate on child care quality. Our understanding of community perceptions is based on media analysis, which found that market/quantity issues (including government subsidy arrangements, market demand, growth in the number of new centres and market supply in general) appear most frequently in reports about child care. We also found that the majority of articles concentrated on issues relating to parents as customers and not on issues directly related to children's experience of child care, particularly those articles that comment on financial issues in child care. Finally, our analysis of the small proportion of articles that do comment on child care quality, whether this formed the article's primary focus or not, revealed that most referred to structural quality dimensions like health and safety of equipment and adult-child ratios.

We argue that these dominant media constructions of child care resonate with the fears and aspirations of parents—with the effect that they have shaped parental perceptions and given pre-eminence to market issues as a measure of quality in child care. We conclude that media constructions distract parents' attention away from the important 'process' dimensions of child care quality that better reflect the child's experience and have been shown to predict child outcomes.

In furthering the goal of establishing a more effective quality regime, we have also discussed the role that non-profit providers could play in driving policy change to address—and effectively regulate—child care quality, with a greater focus on the 'process' quality aspects, which research has identified as so important. We have noted how several economists argue that consumers,are likely to consider non-profit providers as more trustworthy than for-profit providers due to their non-distribution constraint. We have also referred to other political and social theory that emphasises non-profits' roles as vehicles for social and political change. Given their unique characteristics, non-profit providers are well placed to garner widespread support and drive the future child care agenda. But, given the power of self-limiting beliefs, an identity shift from service provider to advocate could be difficult to achieve. Any such changes need to be supported with continuing efforts directed at non-profit advocacy capacity-building.

Without a sustained and well-planned advocacy campaign, non-profits will not effectively engage with dominant constructions of child care quality, and so will fail to place quality of service on the political agenda. In the absence of such efforts, it is likely that corporatisation of the sector will increase, as rising fees and government payments will make for-profits' forays into this market more lucrative. The potential costs of this scenario, where important dimensions of child care quality continue to be neglected, is difficult to overestimate. At best it means the opportunity to maximise the nurturing of our future generations is lost. At worst it may mean we subject our children to sub-optimal and potentially damaging care. Given the high stakes, it is critical that non-profits highlight these issues in a new public discourse on child care quality.

References

Almond, G. & Verba, S. 1989, *The Civic Culture: Political Attitudes and Democracy in Five Nations*, Sage Publications, Newbury Park.

Australian Bureau of Statistics 2006, *Child Care Australia, June 2005*, Cat. No. 4402.0, Australian Bureau of Statistics, Canberra.

Australian Government 2004, *More Help For Families, 2004–05 Budget—Overview*, AGPS, Canberra.

Barnett, W. S. & Ackerman, D. J. 2006, 'Costs, benefits, and the long-term effects of preschool programs', *Community Development: Journal of the Community Development Society*, vol. 37, no. 2, pp. 86–100.

Baum, C. 2002, 'A dynamic analysis of the effect of child care costs on the work decisions of low-income mothers with infants', *Demography*, vol. 39, no. 1, pp. 139–64.

Birnbauer, W. 2006, 'Simple as ABC: Minister, you help us, we'll help you', *Sunday Age*, 6 August.

Blau, D. M. & Mocan, H. N. 2002, 'The supply of quality in child care centers', *Review of Economics and Statistics*, vol. 84, no. 3, pp. 483–96.

Brennan, D. 1998, *The Politics of Australian Child Care: Philanthropy, Feminism and Beyond*, Cambridge University Press, Melbourne.

Brennan, D., Newberry, S. & van der Laan, S. 2007, The corporatisation of Australian child care: As easy as ABC, paper presented at Symposium on For-Profit Providers of Paid Care, University of Sydney, Sydney, 29–30 November.

Brock, W. A. & Durlauf, S. N. 2001, 'Discrete choice with social interactions', *The Review of Economic Studies*, vol. 68, no. 2, pp. 235–60.

Child Care Advocacy Association of Canada 2003, Parent Voices Resource Kit [Online], Available: http://www.ccaac.ca/parent_voices/content/EN/pdf/pv_reskit_pt4.pdf [2008, Mar].

Cleveland, G. & Krashinsky, M. 2002, 'Financing ECEC services in OECD Countries', OECD Occasional Papers [Online], Available: http://www.oecd.org/dataoecd/55/59/28123665.pdf#search=%22Financing%20ECEC%2services%20in%20OECD%20Countries%22 [2007, Nov 25].

Cleveland, G. & Krashinsky, M. 2004, 'The quality gap: A study of nonprofit and commercial child care centres in Canada', [Online] Available: http://childcarepolicy.net/pdf/NonprofitPaper.pdf [2008, Mar 22].

Cleveland, G. & Krashinsky, M. 2005, The nonprofit advantage: Producing quality in thick and thin child care markets, Department of Management, University of Toronto at Scarborough [Online], Available: http://childcarepolicy.net/pdf/non-profitadvantage.pdf [2008, Mar 22].

Davidoff, I. 2007, 'Evidence on the child care market', *Economic Roundup Summer 2007*, Department of Treasury, Canberra [Online], Available: http://www.treasury.gov.au/documents/1221/PDF/04_child_care.pdf. [2007, Nov 15].

DiMaggio, P. J. & Anheier, H. K. 1990, 'The sociology of nonprofit organizations and sectors', *Annual Review of Sociology*, vol. 16, pp. 137–59.

Gamson, W. 1988, 'Political discourse and collective action', in *From Structure to Action: Comparing Movement Participation Across Cultures— International Social Movement Research*, vol. 1, eds B. Klandermans, H. Kriesei, & S. Tarrow, JAI Press, Greenwich, Conn., pp. 219–47.

Ghazvini, A. & Mullis, R. 2002, 'Center-based care for young children: Examining predictors of quality', *Journal of Genetic Psychology*, vol. 163, no. 1, pp. 112–25.

Gornick, J. & Meyers, M. 2003, *Families That Work: Policies for Reconciling Parenthood and Employment*, Russell Sage Foundation, New York.

Hall, J. (ed.) 1995, *Civil Society: Theory, History, and Comparison*, Polity Press, Cambridge.

Hansmann, H. B. 1980, 'The role of nonprofit enterprise', *Yale Law Journal*, vol. 89, no. 5, pp. 835–902.

Hansmann, H. B 1987, 'Economic theories of nonprofit organization', in *The Nonprofit Handbook*, ed. W. W. Powell, Yale University Press, New Haven, pp. 27–42.

Helburn, S. W. & Howes, C. 1996, 'Child care cost and quality', *The Future of Children: Financing Child Care*, vol. 6, no. 2, pp. 62–82.

Hill, E. 2007, 'Making child care count is not just about cost', *The Sydney Morning Herald*, 13 November.

Hill, E., Pocock, B. & Elliott, A. (eds) 2007, *Kids Count: Better Early Childhood Education and Care in Australia*, Sydney University Press, Sydney.

Howes, C., Burchinal, M., Pianta, R., Bryant, D., Early, D., Clifford, R. & Barabin, O. 2008, 'Ready to learn? Children's pre-academic achievement in pre-Kindergarten programs', *Early Childhood Research Quarterly*, vol. 23, no. 1, pp. 27–50.

Keane, J. 1998, *Civil Society: Old Images, New Visions*, Stanford University Press, Stanford.

Krippendorff, K. 2004, *Content Analysis: An Introduction to Its Methodology*, 2nd edition, Sage, Thousand Oaks, CA.

Lipset, S. M. 1956, *Union Democracy*, Anchor Books, Garden City.

Lyons, M. 2001, *Third Sector: The Contribution of Nonprofit and Cooperative Enterprises in Australia*, Allen & Unwin, Sydney.

Malamuth, N. & Impett, E. 2001, 'Research on sex in the media: What do we know about effects on children and adolescents?' in *Handbook of Children and the Media*, eds D. Singer & J. Singer, Sage Publications, Thousand Oaks, CA, pp. 289–307.

Meyrowitz, J. 1985, *No Sense of Place: The Impact of Electronic Media on Social Behavior*, Oxford University Press, New York.

Meyers, M. & Jordan, L. 2006, 'Choice and accommodation in parental child care decisions', *Community Development: Journal of the Community Development Society*, vol. 37, no. 2, pp. 53–70.

Milkie, M. A. 1994, 'Social world approach to cultural studies: Mass media and gender in the adolescent peer group', *Journal of Contemporary Ethnography*, vol. 23, no. 3, pp. 354–80.

Mocan, H. N. 2007, 'Can consumers detect lemons? Information asymmetry in the market for child care', *Journal of Population Economics*, vol. 20, no. 4, pp. 743–80.

Mósesdóttir, L. 1999, 'Breaking the boundaries: Women's encounter with the state', in *Working Europe: Reshaping European Employment Systems*, ed J. Christensen, P. Koistinen & A. Kovalainen, Ashgate, London, pp. 97–135.

National Institute of Child Health and Development Early Child Care Research Network 1999, 'Child care in the first year of life', *Merrill Palmer Quarterly*, vol. 43, no. 3, pp. 340–60.

National Institute of Child Health and Development Early Child Care Research Network 2002, 'Early child care and children's development prior to school entry: Results from the NICHD study of early child care', *American Educational Research Journal*, vol. 39, no. 1, pp. 133–64.

O'Connor, J., Orloff, A & Shaver, S. 1999. *States, Markets, Families: Gender, Liberalism and Social Policy in Australia, Canada, Great Britain and the United States*, Cambridge University Press, Cambridge.

Organisation for Economic Co-operation and Development 2001, *OECD Country Note: Early Childhood Education and Care Policy in Australia*, OECD, Paris.

Organisation for Economic Co-operation and Development 2006, *Starting Strong II: Early Childhood Education and Care*, OECD, Paris.

Pescosolido, B. M. 1992, 'Beyond rational choice: The social dynamics of how people seek help', *American Journal of Sociology*, vol. 97, no. 4, pp. 1096–138.

Press, F. & Woodrow, C. 2009, 'The giant in the playground: Investigating the reach and implications of the corporatisation of childcare provision', in *Paid Care in Australia: Politics, Profits, Practices*, eds D. King & G. Meagher, Sydney University Press, Sydney.

Radich, J. 2002, Confronting the realities—What next for the quality improvement and accreditation system? Contribution to the environmental scan undertaken by the National Childcare Accreditation Council to support its future strategic planning, September. [Online], Available: http://www.earlychildhoodaustralia.org.au/early_childhood_news/speeches/confronting_the_realities_what_next_for_the_quality_improvement_and_accreditation_system_sep_2002.html [2007, Nov 15].

Rose-Ackerman, S. 1996, 'Altruism, nonprofits, and economic theory', *Journal of Economic Literature*, vol. 34, no. 2, pp. 701–28.

Rush, E. 2006, Child care quality in Australia, *Discussion Paper No. 84*, The Australia Institute, Canberra [Online], Available: http://www.tai.org.au/documents/downloads/DP84.pdf [2007, Nov 15].

Sakai, L., Whitebrook, M., Wishard, A. & Hoews, C. 2003, 'Evaluating the Early Childhood Environment Rating Scale (ECERS): Assessing differences between the first and revised edition' *Early Childhood Research Quarterly*, vol. 18, no. 4, pp. 427–45.

Sawer, M. & Groves, A. 1994, 'The women's lobby: Networks, coalition building and the women of middle Australia', *Australian Journal of Political Science*, vol. 29, no. 3, pp. 434–59.

Sumsion, J. & Goodfellow 2009, 'Parents as consumers of early childhood education and care: The feasibility of demand-led improvements to quality', in *Paid Care in Australia: Politics, Profits, Practices*, eds D. King & G. Meagher, Sydney University Press, Sydney.

Sylva, K., Melhuish, E., Simmons, P., Siraj-Blatchford, L., Taggart, B. & Elliot, K. 2003, The Effective Provision of Pre-School Education (EPPE) Project: Findings from the pre-school period, summary of findings [Online], Available: http://www.ioe.ac.uk/schools/ecpe/eppe/eppe/eppefindings.htm [2006, Oct 10].

Schweinhart, L., Barnes, H. V. & Weikart, D. P. 1993, *Significant Benefits: The High/Scope Perry Preschool Study through Age 27*, High/Scope Press, Ypsilanti MI.

Tarrow, S. 1994, *Power in Movement*, Cambridge University Press, New York.

The Australian Child Care Index 2007, [Online], Available: http://www.echildcare.com.au/about/ [2007, Nov 22].

The University of Sydney 2007, 'Children suffer when politicians put profit and populist policies first', Media release, 12 November [Online], Available: http://www.sup.usyd.edu.au/MediaReleaseKidsCount12nov07.pdf [2008, Jul 10].

Vandell, D, Henderson, V. & Wilson, K. 1988, 'A longitudinal study of children with day-care experiences of varying quality', *Child Development*, vol. 59, no. 5, pp. 1286–92.

Vincent, C. & Ball, S. 2006, *Childcare, Choice and Class Practices: Middle-class Parents and Their Children*, Routledge, London.

Vincent, C. & Martin, J. 2002, 'Class, culture and agency: Researching parental voice', *Discourse*, vol. 23, no. 1, pp. 109–28.

Walzer, S. 1997, 'Contextualizing the employment decisions of new mothers', *Qualitative Sociology*, vol. 20, no. 2, pp. 211–27.

Weisbrod, B. 1978, 'Problems of enhancing the public interest: Toward a model of government failures', in *Public Interest Law,* eds B. Weisbrod, J. Handler & N. Komesar, California University Press, London, pp. 30–41.

Weisbrod, B. 1988, *The Nonprofit Economy*, Harvard University Press, Cambridge MA.

Weisbrod, B. A. 1989, 'Rewarding performance that is hard to measure: the private nonprofit sector', *Science*, vol. 244, no. 4904, pp. 541–46.

Wylie, C., Hogden, E., Ferral, H. & Thompson, J. 2006, Contributions of early childhood education to age-14 performance: Evidence from the longitudinal competent children, competent learners study [Online], Available: http://www.educationcounts.govt.nz/__data/assets/pdf_file/0003/7716/cc-contributions-ece14.pdf [2006, Apr 1].

9

The giant in the playground: investigating the reach and implications of the corporatisation of child care provision

Frances Press and Christine Woodrow

Prologue

This paper is a case study of an Australian corporate child care provider, ABC Learning Ltd, when the corporation was at its height. In the months after this paper was first completed, ABC Learning was dramatically affected by a volatile financial market. In March 2008, a financial crisis involving calls on margin loans held by the directors of the parent company quickly resulted in a massive sell-off of international holdings, including 60 per cent of US kindergartens, to Morgan Stanley Private Equity (Korporaal 2008), in a context of tumbling share prices for the company. Margin calls resulted in stock sell-off by members of the board of directors, three of whom have now vacated the board. These include the previous chair of the board, Sallyanne Atkinson, as well as Martin Kemp and William Bessemer. The CEO, Groves retained only 3,186 of his previous 20 million shares. It is understood that the major shareholder of ABC Learning is now Singapore-based Temasek holdings, and that one of the remaining directors, LeNeve Groves now holds no shares in the company.

Several months after this turn of events, ABC Learning once more hit the Australian headlines in August and September 2008. Its shares were suspended from trading and a shareholder class action was prepared against the company on the basis of misstated earnings over previous years (John 2008).

Although the financial structure and wellbeing of ABC Learning and its current and former directors has significantly changed, ABC Learning's domination of the landscape of child-care provision in Australia is a worthy case study. According to the ABC Learning website, 'ABC is the largest publicly listed childcare operator in the world, based on centre numbers' (ABC Learning Centres 2007a). Some of the information presented in this paper has been superseded by events. Nevertheless, the analysis continues to be relevant to the policy context of children's early education and care both in Australia and internationally, because of its illumination of the development, role and potential impact of commercial relationships in the framing and delivery of education and care for young children.

Introduction

Increasingly the landscape of child care service provision in Australia is characterised by the dominance of a large, publicly listed for-profit corporation. Whilst corporations are well placed to respond quickly to shortfalls in child care supply and position themselves through their marketing as caring, trustworthy organisations, there has been little public debate about what is at stake in this changed landscape. We argue, however, that the ascendancy and apparent entrenchment of corporate child care is a phenomenon with far-reaching implications related to the positioning of the care and education of young children in the social policy landscape.

In previous papers (Press & Woodrow 2005; Woodrow & Press 2007) we have traced the rise of privatised and corporate provision and the ways in which it has commodified and transformed child care, creating a discursive space in which the care and education of young children has become an act of consumption. This paper extends these previous analyses by investigating how corporatisation has not only reshaped how we view child care (its purpose and how it is situated within the community), but also diminished the space for discussion, contention and articulation of what society wants for, and from, young children's care and education. By locating and cross referencing an extensive range of documents relating to Australia's largest child care provider ABC Learning (annual reports, prospectuses, court cases, newspaper articles, company websites, et cetera), the paper traces the impact of corporatisation on the shaping of children's services and the professional identities of the teachers and carers who work in them. Encompassed in these considerations are questions concerning what counts as knowledge (curriculum) and what knowledge counts (what curriculum is).

However, we are mindful that discussion of corporate child care within Australia is dominated by one major player, ABC Learning. Its domination of the Australian child care market is such that corporate child care and ABC Learning have almost become synonyms and the company's activities colour our understanding of corporatisation's nature and impact. ABC Learning may, or may not be, a typical child care corporation. However, its market share means that its impact cannot be considered an aberration, and its once rapidly increasing international reach gives rise to implications that extend beyond Australia. Nor is it possible to discuss the impact of corporatisation as if it sits disentangled from issues concerning privatisation. Previously, we have referred to corporatisation as a consolidation of child care privatisation (Press & Woodrow 2005), with the latter giving rise to corporate provision. Nevertheless, the interests of the corporate sector and smaller private providers are at times divergent, for example, as they compete for market share. Thus, the corporatisation of child care is also a distinct phenomenon, the effects of which require particular attention.

The giant in the playground of the paper's title illustrates our contention that corporatised child care, literally and metaphorically, encroaches upon the space of other child care providers and our imaginings of what child care might be, and overshadows alternative policy arrangements to the point that these are rendered almost invisible. This paper traces the resulting diminution of the space available for the maintenance and development of other approaches to early childhood care and education, and speculates upon its existing and possible ramifications. In doing so, we explore the literal engulfing of space by the geographic dominances of ABC Learning and its takeover of other players; the whittling away of the mainstream policy discourse; the attempted containment of government policy instruments; the marginalisation of alternative voices and perspectives; and the creation of a conglomerate which manages and/or excludes outside influences upon its internal functioning through a highly sophisticated vertical and horizontal integration strategy.

Market domination

Despite the exhortation of ABC Learning's Chief Executive Officer, Edmund Groves, that he didn't set out to get rich: 'all I ever wanted to do was pay off my house' ('Playtime's over, says Groves' 2007, p. 9), there is no doubt that ABC Learning has aggressively set out to be a big player in the child care market. Yet Groves presents ABC Learning in an altruistic light, almost as the saviour of child care:

> People struggling with legislation and regulation from all different areas started calling us up saying "we want to sell our centre" … My fear was that there would be 300–400 centres in the group that would go broke. If that had of happened the effects could have been catastrophic. Fingers would have been pointed at the Government for letting … corporates into the industry ('Playtime's over, says Groves' 2007, p. 10).

This quote shrewdly positions ABC Learning in a number of ways. Firstly, it places the blame for smaller corporations exiting the field on their 'struggle' with legislation and regulation (many of which are designed to protect children from harm, and at best, facilitate children's wellbeing and development), and not on factors such as increased competition or poor planning choices. Secondly, rather than acting out of self-interest, ABC Learning staves off the 'catastrophic' consequences of market failure. Thirdly, in preventing this potential catastrophe, it becomes the defender of all corporate child care and safeguards a government policy which directs a large proportion of federal child care funding, via subsidies to parents, to for-profit child care through the Child Care Benefit Scheme (Rush 2006). Thus the fairytale of neoliberalism is embodied and secured: governments should stimulate, not regulate business, and leave the market to effectively respond to consumer demand.

In its Prospectus however, ABC Learning's continued expansion is presented as less ad hoc and is attributed to 'organic growth and strategic acquisitions' (ABC Learning Centres Ltd 2007b, section 3.1). To get a tangible sense of its market growth and dominance it is worthwhile outlining the companies that ABC Learning has acquired. In Australia these include: Peppercorn Child Care Centres Australia; Just Little People; Kids Campus Ltd; Universal Group; and Hutchison's Child Care. In the United States, it purchased the Learning Care Group and, under the umbrella of the latter, acquired Tutor Time Centres, La Petite Academy, Montessori Unlimited and was contracted to buy Children's Courtyard. At its height the company owned over 1,000 centres in the United States (ABC Learning Centres Ltd 2007c). In the United Kingdom, ABC Learning acquired the Busy Bees group which is the United Kingdom's fifth largest provider, and following this, it obtained the Leap Frog Nurseries Group (Moore 2007). In 2004, it gained a foothold in New Zealand-Aotearoa when it bought ten centres, consolidating this in early 2007 with the purchase of New Zealand's Forward Steps. It now owns over 100 centres in New Zealand-Aotearoa, and its 2007 Annual Report proclaimed its intention to increase its New Zealand and Australian holdings by 40–50 per cent (ABC Learning Centres Ltd 2007b). According to its 2006 Annual Report, the company acquired 192 centres in small groups or individually during the preceding year, but this list excludes the individual centres bought previously (ABC Learning Centres Ltd 2006). Given this list, it is not surprising that ABC Learning is the biggest single player in the Australian market, and the self-proclaimed largest corporate child care provider in the world.

Although these figures give some sense of its market domination, it is the local level that gives a real sense of what this control means for communities. In her study of child care in the Townsville region, Harris estimates that ABC Learning provides 50 per cent of child care (Harris 2007). In regional NSW its presence is also significant. Bathurst, with a population of just under 32,000 people has three ABC centres; Orange, with a population of 40,000 has five centres; Dubbo, with a population of 40,000 has three; Albury-Wodonga, with a combined population of 90,000 has nine; and Wagga Wagga, with a population of just under 57,000, has eight. Other centres, both non-profit and private, do exist in these areas. Bathurst for instance, has six other long day care centres. Nonetheless, there is no doubt that in some regions the choice of provider has been severely diminished. In a number of regions ABC Learning provides more child care centres than the other centres combined (for instance, Orange and Canberra) and in centres such as Wagga Wagga and Dubbo, ABC Learning's market domination is almost total, with each township having only two other long day care centres (National Child Care Accreditation Council 2007).

This reach within the Australian context has a number of implications both for families and the shape of early childhood policy. Despite the rhetoric of choice espoused by the then Minister for Families, Communities and Indigenous Affairs, Mal Brough, it is clear that in many regions families have no choice, and place their children in the centre that is available to them, even though this may not be their preferred option ('Caring for Kids' 2006; Harris 2007). The strategy of opening up a number of centres in a particular locality increases the likelihood that, for some regions at least, ABC Learning may be the only provider in the immediate area, or the only provider with a vacancy. Further, by saturating a local market with child care places, ABC Learning can threaten the financial viability of other, already existing centres (Birnbauer & Dowling 2004a). Smaller stand-alone centres find it difficult to underwrite the increased vacancy rates that can result from increased competition—and as these centres become vulnerable to takeover, the range of providers is further reduced. Additionally, ABC Learning has at times aggressively tried to defend its market share through court actions designed to prevent the establishment of other child care providers. For example, in *ABC Developmental Learning Centres Pty Ltd vs City of Tea Tree Gully & ORS, 2004,* the company appealed against the granting of a development application to another child care provider in an action which the judge ruled to be solely instituted for the purpose of delaying or preventing the latter being set up in competition with ABC Learning. Such market control then creates its own momentum. Domination of the market leads to more domination as its relatively comprehensive reach places it in a highly strategic position to secure contracts to provide child care for government departments and corporations. Thus ABC Learning has contracts for the provision of child care for the Defence Force, the Commonwealth Bank, TYCO, OPTUS, ANZ Corporate Care, WESTPAC, Chisholm Institute of TAFE, and Homes Glen Institute of TAFE (ABC Learning Centres Ltd 2006).

Interrelationships

Equally significant for understanding the corporation's capacity to reshape the provision of child care is its control of, and links with, other entities and its development of new markets. It wholly owns the National Institute of Early Childhood Education (NIECE). NIECE is a Recognised Training Organisation which provides training to ABC Learning staff up to Diploma level. ABC Learning has a multi-business agreement with the University of Southern Queensland (USQ) for NIECE Diploma graduates to receive two years credit into its Bachelor of Education. The former Dean of Education at USQ, Professor Frank Crowther is on the board of Independent Colleges Australia (ICA), keeping company with Le Neve Groves and Martin Kemp, who until recently, were both on the board of ABC Learning. As well as being on these boards, Le Neve Groves is the Principal of NIECE.

Other relationships are less directly traced but equally cosy. For instance, IdeaLogical states that it is the online department store for 'ABC Families' and in partnership with ABC Learning provides Too cute! Photos (IdeaLogical—About us 2007). Brendan Riley, the Managing Director of TooCute! Photos, was formerly the National Brand Manager for ABC Learning (Too Cute! Photo Co. 2007). ABC Learning appears to be IdeaLogical's only client. Similarly, the Recruitment agency, '123Careers' is the 'key recruiter for ABC across Australia and NZ', and again, ABC Learning appears to be its only client (Welcome to 123careers 2007).

In 2005 ABC Learning bought Judius, a toy and equipment supplier to early childhood services and schools. In late 2006, ABC Learning sold Judius to Funtastic (Funtastic Limited 2006). However, it did not divest its interest completely, as the sale involved the transfer of 29 million shares to ABC Learning, making the latter a significant shareholder in the company (17.99 per cent) with an additional 1,000,000 shares owned by Edmund Groves. In addition, Funtastic negotiated a twenty-year exclusive global supply agreement with ABC Learning, describing this arrangement in its message to shareholders as a 'truly transformational opportunity' (Funtastic Limited 2006, p. 5).

ABC Learning has, in the past, also expressed its interest in schools. In 2004 it attempted to establish a school in Queensland in the hope of channelling children from its centres into the school (Birnbauer & Dowling 2004b). This bid failed because of ABC Learning's for-profit status and so it set up the not-for-profit subsidiary Independent Colleges Australia (ICA). This arrangement also generated controversy (Norrie 2005). Although ICA now publicly distances itself from ABC Learning (Patty 2006), both organisations shared two board members (Le Neve Groves and Martin Kemp). ICA currently has a registered primary school in Casey, Victoria, and is applying for registration in Victoria for a school it has established at Melton. Its website features proposals for schools in Penrith and Kurri Kurri (Independent Colleges Australia 2007).

Although such arrangements may be read as business savvy, they also have other ramifications, including cementing the construction of child care as both an act, and point of, consumption. Whilst our previous analysis of corporatisation drew attention to the way in which child care is now marketed to parents as a consumer item through which they can express their love and aspirations for their children (Woodrow & Press 2007), companies such as IdeaLogical and Funtastic establish the corporation as a major point of sale.

Here we see the creation of an almost self-contained corporate entity. Training, professional development, equipment supplies, annual photographs, and toy catalogues are either developed 'in house' or obtained through organisations commercially linked to the provider organisation.

Such mutually beneficial corporate arrangements take on wider public significance because of their possible implications for children's and families' experiences of child care, and the very real possibility that decisions about young children's learning and wellbeing are conflated with financial interests in returning the strongest possible dividends to shareholders, and particularly principal share holders. Additionally, many parents may be unaware that their consumption (purchasing) of goods and services is being manipulated to serve the interests of the companies and their shareholders. Under its commercial agreement with Funtastic, ABC is entitled to a percentage of revenue on sales made to and through ABC centres. A recent parent newsletter advised parents of an upcoming opportunity to purchase toys and other items from a catalogue, with 20c from every $1 spent going to the centre. We wonder to what extent parents are aware that their purchasing power further subsidises the business through its shareholdings.

Professional identity

Across the world, the discourses of early childhood professionalism have been strongly characterised by values related to caring, collectivism and collegiality. Evidence for these values consistently recurs in research accounts of early childhood teachers' work, and can be found in curriculum planning documentation, conference programs and other professional development activities, and in codes of ethical practice. These dominant values may simultaneously be strengths and weaknesses of the profession and the problematic nature of these 'caring' discourses has been well discussed (Petrie 1992; Moyles 2001; Grieshaber 2001; Woodrow 2002). Nevertheless, also evident in the literature is a search for more robust frameworks for caring, collective activism and collegiality (Sumsion 2006). In the context of corporate provision of early childhood care, we ask whether discourses of private benefit, individualism, competition and entrepreneurship place these values at risk.

McWilliam, Hatcher and Meadmore explore two distinct understandings about 'enterprise' culture. The first is about the 'paradigmatic status' of the market in relation to the provision of goods and services, which is thus understood as the best way to 'achieve effective organisational arrangements' (1999, p. 2). In keeping with this paradigm, ABC Learning's reach and relationships are described in its Prospectus (n.d.) as providing it 'with scale benefits and, importantly, with the opportunity to offer an enhanced choice of centres for corporate business'. The second understanding revolves around wealth as a marker of success, achieved by highly individualistic orientations to work, in which industriousness though hard work and competitiveness to achieve are fundamental. ABC Learning's maxims—'our "spirit of fun" runs as deep as our "spirit of competition"' and 'Australians Bettering their Children (ABC)' (ABC Learning Centres 2007)—are symptomatic of such orientations.

In previous analyses of the impact of privatisation and corporatisation upon child care, we noted practices reflecting a marketised approach emerging across the sector influenced by commercial practices (Press & Woodrow 2005; Woodrow & Press 2007). This is evident, for example, in an increasing trend across some larger non-profit early childhood providers towards investing heavily in brand identification and marketing, typically expressed through logos and branded clothing for staff. In such ways, practices derived from commercial discourses become normalised and unquestioned, rather than subject to scrutiny about whether they represent the best use of resources. This invites consideration of what other practices might be implicated in shifting understandings of professional identity. Noting the strengthening infusion of commercial discourses in education policy and practice, Sachs (2000; 2001) observes the emergence of a new kind of professional identity that she calls the 'entrepreneurial professional'. Drawing on Casey's (1995) depiction of the designer employee, Sachs (2001) contends that such identity is aligned with elements of standardised procedures, efficiency and accountability, rather than with knowledge-building differentiated across contexts and the exercise of professional autonomy. What professional identities might emerge in the corporate world of child care?

With the establishment of NIECE, ABC Learning has quickly developed the capacity to train a significant proportion of its 17,000-strong work force 'in house', and to integrate another profit-generating element into its operation. Ongoing staff development for employees is facilitated through the college. Such positioning builds the capacity of the entire enterprise to 'authorise' the attributes, dispositions or capacities which professionals should have (McWilliam et al. 1999). Further, the corporation also offers a 'Carers' Share Plan' which, according to the Prospectus, issued 357,905 ordinary shares to carers employed by ABC's licensees in Australia (ABC Learning Centres Ltd 2007b, section 5.4). Thus the professional identity of staff is embedded through in-house training (for example, NIECE), practices such as branding (logos and uniforms), the loyalty program and the 'ABC Carers Share Plan'. In this way, staff are symbolically identified with the organisation, thereby encouraging a shared or collective identification with the company rather than the profession. The consumption and utilisation of products and services also owned by, or affiliated with, the organisation might serve to reinforce this identification. Will such measures privilege privatised concerns over communal and collective discourse, and will a 'culture of production and profit' replace a culture of community (Ball 1994, cited in Groundwater-Smith & Sachs 2002)?

Curriculum

During the time that corporate long day care has been expanding in Australia, there has also been a strengthening discourse of early childhood programs as platforms for early intervention, based on the recognition of the early childhood years as foundational to children's subsequent developmental wellbeing (Press 2006). Of significance to this discussion is the policy attention this has generated, with the question for Australian governments being how best to develop a comprehensive approach to children's early education (Organisation for Economic Co-operation and Development 2006; Press 2006; Elliott 2006). A related issue has been the role and nature of early childhood curriculum. In Australia and internationally, curriculum has been a highly contested space, and has been cast variously as a potential vehicle for social transformation, as a means of maintaining the status quo, or as a platform for social mobility and facilitating private benefit. As a recent OECD study of early childhood policy internationally identified, great diversity exists in approaches to pedagogy and what counts as knowledge within curriculum frameworks (Organisation for Economic Co-operation and Development 2006).

ABC Learning makes strong claims, through its marketing material, about the strength of its educational orientation. One way in which this promise is delivered is through the 'Life Smart Curriculum' developed by the company's self-proclaimed 'Education Department'. The existence and promulgation of this curriculum, which strategically incorporates selective elements of various state-initiated early childhood curricula across Australia and New Zealand-Aotearoa, locates the ABC Learning brand within contemporary discourses of early years provision, and communicates images and notions of 'education', 'quality', and 'professionalism'. However, the complex web of varied relationships between ABC Learning and other companies invites closer consideration of what counts as knowledge in the Lifesmart Curriculum, who 'owns' and produces that knowledge, and what values and interests are privileged or at stake in its ownership, promulgation and implementation.

For instance, in Funtastic's global supply agreement with ABC Learning, the key commercial terms include an ongoing arrangement with Judius supplying toys, furniture and learning and development products, covering 'the complete spectrum of children's development, including literacy, maths, motor skills, arts & crafts and music', on an exclusive basis to all of ABC's child care centres (Funtastic Limited 2006). In 2006, ABC Learning introduced BroadLEARN, an online software program for young children into its centres. In 2007, ABC Learning Centres acquired a 25 per cent share in Mediasphere Holdings, the company that produces BroadLEARN (Certification and training programs 2007).

Such arrangements invite particular kinds of questions about the curriculum. What might be at stake when corporate agreements privilege the use of particular materials and when curriculum ideas emanate from the organisation's web of shareholder relationships? How might curriculum developed centrally, within corporate organisations with strong commercial links to other profit-making organisations, shape and define what counts as knowledge and what knowledge is worth knowing? What risks accompany the commodification of curriculum through these commercial relationships, and how might the resulting education 'product' reflect and privilege populist anxieties about the advancement of one's own children, rather than considerations of collective benefit, citizenship and nation-building (Wong 2007)? 'In an education system where the consumer is king ... education ... is a private good that only benefits the owner, an investment in my future, not yours, in my children, not other people's children' (Labaree, cited in Giroux 2000, p. 90). A further issue to arise from this commodification of curriculum relates to an apparent lack of transparency and contestability. Whereas curriculum devised by the state is public and open to debate and contestation, the curriculum of ABC Learning does not have such transparency. Further, it is reasonable to expect that many parents do not understand the commercial relationships that are embedded in or underpin the curriculum, and its enactment through the various resources such as toys and software.

Policy impact

In the preceding sections we have posed a number of questions pertaining to the possible impact of corporatisation on early childhood professional identity and pedagogies. In this section we examine existing and potential influences upon the broader child care policy context.

In an exploration of the nexus between business and social policy, Farnsworth and Holden trace the ways in which corporate power can be exercised to shape policy. In relation to the provision of welfare services (in which they include child care) they observe: 'Once a corporation is involved … a private interest is created, at the heart of the welfare state, whose primary goal is the accrual of profit' (2006, p. 479). Once they become a provider of welfare services, corporations then have open to them an array of 'means of political engagement and institutional involvement … in order to defend and extend their interests' (2006, p. 479).

Structural power, as well as processes of formal and informal political engagement, becomes the means by which social policy can be subject to the influence of corporate power. Farnsworth and Holden assert that businesses with high structural power are able to influence policy outcomes without resorting to overt action because the decisions of policy makers 'are structurally framed by the imperative to induce companies to invest' (2006, p. 475). The actual influence of structural power is a product of the 'size and relative importance of the business organisation concerned' (2006, p. 476). Direct and overt influence upon social policy can be exercised through the structures of government once the corporation is recognised as a significant service provider. Indirect influence may be exerted through mechanisms such as political donations.

The risk of early childhood policy being shaped by concerns related to business profitability is illustrated by a comment by the previous federal Minister for Families, Communities and Indigenous Affairs that the Australian Labor Party's policy proposal to open child care centres on school grounds was 'a threat hung over the head of every childcare operator today' (Brough 2007, p. 9). Private providers are well aware of the way in which a changed social policy landscape might impact upon their financial viability and/or profitability. Some private child care providers have previously identified the introduction of paid maternity leave as a risk (Brennan 2007, p. 220). In its Prospectus, some of the risks ABC Learning identifies include changes to regulatory regimes, and changes to government subsidies and rebates (section 6.2).

As a major player in child care, and legitimated as an appropriate provider of child care (for example, through government subsidies), ABC Learning earns a place on formal advisory structures. Hence, Le Neve Groves was one of only eight members on the Stronger Families and Communities Partnership established in 2004 by the Commonwealth Government and she was on the National Advisory Group of the National Child Care Accreditation Council. When ABC Learning was in the United States, its annual report referred to its US-based Learning Care Group having a government relations department which 'continues to strengthen its legislative relationships and raise awareness on the issues affecting early education providers' (ABC Learning Centres Ltd 2006, p. 15). ABC Learning has donated to the Queensland Liberal Party (Allen & Ludlow 2006, cited in Brennan 2007) and contributed $50,000 to the National Party, following the appointment of former Nationals minister with portfolio responsibility for child care, Larry Anthony, to its board (Baker 2006).

In addition, the sheer size and scale of the company operations and its financial resources allow it to purchase expensive expert advice on capturing hearts and minds—of parents, of prospective employees, and of policy makers. The 2006 Annual Report records a 12-month expenditure of over $8m on advertising and promotions. This included spending on a highly effective advertising campaign developed by a high-end marketing organisation, focused around the theme of love, which yielded a 300 per cent increase in telephone enquiries over the period of the campaign (Depasquale Advertising 2007).

The size and reach of the company, and its dominance of the sector, affords it a 'positional advantage' (Hirsch 1977, cited in McWilliam et al. 1999) and inevitably leads to normalisation, such that corporate provision becomes entrenched and hard to turn back (Farnsworth & Holden 2006). Giroux (2000, p. 86) writes that market-based approaches to schooling

> share a faith in corporate culture that overrides defending public education as a noncommodified public sphere, a repository for nourishing the primacy of civic over corporate values, and as a public entitlement that is essential for the well-being of children and the future of democracy.

His observations strike a chord with the apparent acceptance of child care corporatisation in Australia. Although it might be overstating the case to say there is a shared faith in corporate child care (for instance, the work of Harris (2007) indicates an active dislike of corporate child care on the part of some parents), there is a sense of its inevitability that moves the policy discourse away from a discussion of the civic values and civic spaces that should be embedded in such provision for young children. This sense of the inevitable (they are here to stay) leads to an unwillingness to debate the rights and wrongs of reliance on corporate provision, and further cements the view of children's earliest education as an act of private parental consumption, rather than as a reflection of collective aspirations for the public good.

Conclusion

Our review has outlined some of the myriad of ways that ABC Learning has legitimated its identity as a responsible child care provider, including its ready capacity to incorporate emerging contemporary language into its promotional and curriculum material. In summary, the corporation presents itself as an authoritative, responsive and caring organisation by deploying sophisticated marketing strategies which appeal to families, governments, potential investors and employees.

Nonetheless, we contend that there are a number of 'signposts' that indicate a need to be less sanguine. International research evidence indicates that the non-profit sector tends to provide higher overall quality than the for-profit sector (Cleveland et al. 2007). Similarly, research in New South Wales indicates that the non-profit sector is more likely to go beyond the minimum regulatory standards in relation to staff-to-child ratios (Fisher & Patulny 2004). In addition, there are a number of Australian reports on parent and staff dissatisfaction with at least some ABC Learning centres (Rush 2006; Harris 2007; Background Briefing 2004), and the *Choice* survey indicated higher levels of parent dissatisfaction with commercial child care ('Caring for Kids' 2006). At the very least, this indicates a need for rigorous research within Australia on the quality of child care and whether levels of quality can be correlated with the type of provider.

Much of the corporation's presentation of itself via its prospectus, annual reports and marketing materials, paints a picture of the apparent success of corporate child care in supplying high quality, safe and responsive education and care for young children. However, our research has illuminated relationships that, although not hidden, are not immediately obvious. The complex web of the corporation's commercial relationships shields much from public view, and demands a new kind of literacy from educational researchers. The interrelatedness of areas such as ABC Learning's staff development, curriculum and equipment supplies have ramifications for the daily decisions and interactions that shape the nature of children's and families' experiences within child care. We are led to ponder—in whose interests are these relationships supported and sustained? Who are the winners and losers from the current arrangements?

Our research to date documents how what previously might have been considered 'public space' has now been taken up and over by commercial interests. This engulfing of space has the effect of residualising institutions that have traditionally been established on principles of community benefit and collectivity. Just as disturbingly, engulfment combines with normalisation to constrain the individual and collective policy imaginings of how provisions for children and families might be 'otherwise' (Moss 2007). By identifying and naming this colonisation of space, we aim to stimulate debate that might resuscitate previous visions related to early childhood provision as a public good and stimulate the production of new ones.

Rather than yield to what Giroux (2001, p. 1) asserts is a 'growing disinterest on the part of the general population in such non-commercial values as empathy, compassion, loyalty, caring, trust, and solidarity that bridges the private and the public and gives substance to the meaning of citizenship, democracy and public life', we want to a claim a right to public space in which to insert alternative understandings and imaginings.

References

ABC Learning Centres Ltd 2006, *Annual Report 2006*, [Online], Available: http://abclcl.republicast.com/ar2006/republicast.asp?page=1&layout=1&control=yes&zoom=100 [2007, Oct 1].

ABC Learning Centres Ltd 2007a, Investor Relations [Online], Available: http://www.childcare.com.au/investors/default.php [2007, Aug 28].

ABC Learning Centres Ltd 2007b, ABC Notes Prospectus, [Online], Available: www.childcare.com.au/files/ABC-Notes-Prospectus.pdf [2007, Aug 28].

ABC Learning Centres Ltd 2007c, *Annual Report 2007*, [Online], Available: http://abclcl.republicast.com/ar2007/republicast.asp?page=1&layout=1&control=yes&zoom=100 [2007, Oct 1].

Background Briefing 2004, 'Child care profits', ABC Radio National, 3 October.

Baker, R. 2006, 'Are our politicians for sale?', *The Age*, 24 May.

Birnbauer, W. & Dowling, J. 2004a, '$3.6bn child's game where it's play for keeps', *Sunday Age*, 5 December.

Birnbauer, W. & Dowling, J. 2004b, 'For-profit school sparks outrage', *Sunday Age*, 5 December.

Brennan, D. 2007, 'The ABC of child care politics', *Australian Journal of Social Issues*, vol. 42, no. 2, pp. 213–225.

Brough, M. 2007, Extract of address to Child Care NSW Conference, Hilton Hotel, Sydney, April.

'Caring for Kids' 2006, *Choice*, November.

Casey, C. 1995, *Work, Self and Society: After Industrialism*, Routledge, London & New York.

Certification and training programs 2007, Mediasphere [Online], Available: http://www.mediasphere.com.au/elearning_certification training.htm [2007, Oct 1].

Cleveland, G., Forer, B., Hyatt, D., Japel, C. & Krashinsky, M. 2007, Final Report. An Economic Perspective on the Current and Future Role of Non-profit Provision of Early Learning and Childcare Services in Canada,

Childcare Resource and Research Unit, University of Toronto, Montreal, Canada.

Depasquale Advertising 2007, [Online], Available: http://www.depasquale.com.au/ [2007, Oct 1].

Elliott, A. 2006, *Early Childhood Education: Pathways to Quality and Equity for All Children*, ACER Press, Camberwell, Victoria.

Farnsworth, K & Holden, C. 2006, 'The business-social policy nexus: Corporate power and corporate inputs into social policy', *Journal of Social Policy*, vol. 35, no. 3, pp. 473–94.

Fisher, K. & Patulny, R. 2004, Impact of Staff Ratios on Under 2 year olds in Children's Services, report prepared for the National Association of Community Based Children's Services (NSW), Early Childhood Asutralia (NSW), Local Government Children's Services Association (NSW) and Community Child Care Cooperative, May.

Funtastic Limited 2006, 'Message to Shareholders' *Annual Report 2006* [Online], Available: http://www.funtastic.com.au/docs/pdf/agm//ARper cent202006per cent20Finalper cent20Apr30.pdf [2007, Oct 1].

Giroux , H. 2000, *Stealing Innocence: Youth, Corporate Power, and the Politics of Culture*, Palgrave, New York.

Giroux, H. 2001, 'Pedagogy of the depressed: Beyond the new politics of cynicism', *College Literature*, vol. 28, no. 3, pp. 1–32.

Grieshaber, S. 2001, 'Advocacy and early childhood educators: Identity and cultural conflicts', in *Embracing Identities in Early Childhood Education*, eds S. Grieshaber & G. Cannella, Teachers College Press, New York, pp. 60–72.

Groundwater-Smith, S. & Sachs, J. 2002, 'The activist professional and the re-instatement of trust', *Cambridge Journal of Education*, vol. 32, no. 3, pp. 341–58.

Harris, N. 2007, The rise of the for-profit child care sector: Implications for choosing quality child care in a regional community, paper presented to the Australia Social Policy Conference, University of New South Wales, Sydney, 11-13 July.

IdeaLogical—About us [Online], Available: http://www.idealogical.com.au/idea_main/about.htm [2007, Oct 3].

Independent Colleges of Australia [Online] Available: http//www.icacolleges.com.au [2007, Sep 28].

John, D. 2008, 'End of a fairy tale', *The Sydney Morning Herald*, 6 September.

Korporaal, G. 2008, 'Investors give ABC Learning's US sell-off deal a poor mark', *The Australian*, 7 March.

McWilliam, E., Hatcher, C. & Meadmore, D. 1999, Corporatising the teacher, new professional identities in education, paper presented to Australian Association for Educational Research (AARE) Annual Conference, University of Melbourne, Melbourne, Nov 30–Dec 2.

Moore, A. 2007, 'ABC Learning buys British-based Leapfrog Nurseries', Lateline Business, Australian Broadcasting Corporation, 13 August.

Moss, P. 2007, 'Bringing politics into the nursery: Early childhood education as a democratic practice', *European Early Childhood Education Research Journal*, vol. 15, no.1, pp. 5–20.

Moyles, J. 2001, 'Passion, paradox and professionalism in early years education', *Early Years*, vol. 21, no. 2, pp. 81–95.

National Childcare Accreditation Council 2008, Search for Child Care, Available: http://www.ncac.gov.au/Search/Search1.asp [2008, Sep 9].

Norrie, J. 2005, 'And look who has an eye on their schooling', *The Sydney Morning Herald*, 1 December.

Organisation for Economic Co-operation and Development 2006, *Starting Strong11: Early Childhood Education and Care*, OECD, Paris.

Patty, A. 2006, 'Banned school steps up NSW push', *The Sydney Morning Herald*, June 24.

'Playtime's over, says Groves', 2007, *Childcare Australasia*, June.

Petrie, A. 1992, 'Chasing ideologies in early childhood: The past is still before us', in *Changing Faces: The Early Childhood Profession in Australia*, ed. B. Lambert, Australian Early Childhood Association, Canberra.

Press, F. 2006, *What About the Kids? Improving the Experiences of Infants and Young Children in a Changing World*, Commission for Children and Young People, Sydney.

Press, F. & Woodrow, C. 2005, 'Commodification, corporatisation and children's spaces', *Australian Journal of Education*, vol. 49, no. 3, pp. 278-97.

Rush, E. 2006, Child care quality in Australia, *Discussion Paper No. 84*, Australia Institute, Sydney.

Sachs, J. 2000, 'The activist professional', *Journal of Educational Change*, vol. 1, no. 1, pp. 77-95.

Sachs, J. 2001, 'Teacher professional identity: Competing discourses, competing outcomes', *Journal of Educational Policy*, vol. 16, no. 2, pp.149-61.

Stronger Families and Communities Strategy Partnership n.d., [Online], Available: http://www.facs.gov.au/internet/facsinternet.nsf/aboutfacs/programs/sfsc-sfcs_partnership.htm [2007, Oct 5].

Sumsion, J. 2006, 'From Whitlam to Economic Rationalism and beyond: A conceptual framework for political activism in children's services', *Australian Journal of Early Childhood*, vol. 31 no. 1, pp. 1-10.

Too Cute! Photo Co. 2007, [Online], Available: http://www.idealogical.com.au/tc_photo/overview.htm [2007, Oct 3].

Welcome to 123Careers 2007, [Online], Available: http//www.123careers.com.au [2007, Aug 21].

Wong, S. 2007, 'Looking backward and moving forward: Historicising the social construction of early childhood education and care as national work', *Contemporary Issues in Early Childhood Education*, vol. 8, no. 2, pp. 144-56.

Woodrow, C. & Press, F. 2007, '(Re)Positioning the child in the policy politics of early childhood', *Educational Philosophy and Theory*, vol. 39, no. 3, pp. 312-25.

Woodrow, C. 2002, 'Living Ethics in Early Childhood Contexts', Unpublished PhD thesis. Central Queensland University.